101 933 443 6

Jo**...**sm

ONE WEEK LOAN

Journalism

principles & practice

second edition

Tony Harcup

Los Angeles | London | New Delhi
Singapore | Washington DC

© Tony Harcup 2009

First edition published 2004
Reprinted 2005 (twice), 2006, 2007, 2008, 2009

SAGE Publications Ltd
1 Oliver's Yard
55 City Road
London EC1Y 1SP

SAGE Publications Inc.
2455 Teller Road
Thousand Oaks, California 91320

SAGE Publications India Pvt Ltd
B 1/I 1 Mohan Cooperative Industrial Area
Mathura Road, New Delhi 110 044

SAGE Publications Asia-Pacific Pte Ltd
33 Pekin Street #02-01
Far East Square
Singapore 048763

Library of Congress Control Number: 2008930189

British Library Cataloguing in Publication data

A catalogue record for this book is available from the
British Library

ISBN 978-1-84787-249-4
ISBN 978-1-84787-250-0

Typeset by C&M Digitals (P) Ltd, Chennai, India
Printed in Great Britain by Asdford Colour Press Ltd, Gosport, Hampshire

To my mum, Beth,
and in memory of my dad, Fred.

contents

acknowledgements

Thanks to everyone who has helped in one way or another over the years, including: Jamilah Ahmed, Michael Ainsley, Huw Alexander, Ian Antcliff, Miles Barter, Kate Betts, Colin Bourne, Quintin Bradley, Paddy Brennan, Paul Breslin, Vanessa Bridge, Sarah Bury, Bill Carmichael, Sev Carrell, Helen Carroll, Trevor Cave, Adam Christie, Peter Cole, Andy Comber, Anne Creyke, Rachel Crolla, Katie Cronin, Jenny Cuthbertson, Jeremy Dear, Tony Earnshaw, Lindsay Eastwood, Richard Edwards, Seth Edwards, Jackie Errigo, Max Farrar, Paul Foot, Jonathan Foster, Bob Franklin, Chris Frost, Gang of Four, Trevor Gibbons, Mike Glover, Tim Gopsill, Quentin Gray, Julia Hall, Mark Hanna, Jackie Harrison, Sarah Hartley, David Helliwell, Rachel Hendrick, Michael Higgins, Mat Hill, David Holmes, Pete Johnson, Brian Kay, Richard Keeble, Ronnie Kershaw, Saeeda Khanum, Marie Kinsey, Jemima Kiss, Peter Lazenby, Tanja Lederer, Cathy Leman, Tony Lidgate, Keith Lomax, Gurdeep Mattu, Rosie Maynard, Lauren McAllister, Derek 'Mac' McKiernan, Archie McLellan, Mekons, Jane Merrick, Alan Maloney, Liz Nice, Richard North, Deirdre O'Neill, Susan Pape, Kevin Peachey, Chris Searle, John Short, Jon Snow, Mila Steele, Katie Stewart, Sean Stowell, Sally Symondson, Abul Taher, Fiona Thompson, Colin Thorne, Julie Thorpe, John Toner, Tony and Matt (*KDIS*), Gill Ursell, Deborah Wain, Martin Wainwright, Chris Wheal, Brian Whittle, Granville Williams, Gordon Wilson, Roger Worth, Terry Wragg, Emily Ye, Philip Young, Waseem Zakir.

list of boxes

notes to the reader

Layout

The design of this book may look unusual but it is easy to follow and is explained in Chapter 1. Start at the top of page one and continue reading the untinted text until all becomes clear…

References

For the benefit of anyone unfamiliar with the Harvard style of academic referencing, when you see something like this in the text (Bloggs, 2009: 10) it means that you can easily find out the source by turning to the alphabetical list of references at the back and looking up the name Bloggs, followed by the year of publication, in this case 2009. The number 10 in the above example refers to the page number in the original source.

preface

The book in your hands can be used as a textbook, but I hope it is much more than that; the idea is that it introduces the voices of practising journalists and of journalism studies academics, and gets them to talk to each other. For this second edition, each chapter has been revised and updated to take account of developments since the publication of the first edition as well as feedback from readers. Every word has been revisited, which is not to say that every word has changed – although many have.

New features include details of the ways in which journalists have been using the UK's Freedom of Information legislation, and there is far more here than in the first edition on the use of blogs, video and audio on the web, non-linear packages, interactive maps and other ways of doing journalism online. To reflect the reality that online journalism is increasingly part of the job for *all* journalists, the online elements are embedded throughout the book as a part of everyday journalism rather than treated separately; however, there is a new chapter specifically on telling stories via pictures, whether on TV or online. The concluding chapter has been expanded to address in more detail the converged nature of much 21st century journalism and to remind readers that, even as the technology changes all around us, the fundamentals of journalism remain crucial.

This edition features several new interviews with different journalists, most of whom are introduced in Chapter 1 and all of whom are listed in the References. Interviews conducted for the first edition remain but most have been updated by fresh interviews with the same journalists. Sadly, two of the original interviewees were no longer with us when work on this edition began.

Paul Foot died at the age of 66 in July 2004, not long after publication of the first edition of this book, and his funeral was attended by an estimated 2,000 people (Ingrams, 2005: 6). The Paul Foot Award is awarded in his memory each year, and one of the new interviewees for this edition is Deborah Wain, joint winner of the prize in 2007.

A very different type of journalist from the Oxford-educated Foot was Brian Whittle, who started out on a local paper as a 17-year-old. They may have had different backgrounds and attitudes, but they were cracking reporters and both were generous with their ztime, willingly discussing their craft with me for the benefit of future generations of journalists. When, subsequently, I bumped into Brian at a press do, he told me he had finally got around to reading the book and had enjoyed it – rather to his surprise, I suspected. I told him that, if the book ran to a second edition, I would be contacting him to update his contributions. Sadly, that was not possible because, in December 2005, he collapsed and died at a party held to mark the departure of the *Express* and *Star* national newspapers from Manchester. As former colleague Peter Reece (2005) commented: "It was fitting that he was in the company of journalists, for tabloid ink ran through Brian's veins." He was aged just 59.

The words of Paul Foot and Brian Whittle are as pertinent today as when they were spoken, which is why they remain in this revised edition.

one

who, what, where,
when, why and how?

an introduction to
journalism

Journalism or churnalism?

"Journalism is a chaotic form of earning, ragged at the edges, full of snakes, con artists and even the occasional misunderstood martyr," writes Andrew Marr in his book *My Trade*. "Outside organised crime, it is the most powerful and enjoyable of the anti-professions" (Marr, 2005: 3). So journalism is a trade, or a craft, rather than a "proper" profession such as medicine or the law. But what is journalism *for*? To pay the mortgage, if you ask many hacks. But journalism is about more than that. It is a form of **communication** based on asking, and answering, the questions Who? What? Where? When? Why? How? Of course, journalism *is* a job, journalists *do* need to feed their kids or pay off student loans, and they have been known to refer to their workplaces as "word factories". Yet being a journalist is not the same as working in other types of factory because journalists play a *social* role that goes beyond the production of commodities to sell in the marketplace. *Journalism* informs society about itself and makes public that which would otherwise be private.

Rather an important job, you might think. But public opinion polls relentlessly remind journalists that we vie for bottom place with politicians and estate agents in the league table of trustworthiness. A typical poll of more than 2,000 adults in 2006 found just 19 per cent saying they trusted journalists to tell the truth – we were the least trusted occupation – whereas 92 per cent said they trusted doctors, who topped the poll of trustworthiness despite the best efforts of serial killer Dr Harold Shipman (Hall, 2006). A YouGov poll for *British Journalism Review* in 2008 found that public trust

Communication

The basic questions of journalism highlighted in the title of this chapter – Who? What? Where? When? Why? How? – are echoed in an early model of the mass communication process, formulated by Harold Lasswell in 1948. For Lasswell, analysis of the media begins with the question: "Who says what to whom, through what channel and with what effect?" (McQuail, 2000: 52–53). This has been termed a "transmission" model of communication, because it is essentially one-way, from sender to receiver. This and later versions of the transmission model have been challenged in recent decades as too simplistic, too linear, too mono-directional to explain the complexities of communication. It has been argued that an "active audience" can filter messages through our own experiences and understandings, sometimes producing readings "against the grain", or even suggesting multiple meanings. Increasingly, too, audiences are contributing to journalism directly via the phenomenon of user-generated content.

Journalism

Journalists may indeed inform society about itself, and much journalism may be concerned with making public that which would otherwise be private, as suggested in this chapter. But such a formulation falls far short of an adequate definition. For a start, journalists also supply information, comment and amplification on matters that are *already* in the public domain.

Journalism is defined by Denis McQuail as "paid writing (and the audiovisual equivalent) for public media with reference to actual and ongoing events of public relevance" (McQuail, 2000: 340). Like all such definitions, this raises many questions – Can journalism never be unpaid? Can media be other than public? Who decides what is of public relevance? – but it remains a reasonable starting point for any analysis of the principles

in journalists had declined since the same question was asked five years earlier; this was for every sector of journalism except the redtop tabloids, where trust was already so low it could hardly decline any further (Barnett, 2008). Mistrust of the *fourth estate* starts early, it seems. When 11 to 21-year-olds were asked how much they trusted journalists, just one per cent said "a lot", 19 per cent "a little", and a whopping 77 per cent replied "I do not trust them" (*Observer*, 2002).

Such attitudes have become all too familiar to online journalist Jemima Kiss, who told me that one of the disappointments in her short career to date has been "some people's assumptions and prejudices about you if you say you are a journalist". Such as?

> It has happened more times than I could count. It seems pretty much anyone outside the industry takes a sharp intake of breath when you say you're a journalist, which means I often feel the need to say, "I'm not *that* kind of journalist." The assumption is the cliche of a ruthless, doorstepping tabloid hack, I suspect, the type perpetuated in cheesy TV dramas.

Yet despite this image problem, a never-ending stream of bright young and not-so-young people are eager to become journalists. Why? Because it can be one of the most exciting jobs around. You go into work not necessarily knowing what you are going to be doing that day. You get the chance to meet powerful people, interesting people, inspiring people, heroes, villains and victims. You get the chance to ask stupid questions; to be one of the first to know something and to tell the world about it; to indulge a passion for writing, maybe to travel, maybe to become an expert in a particular field; to seek truth and campaign for justice; or, if you must, to hang out with celebrities.

Then there's the thrill of seeing your byline in a newspaper, a magazine or on a website; the excitement of seeing your footage on TV or online; and the odd experience of hearing your voice on the radio or via a podcast. You can then do it all over again. And again. Little wonder,

and practices of journalism. McQuail goes on to differentiate between different types of journalism: "prestige" (or quality) journalism, tabloid journalism, local journalism, specialist journalism, "new" (personal and committed) journalism, civic journalism, development journalism, investigative journalism, journalism of record, advocacy journalism, alternative journalism, and gossip journalism (McQuail, 2000: 340).

Such differentiation is rejected by David Randall, who recognises only the division between *good* and *bad* journalism:

> The bad is practised by those who rush faster to judgement than they do to find out, indulge themselves rather than the reader, write between the lines rather than on them, write and think in the dead terms of the formula, stereotype and cliché, regard accuracy as a bonus and exaggeration as a tool and prefer vagueness to precision, comment to information and cynicism to ideals. The good is intelligent, entertaining, reliably informative, properly set in context, honest in intent and effect, expressed in fresh language and serves no cause but the discernible truth. (Randall, 2000: viii)

Whether it is as simple as that is a question we will explore further in this and subsequent chapters.

Fourth estate

The notion of the press as a "fourth estate of the realm" – alongside the Lords Spiritual (clergy sitting in the House of Lords), the Lords Temporal (other peers), and the House of Commons – appears to have first been used by Edmund Burke in the 18th century. Recalling this usage in 1840 – believed to be the first time it had appeared in print – Thomas Carlyle had no doubt of its meaning:

> Burke said there were three estates in parliament; but, in the reporters' gallery yonder, there sat a fourth estate more important far than they all. It is not a figure of speech, or a witty saying; it is a literal fact, very momentous to us in these times. Literature is our parliament too. Printing, which comes necessarily out of writing, I say often, is equivalent to democracy: invent writing, democracy is inevitable. (Carlyle, 1840: 194)

Ideas about democracy and a free press have to a large extent grown alongside each other and come together in the concept of the fourth estate. Although initially referring specifically to the parliamentary

perhaps, that so many people are prepared to make sacrifices for a career in journalism. Sacrifices such as paying for your own training before even being considered for a job, unless you are either extremely lucky or are the offspring of an editor; then being paid less than many of the people whose own complaints about low pay might make news stories.

Almost a century ago journalists staged the first strike in the history of the National Union of Journalists, when they walked out of the *York Herald* in 1911 to protest against working hours and conditions that were described as like something from *Nicholas Nickleby* by Charles Dickens (Mansfield, 1943: 159; Gopsill and Neale, 2007: 84–85). Then, 97 years later in May 2008, journalists on the same newspaper's current incarnation as the *Press* walked out in protest at low pay. The *Press* is now part of the Newsquest group, which in turn is owned by Gannett, a US-based giant that made more than $1 billion profit in 2007 from a turnover of $7.4 billion. A group of strikers wore Edwardian costumes borrowed from York Theatre Royal to help draw parallels with their 1911 predecessors and, in a very 21st century touch, they also set up a group on the social networking site Facebook as well as their own blog. One explained their grievance: "We often feel as if we are still working in Dickensian conditions, our pay is certainly something which is stuck in the past. Trainee journalists start on just £13,500 a year" (http://nujyork.blogspot.com).

The pay of most journalists, particularly those just starting out and particularly those working in the local or regional media, is shameful. As one trainee reporter put it:

> Young people with a strong enough passion for writing will suffer low wages for the chance to work in journalism. But it is a disgrace to the industry as a whole that

> 6 I always tell them start-off pay is abysmal and if they are lucky it will move on to disgraceful after a year, and by the end of the training it will be only just short of appalling. 9
>
> – *Sean Dooley, former Northcliffe editor.*

press gallery, the term has become a more general label for journalism, locating journalists in the quasi-constitutional role of "watchdog" on the workings of government. This is central to the liberal concept of press freedom, as Tom O'Malley notes:

> At the centre of this theory was the idea that the press played a central, if unofficial, role in the constitution. A diverse press helped to inform the public of issues. It could, through the articulation of public opinion, guide, and act as a check on, government... The press could only fulfil this function if it were free from pre-publication censorship and were independent of the government. (O'Malley, 1997: 127)

Public sphere

The idea of the public sphere rests on the existence of a space in which informed citizens can engage with one another in debate and critical reflection; hence its relevance to discussions of the media. Jürgen Habermas traces the rise of the public sphere in Europe in the late 17th and early 18th centuries and argues that increasing commercialisation led subsequently to the decline of the public sphere and the press as a space that enabled "the people to reflect critically upon itself and on the practices of the state" (Stevenson, 2002: 49). Today, according to this analysis, such reasoned public discussion has been replaced by "the progressive privatisation of the citizenry and the trivialisation ... of questions of public concern" (Stevenson, 2002: 50). But, in turn, Habermas has been accused of idealising "a bygone and elitist form of political life" (McQuail, 2000: 158).

Free press

Editors and owners alike are often heard extolling the virtues of a "free press", a liberal model based on the idea that everyone is free to publish a newspaper without having to be licensed by those in power. Although publishers must act within the constraints of the law, they do not have to submit to censorship in advance. Newspapers are said to be in the business of truth-telling and serving only their readers. Thus,

they should have to. The industry cynically manipulates our ambition. (Quoted in Journalism Training Forum, 2002: 57)

Some wannabe journalists *are* put off when they discover the awful truth about pay. Others become disillusioned by work experience in newsrooms, observing that too many journalists seem to be chained to their desks in a culture of "presenteeism", processing copy and checking things out – if at all – on the telephone or the internet. Waseem Zakir, a business journalist with BBC Scotland, came up with the word "churnalism" to describe too much of today's newsroom activity. He told me what he meant:

Ten or 15 years ago you would go out and find your own stories and it was proactive journalism. It's become reactive now. You get copy coming in on the wires and reporters churn it out, processing stuff and maybe adding the odd local quote. It's affecting every newsroom in the country and reporters are becoming churnalists.

An ever-increasing workload may reduce the chances of doing the very things that made journalism seem so attractive in the first place. On top of all that, young journalists have to listen to more experienced hacks grumbling that "it wasn't like this in my day". The old-timers may have a point, but even the journalists of 100 years ago looked back fondly on a supposed "golden age" of journalism circa 1870 (Tunstall, 2002: 238).

Even when disabused of romantic illusions about travelling the world on huge expense accounts, pausing between drinks to jot down the occasional note, large numbers of people are attracted by the fact that journalism remains an occupation in which no two days are exactly the same and where the big story may be only a phone call away. And by the fact that journalism *matters*.

If it didn't matter, why would there be so many laws restricting how journalists can do their jobs? Why would government and opposition alike spend so much time courting the media? Why would Shiv Malik, Bill Goodwin and others have been threatened

through the democracy of the free market, we get the press we both desire and deserve.

However, this concept of a press selflessly serving the public does not go unchallenged. Colin Sparks, for example, points to increasing concentration of ownership and to economic barriers on entry, keeping out competitors. He argues:

Newspapers in Britain are first and foremost businesses. They do not exist to report the news, to act as watchdogs for the public, to be a check on the doings of government, to defend the ordinary citizen against abuses of power, to unearth scandals or to do any of the other fine and noble things that are sometimes claimed for the press. They exist to make money, just as any other business does. To the extent that they discharge any of their public functions, they do so in order to succeed as businesses. (Sparks, 1999: 45–46)

For Sparks, a truly free press – presenting objective information and a range of informed opinions while acting as a public forum – is "an impossibility in a free market" (Sparks, 1999: 59).

Ideology

By ideology is meant "some organised belief system or set of values that is disseminated or reinforced by communication" (McQuail, 2000: 497). Marxists believe that a ruling-class ideology is propagated throughout western, capitalist societies with the help of the media. Ideology may be slippery and contested, but it is argued that the principle remains essentially as expounded by Karl Marx and Friedrich Engels more than 160 years ago:

The ideas of the ruling class are in every epoch the ruling ideas: ie, the class which is the ruling material force of society, is at the same time its ruling intellectual force. The class which has the means of material production at its disposal, has control at the same time over the means of mental production, so that thereby, generally speaking, the ideas of those who lack the means of mental production are subject to it. The ruling ideas are nothing more than the ideal expression of the dominant material relationships, the dominant material relationships grasped as ideas; hence of the relationships which make the one class the ruling one, therefore, the ideas of its dominance. (Marx and Engels, [1846] 1965: 61)

Ideological power has been described as "the power to signify events in a particular way", although ideology

with jail for protecting their sources? As we shall see in the next chapter, many journalists around the world pay with their lives precisely because journalism matters.

Explanations of *how* and *why* journalism matters depend, like so many things, on *who* is speaking. Journalism is variously said to be the fourth estate of the realm, to be part of a **public sphere**, to support a **free press** or to inculcate us with the **ideology** of the ruling class. The reality is that journalism is probably all those things and more because, as we shall see below, there is not *one* journalism.

> ❝ The business of the press is disclosure. ❞
> – *John Thaddeus Delane, 19th-century editor of the Times.*

is also "a site of struggle" between competing definitions (Hall, 1982: 69–70). To illustrate the point, Stuart Hall refers to media coverage of industrial action in the UK public sector in the late 1970s:

> [One] of the key turning-points in the ideological struggle was the way the revolt of the lower-paid public-service workers against inflation, in the "Winter of Discontent" of 1978–9, was successfully signified, not as a defence of eroded living standards and differentials, but as a callous and inhuman exercise of overweening "trade-union power", directed against the defenceless sick, aged, dying and indeed the dead but unburied "members of the ordinary public". (Hall, 1982: 83)

Viewed from this perspective, the "news values" employed by journalists in the selection and construction of stories can be seen, not as the neutral expression of professional practice, but as ideologically loaded (Hall et al., 1978: 54). Thus, for all the apparent diversity of the media, and taking into account various exceptions, the routines and practices of journalists *tend* to privilege the explanations of the powerful and to foreclose discussion before it strays too far beyond the boundaries of the dominant ideology (Hall et al., 1978: 118).

An emphasis on the ideological content of journalism is frequently challenged for downplaying the agency of journalists and/or for failing to take account of the complex ways in which audiences may actually "read" media texts.

What's in this book?

Individual journalists have their own tales to tell, their own beliefs about what they do, their own reasons for pursuing a career in whatever field of journalism they work in. For this book I have interviewed a range of journalists from different generations, different backgrounds and different media; their comments are taken from these interviews unless otherwise indicated. Here are some of those you will meet in subsequent chapters:

- Lindsay Eastwood, a reporter for ITV Yorkshire's *Calendar* news programme since 1998, began work on her local newspaper, the *Craven Herald*, straight from school. She moved to the *Watford Observer* and worked shifts on the nationals before returning north to the *Yorkshire Evening Post* and then switching to broadcasting. In addition to reporting for *Calendar* she also makes TV documentaries.
- Paul Foot joined the *Daily Mirror* in 1961 and worked on the *Daily Record* in Glasgow before moving on to *Private Eye* and then *Socialist Worker*. He left when he was offered his own page in the *Daily Mirror* but eventually fell foul of the post-Maxwell regime at the paper and returned to his spiritual home at *Private*

Agency

Within the study of journalism, agency means the extent to which individual journalists can *make a difference* to media practices and content: "To have agency is defined by the ability to be able to actively intervene" (Stevenson, 2002: 226). To say that journalists have agency is not to deny that journalists operate in a world of constraints (see Chapter 2), nor to ignore the political and economic pressures to replace journalism with churnalism; it is to argue that structural forces do not totally determine all the actions of individuals. Yet many academic critics of the media seem to allow little room for agency. Take Sparks' explanation for the "lurid, sensational and

Eye. When he was interviewed for this book he was on the staff of *Private Eye* magazine, a columnist for the *Guardian* newspaper, and a freelance contributor to a range of other publications. He died in 2004.

- Sarah Hartley is head of online editorial at MEN Media in Manchester, where she helps run a converged editorial operation that includes print, TV, radio and the web; she is also an experienced blogger. She took her National Council for the Training of Journalists (NCTJ) exams at Darlington, started out as a trainee on the weekly *Leamington Spa Observer*, and later became news editor of the *Northern Echo* newspaper. She switched to the *Echo's* website in 1999 before moving to the website of the *Manchester Evening News* two years later.

- Jemima Kiss is the new media reporter for the *Guardian* website, writing news stories for the website's media section plus occasional pieces for the media pages of the newspaper as well as maintaining a blog, all on the specialist area of media and technology. She did not train as a journalist but studied fine art at college before working at the Brighton Media Centre, where she helped develop the centre's website. Jemima began writing freelance technology-based features for websites produced by a company based at the centre before becoming a full-time journalist for www.journalism.co.uk in 2003, writing about the digital publishing industry. She mostly learned on the job but was also sent on several short training courses about writing for the web and media law. She joined www.mediaguardian.co.uk in 2006.

- Jane Merrick became political editor of the *Independent on Sunday* in 2008, but she was interviewed for this book while she was a lobby correspondent for the *Press Association*. After completing a postgraduate training course in Leeds, she worked as a reporter for the *Mercury* news agency based in Liverpool and then for

sometimes offensive material" he finds in much of the media:

> None of these elements can be traced to the shortcomings of individuals. Newspaper proprietors may be, in the main, bullying reactionary bigots who force their editors to print politically biased material. But even if they were self-denying liberal paragons, it would still make sense for editors to act in the same way, because that is the best business model available to them. Again, editors and journalists may well be moral defectives with no sense of their responsibility to society and to the people upon whose lives they so pruriently report. But even if they were saintly ascetics, it would still make sense for them to publish the same sorts of material, because that is what best secures the competitive position of their newspapers. (Sparks, 1999: 59)

Little sense there of the flesh-and-blood journalists we will hear from in this book. Yet, if journalism matters – as is argued in this book – then the actions of individual journalists must matter too.

the *Press Association* both in the north and at Westminster. She moved from there to the *Daily Mail*, where her scoops included exposing an expenses scandal involving Tory MP Derek Conway: SNOUTS IN THE TROUGH (CONT.) and NICE WORK IF YOU CAN GET IT! (*Daily Mail*, January 29 and 30 2008).

- Kevin Peachey, as the consumer affairs correspondent of the *Nottingham Evening Post*, has won a range of awards for his campaigning journalism on behalf of the paper's readers, including Campaign of the Year in the 2005 Regional Press Awards. He trained to be a journalist on a postgraduate course in Preston.
- Abul Taher has been a reporter for the *Sunday Times* since 2004. After gaining an MA in Journalism Studies from Sheffield, he worked as news editor of *Eastern Eye* newspaper. He has also freelanced for the *Daily Mail*, the London *Evening Standard* and *Metro*.
- Deborah Wain works as a reporter for the *Doncaster Free Press* which, despite its title, is a paid-for weekly newspaper (plus website, of course). She went into journalism straight from school, taking NCTJ exams at a local college and starting out on the *Matlock Mercury*. After a stint on the *Derby Evening Telegraph* she went to university to study drama and fine arts, and she now combines journalism with script writing. In 2007 she was joint winner of the Paul Foot Award for investigative journalism.
- Martin Wainwright, northern editor of the *Guardian*, on which he has worked since 1976, having previously been on the *Evening Standard* and local newspapers in Bath and Bradford. He is a frequent broadcaster and is a regular contributor to the *Guardian's* online presence with written, audio and even video contributions.
- Brian Whittle started on the weekly *Harrogate Herald* at the age of 17 and went on to work

for the Bradford *Telegraph and Argus*, the *Northern Echo*, the *Sun*, the *Daily Sketch*, the *Sunday People*, the *National Enquirer* and the *Daily Star* before launching his successful *Cavendish Press* news agency in Manchester. He died in 2005.

Other journalists featured in this book include Trevor Gibbons, who works for BBC online as well as presenting a radio show and David Helliwell, who was interviewed while assistant editor of the *Yorkshire Evening Post* (later becoming editor of the *Gazette* in Blackpool).

Another presence felt throughout this book will be that of the author. As a journalist for upwards of three decades now, I have first-hand experience of working for a range of media large and small, mainstream and alternative. As a long-standing member of the National Union of Journalists, I have engaged with the ethics and social role of journalism as well as the industrial issues that impact upon the working conditions of journalists, including staffing and pay. As someone who now teaches on vocational courses accredited by the NCTJ along with the Broadcast Journalism Training Council (BJTC) and the Periodicals Training Council (PTC), I have first-hand experience of practical journalism training. And as someone who has tried my hand at research, I am aware of the insights that can be achieved by academic scholarship about, critical engagement with, and reflection upon the principles and practices of journalism.

> ❛ Journalism largely consists in saying "Lord Jones Dead" to people who never knew that Lord Jones was alive. ❜
>
> – GK Chesterton.

However, I am also aware of the gap of understanding that too often separates those who *study* media from those who *produce* media. In the UK, as Richard Keeble (2006: 260) notes with regret, "mutual suspicion persists between the press and academia. ... Scepticism about the value of theoretical studies for aspiring reporters remains widespread". Similarly, in the USA, Barbie Zelizer highlights this disconnection:

> As a former journalist who gradually made her way from wire-service reporting to the academy, I am continually wrestling with how best to approach journalism from a scholarly point of view. When I arrived at the university – "freshly expert" from the world of journalism – I felt like I'd entered a parallel universe. Nothing I had read as a graduate student reflected the working world I had just left. Partial, often uncompromisingly authoritative, and reflective far more of the academic environments in which they'd been tendered than the journalistic settings they described, these views failed to capture the life I knew. … My discomfort was shared by many other journalists I knew, who felt uneasy with the journalism scholarship that was fervently putting their world under a microscope. (Zelizer, 2004: 2–3)

Under a microscope is perhaps not the most comfortable place to be, which might explain why so many who earn their livings within the media in general and journalism in particular feel the need to either ignore or attack those looking down the lens. As David Walker (2000: 236–237) notes: "The academic literature of sociology, media studies or cognate disciplines nowadays goes almost entirely unread by journalists." Many journalists seem happy to cover stories about the work of academic researchers on a vast range of subjects, from the health effects of drinking coffee to the psychology of sexual attraction, but when journalism itself comes under scrutiny, such academic study is suddenly deemed to be a waste of time and money. "It's difficult to think of another field … in which practitioners believe that the study of what they do is irrelevant to their practice," observe Simon Frith and Peter Meech (2007: 141 and 144): "If journalists look at university journalism courses and find evidence that academics simply don't understand the realities of journalism, so academics look at journalists'

> ❛ All human life is there. ❜
> – old News of the World motto.

accounts of themselves and find evidence of a striking amount of myth-making."

This mutual suspicion was emphasised one day in the autumn of 2007 when I happened to read the academic journal *Journalism: Theory, Practice and Criticism* and the journalists' trade magazine *Press Gazette*. The former included a review in which a book about news was derided for lacking "academic rigour" because, "of the 480 endnote citations in the book, only six are either from academic books or from peer-reviewed articles"; the bulk of references were to newspaper articles which, sniffed the reviewer, were "pretty dicey" as a source (Berenger, 2007: 477). Contrast such fetishisation of peer-reviewed academia with the following letter that appeared in *Press Gazette*, prompted by an article concerning academic research into the small number of sources cited in most local newspaper stories: "Haven't the researchers got anything better to do? A few months in the newsroom of one of the titles they criticise might knock a bit of reality into them" (Thom, 2007). As it happens, the researchers in question were both former journalists, one of whom had spent years not months working in the very newsrooms under scrutiny; and even if they had not worked as journalists themselves, would it automatically render their research useless? Yes in the eyes of many, because the press "is fearful of being dissected", in the words of one national newspaper reporter (Journalism Training Forum, 2002: 46). Yet surely there are *some* insights to be gained from such dissection and from what has been described as "the melding of theory and practice in a judicious mix of skills and experience along with scholarly study" (Errigo and Franklin, 2004: 46)?

I believe there are, and I think that journalists and academics alike have something useful to contribute to the process of understanding; that is why I wrote this book. The aim is to help bridge the conceptual divide between those journalists (practitioners) who feel academics have little to teach them, and those academics whose focus on theory is in danger of denying journalists any degree of autonomy (or **agency**). This book makes explicit some of these different ways of exploring the principles and practices of journalism. In a dialogic approach, each chapter begins from a practitioner viewpoint but includes a parallel analysis from a more academic perspective. These two ways of seeing are not to be read in isolation, as each engages in dialogue with the other; they talk to each other, as do the best journalists and scholars.

The chapters can be read in a number of ways: by reading the practitioner section first, followed by the more theoretical section; by reversing the order; or by flitting between the two, following the bold words in the initial text to the relevant accompanying section – much in the way we follow hyperlinks on a website. As well as providing useful practice in the journalistic art of keeping an eye on a number of things at once, this should also mean that the book will repay repeated visits.

This book does not attempt to go into too many of the specifics of, for example, being a foreign correspondent, a war correspondent, a sub, a sports reporter, a showbiz diarist, a motoring correspondent, or most of the other specialisms that all have their own rules and folklore; nor does it cover the ins and outs of that peculiar phenomenon, the David Beckham correspondent. Call me old-fashioned, but I believe the fundamentals of journalism must be grasped before more specialised roles can be either accomplished or understood. The experience of Edward Behr rings a bell that echoes down the years. As a young reporter, Behr went to work for the *Reuters* agency in Paris:

> In London, Agence France-Presse (AFP) correspondents rewrote Reuters' copy, as fast as they could, and the finished product ended up as part of the AFP news service. In Paris we shamelessly rewrote Agence France-Presse copy, serving it up as Reuters' fare. All over the

world lesser news agencies were writing up *their* versions of Reuters' stories and serving them up as authentic Indian, Spanish, or Brazilian news agency stories. Somewhere, at the bottom of this inverted pyramid, someone was getting a story at first hand. But who was he, and how did he set about it? (Behr, 1992: 72)

He may not be a "he", of course, but it is this reporter – the reporter who goes out and gets the story – who will be the focus throughout this book. Virtually anyone can cut and paste text from the internet. Real reporting requires something more.

> ❝ By journalism is to be understood, I suppose, writing for pay about matters of which you are ignorant ❞
> – Leslie Stephen, father of Virginia Woolf.

Journalism education

This book is designed to help readers produce such reporting, with a necessary emphasis on the basics. Therefore, many of the practices discussed here will be those that developed within print journalism in general, and newspapers in particular, because they remain a solid foundation for a career in journalism that today embraces online, television, radio, magazine and other formats. The practical emphasis will be on the *core* journalistic skills that will be part of any good training course covering journalism in any – or all – media. Such skills cannot be allowed to diminish in importance, even if too many media organisations have in recent years made themselves dazed and confused by trying to leap aboard every passing technological bandwagon, even before they have a clue where it might take them. "There is no possibility of standing still," argues media commentator Roy Greenslade (2008), because "what is state-of-the-art today will be old hat by tomorrow."

This book goes beyond practical instruction to encourage understanding of, and critical reflection upon, our practice. It does so because skills alone are not enough. Media employers have been accused of wanting cheap young journalists to be schooled in the routines of work through "basic skills, relevant knowledge and an unquestioning attitude", unencumbered by engagement with ideas from critical theory (Curran, 2000: 42). This book is certainly aimed at supporting students and trainee journalists in the acquisition and application of reporting and writing skills to complement the other necessary elements of journalism training, such as shorthand, media law, and knowledge of public affairs. Yet, at the same time, it will introduce and engage with some of the more academic analysis that aids our understanding of how journalism works. To this end, the book is aimed at supporting *journalism studies* as well as *journalism training*. Taken together, the two elements can be said to constitute *journalism education* (Bromley, 1997: 339). By asking Why journalists do certain things – as well as the Who, What, Where, When and How – it seems to me that the study of journalism can offer insights that complement journalism training and encourage a questioning attitude and a more reflective practice.

Much of the material discussed in these pages may be seen as culturally and historically specific to the UK in the 21st century, but there will be many points of wider relevance. Each chapter will raise questions that could form the basis of individual reflection and/or group discussion. Each chapter also suggests further readings that, together with the references listed in the extensive bibliography, will provide a wealth of stimulating material to encourage further exploration of the issues discussed here.

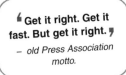

> ❛ Get it right. Get it fast. But get it right. ❜
> – old Press Association motto.

> ❛ Most of journalism, and all of the interesting part, is a disreputable, erratic business which, if properly conducted, serves a reputable end. ❜
> – Max Hastings.

Ethical journalism

There is a rapidly growing literature on the ethics of journalism, informed by ideas of right and wrong, good and bad (Harcup, 2002b and 2007), but you will not find a separate chapter on ethics in this book. That is not an oversight. It stems from a belief that a concern for ethical issues is not something to be compartmentalised, a curriculum item to be ticked off and conveniently forgotten. Because ethical issues have implications for *all* aspects of journalistic practice, questions about ethical issues will be raised at appropriate points throughout the text, just as ethical issues crop up throughout a journalist's working life – often when least expected.

Journalism is sometimes said to be a mirror reflecting society; on occasions, a distorting mirror. But journalism is not a simple *reflection* of everyday reality. As Walter Lippmann observed as long ago as 1922, reporting is not "the simple recovery of obvious facts", because facts "do not spontaneously take a shape in which they can be known. They must be given a shape by somebody" (quoted in McNair, 2000: 71). That's where journalists come in. Journalism is not simply fact-gathering. It involves dealing with sources, selecting information and opinion, and telling stories – all within the framework of the constraints, routines, principles and practices discussed in the following chapters.

▓ ▓ Summary ▓

Journalism is not simply another product but a process of communication, although not necessarily a one-way or linear process. Journalism is said to play a social role in informing society about itself, yet there is a gap of knowledge and understanding between vocational journalism training and academic journalism study. This book will describe the practices of practitioners while engaging with the principles that inform both practice and analysis. A number of theoretical models or concepts are introduced in this chapter.

▓ Questions

What role does journalism play in society?

Why are journalists apparently so mistrusted by the public?

What skills does a good journalist need?

Is a journalist a professional or a worker?

Why do media studies get such a bad press?

▓ ▓ Further reading ▓

One of the more thoughtful introductions to journalism from the perspective of a reflective practitioner is David Randall's (2007) *The Universal Journalist*, now in its third edition. Other useful introductions to journalism – these ones from journalists-turned-academics – are those by Keeble (2006) and Sissons (2006). The edited collection by Allan (2005) brings together a range of contemporary contributions to the state of journalism in the 21st century, while the Bromley and O'Malley (1997) reader includes more historical accounts that should help to stimulate students, producers and consumers of journalism alike. McQuail (2000) is a comprehensive and largely comprehensible introduction to media and mass communication theories, including a glossary of almost 100 key concepts. Franklin and others (2005) have produced an invaluable A to Z (well, A to Y, actually) of key concepts within journalism studies. Further suggestions will be made at the end of each chapter.

Sources for soundbites

Sean Dooley, quoted in Slattery, 2005; Delane, quoted in Wheen, 2002: xi; Chesterton, 1981: 246; Stephen, quoted in Glover, 1999: 290–291; Hastings, 2004.

two

constraints and influences on journalists

key terms

Advertising; Audience; Codes of conduct; Constraints; Free press; Legislation; Ownership; Propaganda; Pseudo-events; Public relations; Regulation; Routines; Self-censorship; Self-regulation; Social composition; Socialisation

It was a Saturday afternoon and Anna Politkovskaya had taken a break from her computer keyboard to go shopping for groceries. On her return she took a couple of bags up to her seventh-floor flat, then went back down to collect the others from her car. It was her final journey because, as the lift doors opened at the ground floor, Anna Politkovskaya was shot dead. She may not have been working on the afternoon of October 7 2006, but few doubt that it was her work that prompted someone to kill her – or to order her death. She was a journalist.

Anna Politkovskaya worked for the relatively small circulation Russian newspaper *Novaya Gazeta* and her reports about war, terrorism and their attendant human rights abuses had earned her countless death threats. Her journalism also won her praise from supporters of democracy and free speech around the world, although she was something of a marginal figure in her own country and was virtually never invited to appear on television, from which most Russians get their news (Parfitt, 2006). Her death was shocking yet in many ways unsurprising; she was one of an estimated 20 Russian journalists to have been killed or to have died in suspicious circumstances since 2000 (Osborn, 2007). And she was aware of the dangers of making powerful enemies by her courageous reporting, as her sister Elena Kudimova later recalled:

> Anna knew the risks only too well. We all begged her to stop. We begged. My parents. Her editors. Her children. But she always answered the same way: "How could I live with myself if I didn't write the truth?" (Quoted in Specter, 2007)

> ❝ How could I live with myself if I didn't write the truth? ❞
>
> – *Anna Politkovskaya.*

Constraints

Journalism is not produced in a vacuum. Journalists work within a range of constraints and influences; structural factors that affect their output (McQuail, 2000: 244). Media theorists argue that journalists "have to make decisions at the centre of a field of different constraints, demands or attempted uses of power or influence" (McQuail, 2000: 249). These range from legal constraints and regulatory codes of practice to the less visible influence of proprietors, organisational routines, market forces, cultural bias, patriotism, professional ethos, and a gender, racial or class imbalance in the workforce. Further constraints – time, sources, subjectivity, audience, style, advertisers – are addressed in David Randall's suggestion that every newspaper might consider publishing the following disclaimer:

> This paper, and the hundreds of thousands of words it contains, has been produced in about 15 hours by a group of fallible human beings, working out of cramped offices while trying to find out about what happened in the world from people who are sometimes reluctant to tell us and, at other times, positively obstructive. Its content has been determined by a series of subjective judgements made by reporters and executives, tempered by what they know to be the editor's, owner's and reader's prejudices. Some stories appear here without essential context as this would make them less dramatic or coherent and some of the language employed has been deliberately chosen for its emotional impact, rather than its accuracy. Some features are printed solely to attract certain advertisers. (Randall, 2000: 21)

Journalists work in a field of conflicting loyalties, all of which have the potential to influence their work. They may feel a sense of duty towards their audience, editors, advertisers, proprietors, the law, regulatory bodies, contacts, colleagues, fellow

The Moscow Union of Journalists immediately condemned the murder of Anna Politkovskaya as "a new attack on democracy, freedom of speech and openness in Russia", and Alexei Simonov of the Glasnost Defence Foundation warned: "The result of Anna's death is simple. Every journalist will now practise self-censorship: think twice, before you write" (Quoted in Parfitt, 2006). Such things do not happen only in faraway countries. Ten years earlier the *Sunday Independent's* crime reporter Veronica Guerin had been shot dead in Dublin; more recently, within the jurisdiction of the UK, *Sunday World* journalist Martin O'Hagan was shot dead outside his Lurgan home in 2001. And in 2007 the editor of the *Andersonstown News* in Belfast was the subject of a message from the "Red Hand Defenders" sent to Ulster Television, containing his name, address, car registration number, a threat to kill him – and a bullet (*Journalist*, 2007a).

Killings, attacks, and threats are the most brutal examples of **constraints** on the work of journalists and, as Simonov points out, their effects can be pervasive. For every journalist killed, and for every dozen threatened, there may be hundreds or even thousands of journalists who – consciously or otherwise – are more likely to stick to safer stories as a consequence. This is what is meant by the phrase self-censorship.

More visible forms of censorship and constraint include the prosecution and jailing of journalists, the deportation of troublesome foreign correspondents, the banning of particular outlets, police raids on TV studios and newspaper offices, and the confiscation of equipment. All these things still go on in various countries around the world towards the end of the first decade of the 21st century, as journalists and their fellow citizens insist on what the English poet John Milton demanded more than 350 years ago: "the liberty to know, to utter, and to argue freely according to conscience" (Milton, [1644] 2005: 101).

In fact, the world is becoming an increasingly dangerous place for journalists, and every year the

citizens, and to themselves and their families (Frost, 2000: 61–64; Harcup, 2002b: 103). Denis McQuail highlights "the tension arising from the following oppositions at the heart of media-making":

- constraint versus autonomy
- routine production versus creativity
- commerce versus art
- profit versus social purpose (McQuail, 2000: 246).

In Chapter 1 we heard the argument that a free press (social purpose) is impossible in a free market, because market forces (profit) work against the objective of supplying the public sphere with a reasoned discourse. But market forces are not the only pressures at work: "[The] relations between media organisations and their operating environment are governed not solely by naked market forces or political power but also by unwritten social and cultural guidelines" (McQuail, 2000: 249). Even when analysed solely in economic terms, it has been pointed out that although media organisations will "naturally gravitate towards oligopoly and monopoly market structures", if unchecked this process may have a negative impact on the journalistic product which could hit sales and advertising income (Doyle, 2002: 125–126).

The constraints and influences discussed in this chapter need to be understood not as totalising systems imposing on journalists certain ways of doing things; rather, they are a range of sometimes conflicting influences, some more powerful than others and some more powerful at certain times, with a *tendency* to influence journalists in certain ways. Constraints on journalists are subject to counter-pressures and can be negotiated and resisted as well as accepted.

Proprietors

Ultimately it is the owners who, "through their wealth, determine the style of journalism we get," argues Michael Foley (2000: 51). Media proprietors set the broad lines of policy for their organisations, and the combination of vertical and horizontal integration (synergy) may increase pressures on journalists to cross-promote other products or to keep their noses out of their company's business. The situation in public

International Federation of Journalists (IFJ) produces a grim list of every journalist and media worker killed in the course of their work. The highest number of deaths in a single year was 177 in 2006, but 2007 was almost as deadly with 172 journalists killed. Since the US-led invasion in 2003, Iraq has been the most dangerous country for journalists, with 65 deaths in 2007 alone – all but one of that year's victims being Iraqi rather than a foreign correspondent. Around the world it is journalists operating in their home countries who are most at risk, particularly when their country is politically unstable (IFJ, 2007 and 2008). Few, if any, journalists go out of their way to become targets for killers or kidnappers, yet no journalist can be certain as to whether or not a particular story might attract unwelcome attention.

The law

The UK boasts of having a "free press" yet journalists' activities are constrained by more than 60 pieces of legislation (see *Box 2.1*) and, at the last count, a further 251 statutory legal instruments (Petley, 1999: 143). Viewers of TV news are given a clue about such legal constraints whenever they see a reporter standing outside a court building, telling us about a brief hearing in which somebody has made their first appearance in the dock, ending with the stock phrase: "Reporting restrictions were not lifted." What restrictions? Those contained in the Magistrates' Courts Act 1980, limiting (with very few exceptions) reports of preliminary court hearings to ten points that should be committed to memory by every trainee journalist:

- The name of the court, and the names of the magistrates.
- Names, addresses, and occupations of the parties and witnesses, ages of the accused and witnesses.

service broadcasting is more complex than in commercial media, with bureaucratic and budgetary control rather than "naked market forces"; nonetheless, public broadcasters operate in an increasingly competitive environment and are certainly not immune from market pressures (McQuail, 2000: 259–261).

In their "propaganda model" of how (US) media operate, Edward Herman and Noam Chomsky identify media owners as the first of five filters through which the wealthy and powerful are able "to filter out the news fit to print, marginalise dissent, and allow the government and dominant private interests to get their messages across" (Herman and Chomsky, 1988: 166). The filters are:

- wealth and concentrated ownership of dominant media firms
- advertising
- reliance on information from the powerful
- punitive action (flak) against transgressors
- anti-communism (Herman and Chomsky, 1988: 166–176).

This model has been dismissed by critics as a conspiracy theory, as too mechanistic, as failing to take account of resistance. Herman counters:

> [The] filters work mainly by independent action of many individuals and organisations. ... [The] propaganda model describes a decentralised and non-conspiratorial market system of control and processing. ... We never claimed that the propaganda model explained everything or that it illustrated media omnipotence and complete effectiveness in manufacturing consent. (Herman, 2000: 102–103)

Media themselves tend not to draw attention to the potential impact of ownership structure on issues such as editorial content and diversity. Indeed, argues Robert McChesney (2000: 294–295): "The news media avoid any discussion of media structure, leaving analysis of media ownership and advertising to the business pages and the trade press, where they are covered as issues that concern investors, not workers, consumers, or citizens."

Routines

Journalists engage in routines, recurrent practices such as working to deadlines, keeping to word or time limits, ensuring that each edition or bulletin is

- The offence(s), or a summary of them, with which the accused is or are charged.
- Names of counsel and solicitors in the proceedings.
- Any decision of the court to commit the accused, or any of the accused, for trial, and any decision on the disposal of the case of any accused not committed.
- Where the court commits the accused for trial, the charge or charges, or a summary of them, on which he or she is committed and the court to which they are committed.
- Where proceedings are adjourned, the date and place to which they are adjourned.
- Any arrangements for bail, including conditions, but not reasons for opposing bail.
- Whether Legal Aid was granted.
- Any decision of the court to lift, or not to lift, these reporting restrictions (Welsh and Greenwood, 2001: 39).

Given the meagre fare offered above, it is remarkable how reports of high-profile court appearances, lasting only a few minutes, are embellished. Extra information often includes the accused's clothing, facial expression and tone of voice, or the presence of the victim's weeping relatives in the public gallery. Jane Colston points out that, because Section 8 of the Magistrates' Court Act 1980 applies only to reports of the proceedings themselves, it would not be a breach to say, for example, that large crowds assembled *outside* the courthouse (Colston, 2002: 149). But what about reporting that the accused was conveyed in an armed convoy, amid tight security, with police marksmen on the roof of the court building? Does that not imply that the defendant is extremely dangerous and, therefore, probably guilty?

Journalists frequently push against legal constraints, stretching the boundaries of what they might report – *a little*. They usually get away with it. Sometimes, however, there are spectacular pratfalls. When the *Sunday Mirror* published an emotional interview with a victim's father

exactly full, conforming to house style, making regular check calls to official sources, and covering diary jobs. There is an occupational pressure on journalists to "bow to the imperative of routine news copy production" (Manning, 2001: 52). Although the unexpected may happen at any time, crises develop patterns so that, for journalists, even "the unexpected becomes the predictable" (Curran and Seaton, 1997: 276). Research has consistently found that "content is systematically and distinctively influenced by organisational routines, practices and goals rather than either personal or ideological factors" (McQuail, 2000: 244–245).

Advertisers

The interests of advertising can influence journalistic product, although such influence does not *normally* take the form of advertisers threatening to take their money elsewhere unless they receive favourable editorial coverage. Direct intervention by advertisers does happen occasionally but much less often than many people would think. A far more prevalent influence is that the content patterns and style of media are matched to the consumption patterns of target audiences (McQuail, 2000: 261). Commercial media operate in a "dual product market" in which the media product sells *itself* to consumers and at the same time sells its *audience* to advertisers (Sparks, 1999: 53; Doyle, 2002: 12). Mass circulation newspapers demand a mass readership for mass advertising, while the "quality" press depend on delivering smaller target audiences for more niche advertising markets. The quest for these different audiences directly affects the journalism offered in different titles, as Colin Sparks notes:

> The popular press are under market pressure to try to reach the widest possible audiences, and thus must prioritise the kinds of material that will sell vast quantities. Quality newspapers are much less interested in maximising circulation, and are concerned to prioritise the kinds of material that will sell to particular kinds of people. ... The products that serve the richest audience are approximations to the newspaper of democratic mythology. The others are quite different commodities. (Sparks, 1999: 53 and 59)

while the jury in a high-profile assault trial was still considering its verdicts, the case was immediately halted. The paper was fined £75,000 for contempt of court and ordered to pay costs of £130,000. Two of the newspaper's lawyers were dismissed and the editor resigned (Hall, 2002; *Media Lawyer*, 2002: 19–20). Not a good day at the office. Journalists sometimes challenge the courts' interpretation of the law in a more formal manner. The journalists' trade rag *Press Gazette* frequently cites cases of reporters persuading courts to lift orders banning publication of defendants' identities and other information that, arguably, should be in the public domain (*Press Gazette*, 2000a and 2002).

Laws that act as a constraint on journalists in England and Wales are listed in *Box 2.1*. The law in Northern Ireland is broadly similar to that in England and Wales, but Scotland has its own legal system (see Bonnington et al., 2000, as recommended by Welsh and Greenwood, 2001: 435).

Not even included in *Box 2.1* is breach of confidence, which has been described by lawyer Joanna Ludlam as "one of the most significant fetters on freedom of expression in the media" (Ludlam, 2002: 89). Journalists have come up against this with increasing frequency in recent years, as governments, employers and celebrities alike have obtained injunctions preventing the media reporting "confidential" information supplied by spies, employees, and even spouses or ex-lovers (Welsh and Greenwood, 2001: 261–279 and 387–410; Grundberg, 2002: 114–130; Ludlam, 2002: 89–103). The use of injunctions citing breach of confidence – by those who can afford to go to court – has drawn public attention to the issue of privacy. Before the Human Rights Act 1998 (which became law in October 2000) there was no specific legal right to privacy in the UK. The Act incorporates the European Convention on Human Rights, Article 8 of which gives everyone "the right to respect for his private and family life, his home and his correspondence". But actions under Article 8 are weighed by the courts against the journalist's defence, enshrined in Article 10, that "everyone has the right

Public relations

At the heart of public relations, according to Daniel Boorstin, is the "pseudo-event", which he defined in the early 1960s as something planned rather than spontaneous, arranged for the convenience of the media, with an ambiguous relation to reality (Boorstin, 1963: 22–23). For Boorstin, the pseudo-event confuses the roles of actor and audience, object and subject. For example, a politician can *compose* a news story by "releasing" a speech to the media, while a journalist can *generate* an event by asking an inflammatory question (Boorstin, 1963: 40).

Since Boorstin described the rise of the pseudo-event, "public relations staffs have expanded while journalists have been shrinking, creating news media's greater editorial reliance on press officers" (Franklin, 1997: 19). Organisations ranging from local charities to multinational corporations now employ press officers who supply journalists with a stream of potential stories, comments and fillers. This process has been described as an "information subsidy" through which media organisations receive a flow of free material that will "favour those, notably business and government, best able to produce strong and effective PR material" (Lewis et al., 2008a: 2 and 18).

Press officers do not just supply information, they also play a role in controlling access. Writing in the context of music journalism, Eamonn Forde argues that the industry press officer has become increasingly powerful as a "buffer zone", gatekeeping access to artists and screening journalists along the lines of "the Hollywood approach to press management" (Forde, 2001: 36–38). For Bob Franklin, the growing power and journalistic reliance on press officers comes at a price because "they are not detached observers and reporters of the world, but hired prize fighters, advocates and defenders of whichever sectional interest employs them" (Franklin, 1997: 20).

Such "hired prize fighters" in the political arena, such as Sir Bernard Ingham and Alastair Campbell, have been key to the process described as "the packaging of politics" (Franklin, 1994: 226). Former BBC lobby correspondent Nick Jones is uncomfortable with political reporting based on unattributable conversations with politicians or advisers, and he has been ridiculed by Campbell himself as being "obsessed with spin" (Gopsill, 2001). But David Walker is critical of the self-conception of Jones and

Box 2.1

Legislation that constrains journalists

These pieces of legislation regulate or restrict the ways in which journalists in England and Wales may *gather* information, what information they may have *access* to, and/or what may be *published*.

Access to Justice Act 1999
Administration of Justice Act 1960
Adoption and Children Act 2002
Anti-Terrorism, Crime and Security
  Act 2001
Broadcasting Act 1990
Broadcasting Act 1996
Children Act 1989
Children and Young Persons Act 1933`
Communication Act 2003
Contempt of Court Act 1981
Copyright, Designs and Patents Act 1988
Courts Act 2003
Crime and Disorder Act 1998
Crime (Sentences) Act 1997
Criminal Justice Act 1925
Criminal Justice Act 1987
Criminal Justice Act 1991
Criminal Justice Act 2003
Criminal Justice and Public Order
  Act 1994
Criminal Procedure and Investigations
  Act 1996
Data Protection Act 1998
Defamation Act 1952
Defamation Act 1996
Disability Discrimination Act 1995
Domestic and Appellate Proceedings (Restriction
  of Publicity) Act 1968
Employment Tribunals Act 1996
Family Law Act 1986
Financial Services and Markets Act 2000
Freedom of Information Act 2000
Human Rights Act 1998
Interception of Communications Act 1985
Judicial Proceedings (Regulation of Reports)
  Act 1926
Libel Act 1843

Local Government (Access to Information)
  Act 1985
Local Government Act 2000
Magistrates' Courts Act 1980
Obscene Publications Act 1959
Obscene Publications Act 1964
Official Secrets Act 1911
Official Secrets Act 1989
Planning (Hazardous Substances)
  Act 1990
Planning (Listed Buildings and Conservation
  Areas) Act 1990
Police Act 1997
Police and Criminal Evidence Act 1984
Police and Criminal Evidence Act 2002
Political Parties, Elections and Referendums Act
  2000
Proceeds of Crime Act 2002
Protection from Harassment Act 1997
Public Bodies (Admission to Meetings) Act 1960
Public Order Act 1986
Racial and Religious Hatred Act 2006
Regulation of Investigatory Powers Act 2000
Rehabilitation of Offenders Act 1974
Representation of the People Act 1983
Representation of the People Act 2000
Serious Organised Crime and Police Act 2005
Sexual Offences (Amendment) Act 1976
Sexual Offences (Amendment) Act 1992
Sexual Offences Act 2003
Terrorism Act 2000
Terrorism Act 2006
Trade Union Reform and Employment Rights Act
  1993
Treason Felony Act 1848
Wireless Telegraphy Act 1949
Youth Justice and Criminal Evidence
  Act 1999

Sources: Crone, 2002; Welsh and Greenwood, 2003; Welsh and Greenwood, 2001; Welsh et al., 2007; Addicott, 2002; plus *Media Lawyer*, No 43, Jan/Feb 2003, No 37, Jan/Feb 2002 and No 33, May/June 2001

to freedom of expression" (Welsh and Greenwood, 2001: 371). Many "victims" of the redtop tabloids now prefer to rush straight to the courts rather than trust the more sedate inquiries of the Press Complaints Commission (see below).

Apart from breach of confidence, the other main legal weapon in the hands of those with money is the law of libel. Ever-present during a journalist's working life is the possibility of being sued for libel because of defaming somebody. The risk is lower than it might be because many potential litigants are put off by the horrendous costs involved, but it would be easier to avoid if there were a hard-and-fast rule of what defamation is. According to the courts, a statement is defamatory if it tends to expose someone to hatred, ridicule or contempt; if it causes someone to be shunned or avoided; if it causes someone to be lowered in the estimation of other people; if it disparages someone in their business or profession. The statement may not actually *have* such effects, only a tendency towards them in the eyes of a "reasonable man" (Welsh and Greenwood, 2001: 186).

Considering the above definition, much of the work of journalists could be considered as defamatory were it not for the defences offered in law. The main ones are:

> ' A solicitor's letter produces a spectacular effect in a newspaper office – editors put work aside, executives are summoned, anxious conferences convened. '
> – Alan Watkins.

- justification (proving that the report is true)
- fair comment (an honest opinion, based on facts, without malice)
- privilege (the right to fairly report parliament, council meetings, court cases and certain other proceedings affording either absolute or qualified privilege) (Welsh and Greenwood, 2001: 211–239).

Despite these defences, the libel courts are notoriously dangerous ground for journalists, and many news organisations err on the side of caution, settling out of court rather than risking

other Westminster journalists: "They believe there is a single truth within and about politics. Battles over it form the staple of political reporting. Victory in this struggle for the single truth gives them their occupational justification" (Walker, 2002: 103). Walker goes on to claim that this "anti-ideological" ideology of political reporters – that is, the idea that political reporting is a battle for truth between journalists and spin doctors – takes no account of the possibility that media organisations might also be political players in their own right: "[T]the power held by journalists and the media organisations for which they work is unperceived or assumed away" (Walker, 2002: 108).

Social environment

New recruits to journalism go through a process of "assimilation of newsroom mythology and socialisation", and those who survive learn "a way of doing things" that results in "a conformity of production and selection" (Harrison, 2000: 112–113). This professionalism "can only be recognised by fellow professionals" (McQuail, 2000: 257). Robert McChesney argues that most journalists are socialised into internalising their role as "stenographers for official sources", with the result that: "When a journalist steps outside this range of official debate to provide alternative perspectives, or to raise issues those in power prefer not to discuss, *this is no longer professional*" (McChesney, 2002: 17, my emphasis).

However, the extent to which journalism is constrained in this way is questioned by Greg McLaughlin's study of reporting the Kosovo conflict. He found that, while many reporters may have internalised Nato's frame of reference, this did not entirely determine how stories were presented, and "it would be wrong to dismiss as irrelevant the resistance of some journalists to Nato spin control" (McLaughlin, 2002a: 258). Paul Manning similarly warns of downplaying agency:

> [There] is a danger that in envisaging the practice of news journalism as a production process, shaped by

huge damages. The net result is what has been referred to as a "chilling" effect, whereby journalists may avoid certain subjects or litigious individuals (Dodson, 2001; Welsh and Greenwood, 2001: 183). Publisher and pensions thief Robert Maxwell was one of the quickest on the draw when it came to issuing writs against anyone probing his business affairs, and during his lifetime he succeeded in preventing most – but not all – journalists from exposing his dubious methods (Spark, 1999: 147). Other powerful figures to make use of the law of libel against inquisitive journalists, only to end up being discredited, were Conservative politicians Jeffrey Archer, Jonathan Aitken and Neil Hamilton (Kelso, 2001). Journalists cannot guarantee they will never be dragged through the courts by the rich and powerful, but Francis Wheen suggests a simple way of reducing the risk when he says: "I don't like to go into print without checking my facts" (Wheen, 2002: xi). That's a pretty sound starting point for any journalist. Furthermore, an important House of Lords ruling has now given journalists a series of pointers – known as the "Reynolds defence" – to help test if a potentially defamatory story could be defended as being in the public interest. The Reynolds defence is discussed further in Chapter 6.

Journalists sometimes find themselves in court not because somebody wants to extract money or an apology, but because somebody wants to know the identity of a confidential source of information. That's what happened to Bill Goodwin after he took a phone call just three months into his first job as a trainee reporter with *The Engineer* magazine. A source told him about a company in financial difficulties. He called the firm for a response and the reply was a faxed

> ❛ If it has fallen to my destiny to start a fight to cut out the cancer of bent and twisted journalism in our country with the simple sword of truth and the trusty shield of British fair play, so be it. ❜
>
> – Jonathan Aitken, launching his ill-fated libel action.

bureaucratic routines and organisational imperatives, we underestimate the extent to which particular journalists *do* make a difference. (Manning, 2001: 53, emphasis in original)

If agency is a crucial consideration when discussing constraints, so too is the extent to which the social composition of the workforce influences journalistic practice. Anne Perkins asserts that, because relatively few women rise to the most senior editorial positions, "a distorted image of women's lives protrudes from the newsstands" (Perkins, 2001). But this assumption is challenged by Karen Ross, who studied women journalists in the UK:

> Gender *alone* will not make a difference in changing the culture of newsrooms or in the type of news produced, inasmuch as a journalist's sex is no guarantee that she or he will either embrace sentiments that privilege equality or hold specific values and beliefs that promote a more equitable and non-oppressive practice. (Ross, 2001: 542, my emphasis)

Similarly, it may indeed be shameful that journalists in the UK – rather like journalism professors – are overwhelmingly white, but can we assume that journalistic practice would be significantly altered merely by the presence of more black journalists? Or more journalists from working-class backgrounds? Research is inconclusive but some studies suggest that journalists owe more of their relevant attitudes and tendencies to "socialisation from the immediate work environment" than to their personal or social backgrounds (McQuail, 2000: 267–269).

Nick Stevenson sounds a cautionary note about the tendency of media theorists to "overstate the incorporating power of ideology" (Stevenson, 2002: 46). Questioning assumptions that the social background of journalists leads automatically to a middle-class perspective in their output, he argues not that class composition has *no* influence, but that there are ideological divisions and conflicts *within* classes, limiting the degree of "ideological closure" achieved by the structural dominance of journalism by white middle-class graduates (Stevenson, 2002: 33).

The prevailing atmosphere in newsrooms, the extent to which dissent can survive and journalists

injunction ordering the magazine not to publish anything about the company. Two days later he was in court facing an order to disclose the identity of his source or be sent to prison (Goodwin, 1996).

Goodwin refused, citing the principle enshrined in the NUJ code of conduct that a journalist should protect a confidential source of information. Over the following seven years the case went before a succession of courts before he won at the European Court of Human Rights, which ruled in 1996 that an order to disclose a source could not be compatible with Article 10 of the European Convention on Human Rights unless there was an overriding requirement in the public interest (Welsh and Greenwood, 2001: 286).

Similarly, freelance journalist Robin Ackroyd fought a long and ultimately successful battle to defend the source of his 1999 *Daily Mirror* story about the treatment of Moors murderer Ian Brady in Ashworth high-security hospital. The Mersey Care NHS Trust, which runs the hospital, launched legal proceedings to force him to identify his source. During eight years of legal pressure he stood by the NUJ code of conduct and, with backing from his union, defended the principle of protecting confidential sources during a series of court cases and appeals. High Court judge Mr Justice Tugendhat ruled in Ackroyd's favour, declaring that the journalist had "a record of investigative journalism which has been authoritatively recognised, so that it would not be in the public interest that his sources should be discouraged from speaking to him where it is appropriate that they do so" (quoted in Gopsill and Neale, 2007: 280–282). Even then, the case was not over until the House of Lords refused the Mersey Care NHS Trust's application for a third appeal in 2007. Ackroyd, who had spent almost a third of his career fighting the case, said afterwards:

> ❝ If one journalist betrays a source, others will be less willing to come forward in the future. ❞
> – *Bill Goodwin.*

have ideological room to breathe, cannot be divorced from the existence or otherwise of an effective collective forum, argues Paul Foot in this chapter. His point is echoed by McChesney, who points out that rocking the boat can be a risky business for journalists. Like Foot, he advocates "strong, progressive unions" as a bulwark to defend journalistic integrity against commercial pressures (McChesney, 2000: 61 and 301–304).

It's had a huge impact on my work. … But journalists ultimately, if they are faced with a position like this, have to make a stand as an individual and I was prepared to do that. You have to be quite strong and prepared to do your utmost to protect your sources, in terms of both saying it and also thinking about how you physically do it. (Quoted in Journalist, 2007b)

There is always a new case just around the corner, it seems. In 2008 freelance journalist Shiv Malik faced police demands under the Terrorism Act 2000 that he hand over notes he had gathered while researching a book on Islamic radicals. Malik resisted, explaining that "protection of sources is a totem of all investigative journalism and almost none of my work to date has been possible without the promise of confidentiality" (Malik, 2008).

Such cases will continue to be fought on their individual merits as journalists resist attempts to identify confidential sources and/or to seize notes or pictures. Meanwhile, the safest way for journalists to be given leaked information probably remains the unmarked photocopy in a plain brown envelope delivered anonymously in the dead of night by somebody wearing gloves on their hands and a scarf over their face; a journalist cannot be forced to reveal the identity of a source they do not know.

Before we leave the powers of the state, let us pause and consider the Defence, Press and Broadcasting Advisory Committee. That's where Whitehall mandarins meet representatives of the UK media and agree to restrain coverage of sensitive military or security issues. From time to time members of the committee will stir from their Earl Grey tea and cucumber sandwiches to issue a Defence Advisory (DA) notice or more commonly to write a polite letter to editors, requesting that some matter be ignored or played down. In these days of so-called open government, the committee

has its own website which includes minutes of its meetings: www.dnotice.org.uk. The whole thing is entirely voluntary on the part of the media, operating as "an unofficial system of censorship involving public officials and senior media executives" (Curran and Seaton, 1997: 367). DA notices are, in effect, a system of *self-censorship* and are not to be confused with *self-regulation*, of which more below.

Regulation and self-regulation

Journalism on television and radio in the UK is subject to what is known as statutory regulation, whereby misdemeanours can be punished with fines and even the withdrawal of licences. Lindsay Eastwood noticed the difference in regulatory regimes as soon as she left newspapers for television:

> TV is much stricter on things like intrusion, and taste and decency. You can't have people saying "God" or "Jesus Christ" in a voxpop, because if one person complains and it's upheld, it counts. They are quite careful at *Calendar* not to upset people, whereas newspapers are not bothered so much about flak. I think the difference is you can lose your licence with TV. They can shut you down, so there's a bit more at stake really.

In contrast to the broadcast system of fines being imposed and licences being revoked, print and online journalism has a system of self-regulation. The Press Complaints Commission (PCC) was set up in 1991 by the newspaper industry itself to ward off the threat of privacy laws or broadcast-style statutory regulation. It covers newspapers, magazines and, since 2007, websites associated with newspapers and magazines – including audio and visual material. A voluntary arrangement with no powers to punish those who transgress its code of practice, the PCC operates by a system of customer

> ❝ Forty years experience of "press self-regulation" demonstrates only that the very concept is an oxymoron. ❞
> – Geoffrey Robertson QC.

complaints. But only a tiny proportion of such complaints are ever adjudicated. Of the 4,340 received in 2007 just 16 were upheld (PCC, 2008). Rather than being the industry's police-man, the PCC is perhaps more like a police community support officer – they look like the police from a distance yet they have little clout when challenged. With the PCC, comments journalist Catherine Bennett, "we get all the benefits of a code of practice, with none of the burden of enforcement" (Bennett, 2001).

> *❛ I did not come all this way not to interfere. ❜*
> *– Rupert Murdoch.*

Despite its relative toothlessness, the PCC does act as some kind of constraint on the activities of journalists. *Sun* editor Rebekah Wade told a committee of MPs in 2003 that the PCC had "changed the culture in every newsroom in the land" (quoted in Rose, 2003). Editors have no desire to be embarrassed by PCC rulings – which they agree to publish – and will not look favourably on journalists who attract too many complaints. Print journalists as a whole, and those on the redtops in particular, also know that a recurrence of press "excesses", such as the perceived harassment of Princess Diana, may result in more stringent state regulation. Tony Blair raised such a possibility in a speech about the "feral" press, but significantly he did so only when he was already on his way out of Downing Street, leaving incoming Prime Minister Gordon Brown to declare:

[A] free press is the hallmark of our democracy. There is no case for statutory regulation of the press. Self-regulation of the press should be maintained and it is for the publishers themselves to demonstrate by their decisions that they can sustain and bolster public confidence in the way information is gathered and used. (Quoted in Rose et al., 2007)

So press self-regulation in the UK looks to be safe – for now.

Media owners

As with self-regulation, so with concentration of ownership: big media **proprietors** are used to getting their own way. That can act as a further constraint on the journalists they employ, critics argue. That helps explain why staff on the *Wall Street Journal* were less than keen on their title being taken over by Rupert Murdoch in 2007; they were nervous about what they had heard about his empire. About Sam Kiley, for example, who spent 11 years as a foreign correspondent on Murdoch's *Times* before resigning in 2001, exasperated by reports on the Middle East conflict being changed in line with the perceived views of the owner:

Murdoch's executives were so scared of irritating him that, when I pulled off a little scoop by tracking, inter-viewing and photographing the unit in the Israeli army which killed Mohammed al-Durrah, the 12-year-old boy whose death was captured on film and became the iconic image of the conflict, I was asked to file the piece "without mentioning the dead kid". After that conver-sation, I was left wordless, so I quit. (Kiley, 2001)

Another journalist who complained of constraints on the same newspaper was former East Asia editor Jonathan Mirsky. He says his coverage was hampered by the *Times*' desire to stay in tune with Rupert Murdoch's business interests in China, so everything was done to avoid upsetting the Chinese authorities:

I saw the paper change from one keenly interested in reporting and analysing China to one so apprehensive that the editor spiked a piece by me on cannibalism during the Cultural Revolution … because he was having lunch that day at China's London embassy. … Of course, the Murdochs do not need to tell their editors what to write about China on every issue; *they just know*. (Mirsky, 2001, my emphasis)

Andrew Neil, former editor of the *Sunday Times*, describes Murdoch's normal methods of control as rather more subtle, beginning with choosing editors "who are generally on the same wavelength as him" (quoted in Sanders, 2003:

134). He can certainly pick them, as demonstrated by the way the editorial line of all 175 Murdoch-owned newspapers on three continents just happened to agree with his own pro-war stance leading up to the 2003 conflict in Iraq (Greenslade, 2003a).

Murdoch has been an easy target for those who claim media owners wield too much power. But it is not only journalists taking the Murdoch shilling who feel proprietorial constraints, explicit or implicit. David Walker confesses:

> ❝ Editors hire in their own image. ❞
> – Gary Younge.

> At the *Independent* I spilled much ink in editorials savaging his [Murdoch's] power and pricing strategy. But such criticism is vitiated by a lack of honesty about one's own organisation. How many *Independent* journalists, myself included, ever wrote in their own newspaper about the effects of ownership by Mirror Group Newspapers? (Walker, 2000: 241)

The *Express* is another title that has published stories in harmony with the commercial interests of its proprietor. Owner Richard Desmond has also been accused of interfering in editorial matters by urging the inclusion of coverage critical of asylum seekers, prompting one of his business correspondents to issue a public attack on "the continual interference of the proprietor in allegedly objective reporting" (quoted in Day, 2001).

There is nothing new in media owners being accused of using *their* journalists to pursue certain agendas. It was in 1931 that Conservative party leader Stanley Baldwin launched his famous attack on press barons Beaverbrook and Rothermere, owners of the then hugely influential *Daily Express* and *Daily Mail* respectively:

> The newspapers attacking me are not newspapers in the ordinary sense. They are engines of propaganda for the constantly changing policies, desires, personal wishes, personal dislikes of two men. What are their methods? Their methods are direct falsehood, misrepresentations, half-truths, the alteration of the speaker's meaning by publishing a sentence apart from the context. … What

the proprietorship of these papers is aiming at is power, and power without responsibility – the prerogative of the harlot throughout the ages. (Quoted in Griffiths, 2006: 251–252)

In 1949 Lord Beaverbrook told the Royal Commission on the Press that he ran the *Daily Express* "merely for the purpose of making propaganda and with no other motive", and in the 1980s Robert Maxwell described the *Daily Mirror* as his personal "megaphone" (Curran and Seaton, 1997: 48 and 76).

Former *Mirror* journalist Paul Foot describes such proprietorial influence on journalism as "absolutely insufferable". Yet he did suffer it in the shape of Maxwell, and he managed to produce much challenging journalism in spite of it. Foot recalls how he pinned up a list of Maxwell's business friends and, whenever he was investigating one of them, made sure he had the story copper-bottomed and "legalled" (checked by lawyers) before the subject would be approached for a comment:

> The minute you put it to him – "is this true?" – he rings Maxwell. That happened on several occasions. So you have to have the story sewn up and prepared for when Maxwell says: "Are you sure this is right?" *But we got most of the stuff published.*

A survey in the USA found that almost one-third of local journalists admitted to softening the tone of a news story in line with their employer's interests, and one in five reporters had been criticised by bosses for stories damaging to their company's financial interests (Pew Research Centre, 2000). In Italy, an employee of Silvio Berlusconi described the atmosphere when the owner was also the country's Prime Minister: "We never hear from him directly, editors don't cite his instructions. But there is a climate of self-censorship. We know we can only go so far. Lines exist and we do not cross them." (Quoted in Carroll, 2002.)

But for most journalists in most newsrooms, most of the time, proprietorial interference probably means little more than an editor's instruction to make sure you don't crop the owner's wife off a photograph or there'll be hell to pay. Many journalists go about their work without giving the wishes of the owner a second thought. Yet proprietors have influence not just by direct intervention or by establishing lines that will not be crossed. They set the tone, they decide which markets to target, they control editorial budgets, and they hire and fire the editors who are their representatives on Earth.

There are some alternative models of media ownership. The publicly owned BBC enshrines the Reithian principles of public service broadcasting (Briggs and Burke, 2002: 160–163); the *Guardian* is owned by the Scott Trust, with a strict separation between financial and editorial matters (Franklin, 1997: 98); and smaller-scale media may be run by *ad-hoc* groups, community organisations or workers' co-operatives (Harcup, 1994 and 2005). Journalists working for such media may escape the owner wishing to use them as a personal megaphone, but they cannot avoid most of the other constraints discussed in this chapter.

Routines

Deadlines, **routines** and the whims of the newsdesk tend to be the most prevalent constraints on journalists. Routines may change as the technology changes, but there are still routines even if online journalism means that a story is never *finished* these days (was it ever really finished even in the old days?). The constant pressure to meet deadlines, including the instant deadlines of online and rolling broadcast news, teaches journalists that an average story delivered on time is of more use than a perfect story that arrives late. Not that the deadline is always bad news. Many journalists welcome deadlines for providing the focus, and the adrenalin rush, necessary to get the job done.

Although the latest technology could mean that newspaper deadlines become later, in practice they have moved forward to cope with smaller staff numbers and the printing of fatter papers with ever more bulky supplements. Time is at

even more of a premium on television, as Lindsay Eastwood discovered when she switched from newspapers to become a TV reporter:

> It takes so long to do everything. You've got to set up the story and organise camera crews, and it takes an hour to film a minute's worth of stuff. There's just so much faffing about and not actually doing the journalism, which I find very frustrating. You're still getting a shot of the house while all the newspaper reporters are knocking on the doors of neighbours, and I'm saying to the cameraman, "Come *on*". Then you've got to get back to the studio to cut it before deadline.

Faced with a constant shortage of time, journalists make many decisions instantly, almost subliminally. News editor David Helliwell says most of the numerous press releases arriving on a newsdesk will receive just one or two seconds' attention before a journalist decides if it might make something. Spending five minutes pondering each one in detail would quickly bring the routines of the newsroom grinding to a halt.

Time constraints can result in inaccurate journalism, believes Martin Wainwright of the *Guardian*:

> You're doing stuff so quickly you don't have time to be absolutely sure about things, and more importantly the people you're talking to don't. So they will say things they believe to be true, about a developing situation, which then turn out not to be. It happened in the [Selby] rail crash when for nearly a week everybody said 13 people had been killed. The police said 13 people had been killed. In fact it now turns out to be 10. A central fact of the whole story was wrong for nearly a week, and somebody coming across a newspaper from that week and not checking a week later will not get the truth.

Lack of time may also lead to journalists falling short of professional standards, as Michael Foley notes: "Much that passes for unethical behaviour takes place because too few journalists are taking too many decisions quickly and without time to reflect. This is because proprietors have not invested in journalism" (Foley, 2000: 49–50). Maybe. But the UK national paper enjoying some of the heaviest editorial investment is the *Daily Mail*, hardly a stranger to complaints of unethical behaviour or inaccurate reporting.

Even on the squeaky-clean *Guardian*, reporters can be constrained by being sent out when somebody else has apparently decided in advance what the story is. Wainwright again:

> During the foot and mouth crisis the newsdesk said to me: "Can you go shopping and see the meat panic? And we do *want* a meat panic." You're always coming up against that kind of pressure. It's a really pernicious aspect of modern journalism, that they don't trust people like myself who are here. They think they know what the story is because they've read it in the *Daily Mail* or heard it on the *Today* programme.

He adds that reporters sometimes feel pressure to deliver the goods simply because the routines of production planning mean that a large space has been allocated in expectation of a major story:

> A colleague had it with drug dealers. The story collapsed but they [still] wanted a big thing about drug dealers. The way they'd designed it and thought about it, it had to be *big*. Lots of journalists I know complain about this and say, "they're not really interested in how *I* am seeing this".

A similar point is made in a telling anecdote from John Kampfner, who recalls a Conservative party meeting he covered for the *Financial Times* during which two politicians outlined their differing views on the UK's relationship with Europe:

> Both had said as much many times before, and I wrote a quiet piece. That evening, the newsdesk at the *FT*, not one usually to follow others' stories, politely enquired if I had been at the same event as my colleagues. They pointed out the screaming "Tories in meltdown" headlines. Somewhat chastened, I ratcheted up my story so as not to feel exposed. I should not have done. It was a non-story. (Kampfner, 2007)

It is not unknown for a newsdesk to put pressure on a reporter to set aside personal or ethical considerations in the pursuit of a story. Even in organisations publicly committed to following ethical codes of practice, there may be an atmosphere of *if you haven't got the story, don't bother coming back*. For example, journalists returning empty handed from "death knocks" – calls on the recently bereaved to pick up quotes and pictures – may be ridiculed for being insufficiently aggressive. A sports reporter on the *Stoke Sentinel* lost his job after refusing to seek an interview with one of his contacts whose son had died (Morgan, 1999).

Audience

Despite the fact that we now have lists of Most Read stories online, and that some people choose to post reactions to Your Comments sections, journalists still have little direct experience of the ways in which audiences consume their work. BBC foreign correspondent David Shukman was invited to join a group of postal workers viewing two of his TV news reports about Angola. The stories – one about landmines and the other about corruption – were understood by the viewers on one level, but only as more or less random happenings in a distant land. "I never know which country is which," said one of the group. Another added: "It's in one ear and out the other" (Shukman, 2000). In discussion, they were asked if they felt indirectly involved in the Angolan conflict; for example, by buying petrol or diamonds that originated there, thereby aiding one side or the other. Suddenly they engaged with the news stories on a different, more personal level, as Shukman notes:

> [It] had taken talk of the possible connections with Britain to raise real concern. ... The discussion had come alive. These were people who could follow the argument and did not want to be short-changed or patronised. ... For this group, foreign news, not always the favourite of the newsrooms, was becoming stimulating. (Shukman, 2000)

His experience is interesting, given the tendency of some journalists to dismiss the audience as stupid (McQuail, 2000: 263). In a survey of US journalists, three-quarters of broadcast reporters said that newsworthy stories were sometimes or often ignored because they were regarded as too complicated for the average person, a factor cited by just under half the print journalists. Almost eight in ten said they at least sometimes ignored stories that the audience might regard as "important but dull" (Pew Research Centre, 2000). In the UK, broadcast journalists report a large turn-off factor during coverage of general elections and newspaper editors complain that sales go down whenever they put election news on their front page. "People are just not interested," said David Yelland of the *Sun* (quoted in Tomlin and Morgan, 2001).

Every now and then journalists will receive injunctions from on high to produce more aspirational human interest stories, based on the findings of surveys or focus groups of the existing or potential audience. At the same time as (supposedly) attracting new readers, such lifestyle copy – entertainment, holidays, health, consumer stories and so on – has been used to attract additional **advertisers**.

Journalists are typically thought of as the active ones in the relationship with their audience, but audiences are not always passive. Take the reaction to the *Sun* front page of April 19 1989, concerning the Hillsborough football disaster in which 95 Liverpool fans died. Under the banner headline THE TRUTH, the paper reported anonymous police officers accusing "drunken Liverpool fans" of robbing the dead and attacking rescue workers. The reaction on Merseyside was based on the fact that so many people knew – via family, friends or personal experience – a different version of "the truth". Anger erupted on a *Radio Merseyside* phone-in, local newsagents put the paper under the counter or refused to stock it at all, and a TV news crew turned up at a shopping precinct just in time to film people burning copies of the

offending *Sun* (Chippindale and Horrie, 1992: 286–289; Pilger, 1998: 445–448). There was nothing passive about this particular audience:

> All over the city copies of the paper were being ripped up, trampled and spat upon. People carrying it in the street found it snatched out of their hands and torn to shreds in front of them; the paper entirely disappeared from Ford's plant at Halewood and dozens of landlords banned it from their premises. ... *Sun* readers in Liverpool had voted spontaneously with their feet and sales of the paper had collapsed. ... From sales before the disaster of 524,000 copies a day, the paper had crashed to 320,000 – a loss of 204,000, or 38.9 per cent. (Chippindale and Horrie, 1992: 289–292)

That strength of reaction was notable precisely because it was so unusual. But hostile audience reaction can act as a potential constraint on *individual* journalists. The plus side is that the reporter who gets something wrong is likely to get calls, emails or letters from irate readers and will learn not to make that mistake again. The less positive side is that the prospect of drowning in a flood of abusive comments from the audience might dissuade some journalists from tackling particularly controversial subjects in the first place.

Public relations

"It's now a very good day to get out anything we want to bury," wrote government spin doctor Jo Moore in her notorious email sent at 2.55pm on September 11 2001, within an hour of the second hijacked plane hitting New York's World Trade Centre. Her memo, to senior colleagues in the Department for Transport, Local Government and the Regions, continued with the helpful suggestion: "Councillors' expenses?" (Clement and Grice, 2001). The department's press office duly rushed out news release number 388 concerning a new system of allowances for local councillors (DTLR,

2001). As predicted, the councillors' expenses story was ignored by a media concentrating on recounting the rather greater horrors of the twin towers.

When her unwise words were leaked, Jo Moore became something of a hate figure and subsequently lost her job. But wasn't she only doing her job? Isn't the whole **public relations** (PR) industry designed not simply to promote good news about clients but to bury bad news? Not according to the Institute of Public Relations, which promotes ethical practice and exhorts its members to "deal honestly and fairly in business with employers, employees, clients, fellow professionals, other professions and the public" (www.ipr.org.uk). But Jo Moore was neither the first nor the last press officer to time the release of information to minimise coverage; Friday afternoons and the beginning of holiday periods seem to be particularly popular times. Others prefer disguising bad news with apparently good news, so that job losses become a footnote in a piece of puffery about an apparent expansion.

It might seem odd to discuss PR within a chapter concerned largely with *constraints* on journalists. After all, the work of the PR industry is visible in the media every day, and some short-staffed newspapers are only too grateful to be stuffed full of scarcely rewritten news releases. But PR is not just about *releasing* information, it is also about *controlling* information. And controlling *access*. Many journalists have an ambivalent attitude to PR. On the one hand, they maintain they are too hard-bitten to listen to PR departments, yet they are also quick to moan about bullying by political spin doctors, demands for copy approval on behalf of celebs, or the freezing out of journalists who don't comply (Helmore, 2001; O'Sullivan, 2001; Morgan, 2002b). Perhaps an ambivalent attitude is only natural. Although many press officers have good working relationships with journalists, based on trust and even grudging respect, the fact remains that they are *working to different agendas*.

6 It's now a very good day to get out anything we want to bury. 9

– Jo Moore, September 11 2001.

Colleagues

If journalists have a social role in informing society about itself, does it matter that journalists are not particularly representative of that society? Newspaper editor Jon Grubb clearly believes so:

For too long newspaper editorial departments have been dominated by white, middle-class staff. If newspapers want to truly connect with the community they must strive to better reflect the multi-cultural nature of their audience. This issue is not just about colour. We need more journalists with working-class roots. Until papers can understand the problems, hopes, aspirations and fears of all sections of the community they will find it difficult to win their hearts and minds. (Quoted in Keeble, 2001b: 143)

Not just newspapers. Witness the prevalence of Oxbridge types at the BBC, particularly on more prestigious programmes, such as *Newsnight*. Research suggests that the **social environment** in which journalists work "does not reflect the diversity of the UK population, either in terms of ethnic mix or social background": 96 per cent of journalists are white and very few are from working-class backgrounds (Journalism Training Forum, 2002: 8). Journalism professor Peter Cole calls it "shameful and disgraceful" that local papers in places such as Bradford, Oldham and Burnley have so few black journalists (Slattery, 2002). Ethnic minority journalists are sometimes seen as *representatives* of the entire black community, or the Muslim community; alternatively, they may be warned against dwelling on race (Younge, 2002). White British journalists, in contrast, are not expected to represent "the white community" – even assuming there is such an entity – and are not warned off "white issues".

As well as being very white, newsrooms had a rather blokey atmosphere in the past. However, the increasing proportion of women entering journalism in recent years has resulted in a more or less even split between the sexes (Journalism Training Forum, 2002: 4). There may be more women in journalism but they are not always in the most powerful positions, as Anne Perkins notes: "The higher up a newspaper hierarchy you travel, the fewer women there are to be seen" (Perkins, 2001). Even a female national newspaper editor told researchers that "much of journalism is still a boys' club, with women struggling for professional acceptance" (quoted in Journalism Training Forum, 2002: 60).

Journalists are recruited from an even more limited pool now that so many have to pay for postgraduate journalism courses on top of normal undergraduate debt. Journalism can look like a closed door to outsiders, as only 30 per cent of journalists get their first job after seeing it publicly advertised; others approach employers on spec, are offered a job after work experience, or hear about vacancies through a range of informal means (Journalism Training Forum, 2002: 33). In the words of a Fleet Street sub:

> Newspaper journalism fosters a culture of the clique. Anyone who does not fit into the prevailing clique's clearly defined pigeon-holes tends to be viewed with suspicion and ends up being marginalised or forced out. People may be tolerated for their usefulness, but few are promoted to the hierarchy, which remains a club that promotes only those who they recognise as younger versions of themselves. (Quoted in Journalism Training Forum, 2002: 60)

The extent to which journalists internalise prevailing attitudes, and reproduce them in their work, is a matter for debate among academics and among some within journalism itself. The issue is at its most acute during times of conflict. Commenting on his own reporting of the Falklands war, Max Hastings, who went on to edit the *Daily Telegraph* and *Evening Standard*, quoted approvingly the words of his journalist father: "When one's nation is at war, reporting becomes an extension of the war effort. Objectivity only comes back into fashion when the black-out comes down" (quoted in Williams, 1992: 156).

It is not necessarily a conscious process. While reporting Nato briefings in Brussels during the bombing of Serbia in 1999, *Sky News* correspondent Jake Lynch felt that most reporters had accepted the US/UK frame of reference:

> Journalists were prepared to accept the fundamental framing of the conflict which Nato was conveying, namely that this was all the fault of Slobodan Milosevic. ... [That] was *internalised*, unexamined, by journalists ... (quoted in McLaughlin, 2002a: 258, my emphasis)

Independent reporter Robert Fisk was rather more blunt about his colleagues' shortcomings: "Most of the journalists at the Nato briefings were sheep. Baaaa Baaaaa! That's all it was." In turn, "mavericks" such as Fisk have been accused by fellow journalists of being more concerned with making "political points" than with straightforward reporting (quoted in McLaughlin, 2002a: 263–264).

In war or peace, journalist colleagues can constrain each other by creating an atmosphere of conformity in which anyone who is a bit different or who challenges the norm is ridiculed, bullied, forced out, marginalised or tolerated as the resident Jeremiah. But colleagues can also support individuals, whether those like Bill Goodwin threatened with the power of the state, or those facing pressure to act in unethical ways. That's why Paul Foot would always urge journalists to band together in a trade union rather than stand alone. "You can only have an alternative to the control of the editorial hierarchy and the proprietor if you've got the discipline of being in a collective body behind you," he argued.

▮▮ ■ Summary ■▮

The work of journalists is influenced by a range of structural factors, such as legal constraints, regulatory regimes, the system of media ownership, organisational routines, shortage of time, market forces, advertising considerations, cultural bias, patriotism, professional ethos, and a gender, racial or class imbalance in the workforce. Constraints and conflicting loyalties lead to claims that individuals have little influence on journalistic output, while others argue that constraints can be resisted or negotiated.

■ Questions ■

Would journalism in the UK be very different if Rupert Murdoch had stayed in Australia?

Why does the law place constraints on journalists?

Why should journalists protect confidential sources?

Are journalists and PR people friends or enemies?

Can a journalist's background influence how they do their job?

▮▮ ■ Further reading ■

To read what Anna Politkovskaya was working on when she was murdered, see *A Russian Diary* (2008). For a journalist's story with a happier ending, see Alan Johnston's (2007) *Kidnapped* for a gripping and inspiring account of his 114 days in captivity in Gaza. Many more everyday constraints are introduced in whistlestop but readable fashion by Keeble (2001b), who also discusses the response of journalists. Also highly readable is Knightley's (2000) classic study of journalism and censorship in wartime. O'Malley and Soley (2000) offer a historical account of press regulation and self-regulation, including case studies of how the Press Complaints Commission has handled particular issues. For legal constraints, Welsh and others (2007) is essential – but make sure you consult the very latest edition, and the 20th edition will be written by David Banks and Mark Hanna, due to be published in 2009. For more on the law, Bloy (2007) and Crone (2002) are useful companions. McQuail (2000) reviews a range of relevant theories and research findings, and Chapter 11 is particularly useful here. Tumber (1999) includes many relevant original readings, including Herman and Chomsky on their propaganda model and Golding and Murdock on the influence of economic power. McChesney (2000) offers a detailed and passionately argued case for journalism being far too important to be left to market forces.

Sources for soundbites

Politkovskaya, quoted in Specter, 2007; Watkins, 2001: 114; Aitken, quoted in BBC, 1999; Goodwin, 1996; Robertson, quoted in Foley, 2000: 44; Murdoch, quoted in Bailey and Williams, 1997: 371; Younge, quoted in Thomas, 2006; Moore, quoted in Clement and Grice, 2001.

three

what is news?

| key terms |

Construction of news; Gatekeepers; Manufacture of news; Market-driven news; News frames; News pegs; News values; Relevance; Selection

The cigarette lighter didn't work when TV journalist Mika Brzezinski tried to set her script on fire, so she simply tore up the story with her bare hands. When the same script was handed to her again she fed it into a shredder, having already told viewers of US cable news channel MSNBC: "I have an apology ... and that is for our lead story, I didn't choose it. ... I hate this story and I don't think it should be our lead. ... We're not covering this..." The story that so enraged her was the release from prison of heiress Paris Hilton; a story that was chosen to lead successive news bulletins in preference to other contenders, such as the fact that a senator had just become the first leading Republican to break ranks and criticise President George Bush over the Iraq war (Tomasky, 2007). By objecting in such a dramatic way to covering the celebrity circus around the "liberation of Paris", not only did Mika Brzezinski quickly become a hit on YouTube (http://www.youtube. com/watch?v=6VdNcCcweL0), but she also opened up for public scrutiny a journalistic activity that usually takes place away from the cameras: the selection of news.

"It was not a story, my gut was telling me that," she explained afterwards. "It's a big problem. I would hope for this to become a bigger conversation that we have to have honestly. We need to have an open discussion about what is news and what is not" (quoted in Harris, 2007). Exhaustive debates about what stories should be covered and with what prominence tend not to be everyday occurrences in most newsrooms, partly because nothing would ever get done if every decision were discussed in detail and partly because prevailing news values are more likely to be

News values

The news values listed in *Box 3.1* are an attempt to update and develop an earlier taxonomy of news values produced by Norwegian academics Johan Galtung and Mari Ruge in the 1960s. Galtung and Ruge's influential list of 12 factors may be summarised as follows:

Frequency: an event that unfolds at the same or similar frequency as the news medium is more likely to be selected as news than is a social trend taking place over a long period of time.

Threshold: events have to pass a threshold before being recorded at all. After that, the greater the intensity, the more gruesome the murder, the more casualties in an accident, then the greater the impact on the perception of those responsible for news selection.

Unambiguity: the less ambiguity, the more likely an event is to become news. The more clearly an event can be understood, and interpreted without multiple meanings, the greater the chance of it being selected.

Meaningfulness: the culturally similar is likely to be selected because it fits into the news selector's frame of reference. Thus, the involvement of UK citizens will make an event in a remote country more meaningful to the UK media. Similarly, news from the USA is seen as more relevant to the UK than is news from countries that are less culturally familiar.

Consonance: journalists may predict that something will happen, thus forming a mental "pre-image" of an event which in turn increases its chances of becoming news.

Unexpectedness: the most unexpected or rare events – within those that are culturally familiar and/ or consonant – will have the greatest chance of being selected as news.

Continuity: once an event has become headline news it remains in the media spotlight for some time

absorbed than challenged (Evans, 2000: 3). That does not – at least, it should not – mean that the selection of news is an automatic or unthinking process. It just sometimes looks that way, as David Randall notes:

> [A] lot of news judgements [are] made swiftly and surely and seemingly based on nothing more scientific than gut feeling. The process is, however, a lot more measured than that. It just appears to be instinctive because a lot of the calculations that go into deciding a story's strength have been learnt to the point where they are made very rapidly – sometimes too rapidly. (Randall, 2000: 24)

What are these calculations about the relative merits of potential stories that can appear so instinctive to the untrained eye? They involve estimated measurements of relevance and interest to an audience – not necessarily the same thing – multiplied by perceptions of importance and then subtracting the logistical difficulties in getting the story. The factors that help journalists make such calculations tend to be called **news values** and they help us to answer the question, what is news?

' **Fact × importance = news** '
– *The Day Today slogan.*

Editors often refer to news as opening a window on the world or as a giant mirror reflecting society, warts and all. But it cannot be as simple as that because news is mostly about what does *not* usually happen – that's why it is news. Few news organisations would stay in business if they featured stories such as this:

> Police reported no major incidents as traffic flowed fairly smoothly along the A61 this morning. Meanwhile, patients in the casualty departments of the city's hospitals were treated without having to wait on trolleys in corridors overnight. Of the thousands of children on the streets yesterday, none was abducted. Finally, on the weather front, the Met Office said that rainfall was average for this time of year, no rivers had burst their banks, and people were going about their business with

because it has become familiar and therefore easier to interpret. Continuing coverage also justifies the attention an event attracted in the first place.

Composition: an event may be included as news less because of its intrinsic news value than because it fits into the overall composition or balance of a newspaper or news broadcast.

Reference to elite nations: the actions of elite nations are seen as more consequential than the actions of other nations. Definitions of elite nations will be culturally, politically and economically determined and will vary from country to country, although there may be universal agreement about the inclusion of the USA.

Reference to elite people: the actions of elite people may be seen as having more consequence than the actions of others, and the audience may identify with them.

Reference to persons: news has a tendency to present events as the actions of named individuals rather than a result of social forces.

Reference to something negative: negative news could be seen as unambiguous and consensual, generally more likely to be unexpected and to occur over a shorter period of time than positive news. (Galtung and Ruge, 1965: 65–71; Harcup and O'Neill, 2001: 262–264)

Additional news values have been suggested by other academics. Allan Bell, for example, adds the importance of *competition*, increasing the desire for a scoop; *co-option*, whereby a story that is only tangentially related can be presented in terms of a high-profile continuing story; *predictability*, that is, events which can be pre-scheduled for journalists are more likely to be covered than events which turn up unheralded; and *prefabrication*, meaning that the existence of ready-made texts (news releases, cuttings, agency copy) will greatly increase the likelihood of something appearing in the news as journalists will be able to process the story rapidly (Bell, 1991: 158–160).

Although the news values identified by Galtung, Ruge and others may be "predictive of a pattern" of which events will and will not be reported, they cannot provide a *complete* explanation of all the irregularities of news composition (McQuail, 2000: 343). While acknowledging that a set of common

little risk of flooding and no need to be rescued by helicopter.

Pretty dull stuff, yet that is the kind of thing that happens most days, indicating that news is a *selective* view of what happens in the world.

For David Randall (2000: 23), news is "fresh, unpublished, unusual and generally interesting". Up to a point. As the word itself implies, *news* contains much that is *new*, informing people about something that has just happened. But it ain't necessarily so. Some stories (the Moors murders, the Yorkshire Ripper, the Soham murders) are always with us, it seems, with or without any new facts to report. Other stories are freshened up by telling us that so-and-so "spoke last night" or "broke their silence" about some ancient scandal or other; or by the apparent discovery of some new information. Take the first three paragraphs of this news story published 97 years after a hanging, perhaps the ultimate example of the "delayed drop" intro:

> ❛ I can handle big news and little news, and if there's no news I'll go out and bite a dog. ❜
> – *Charles Tatum in Ace in the Hole.*

It is one of the most notorious cases in British legal history, the story of an apparently mild-mannered doctor who poisoned and dismembered his showgirl wife, then fled across the Atlantic with his young lover – only to be caught after a sharp-eyed captain recognised him from the newspapers.

Dr Hawley Crippen was hanged in 1910, after an Old Bailey jury took just 27 minutes to find him guilty of murdering his wife, Cora, who had vanished earlier that year.

Nearly a century later, research appears to show that the evidence which sent Crippen to the gallows was mistaken: the human remains discovered under his London house could not be those of Cora. (100 YEARS ON, DNA CASTS DOUBT ON CRIPPEN CASE, *Guardian*, October 17 2007)

Or this intro, published a mere 56 years after the events described:

understandings exists among journalists, Lewis (2006: 309) believes that any rationale for what makes a good story retains an arbitrary quality. For Golding and Elliott (1979: 114–115), stories must fit with the routines of news production as well as the expectations of the audience, and news values "are as much the resultant explanation or justification of necessary procedures as their source. … They represent a classic case of making a virtue out of necessity." John Richardson (2005: 174) argues that identifying something as "newsworthy" does not necessarily explain *why* it is so and, as John Hartley (1982: 79) points out, identifying news values may tell us more about how stories are covered than about why they were chosen in the first place.

It is also argued that lists such as those above fail to address what lies behind news values in terms of *ideology* (a concept introduced in Chapter 1). The news offers a highly selective version of events influenced by the "ideological structure" of prevalent news values, argues Stuart Hall (1973: 235). He explains:

> "News values" are one of the most opaque structures of meaning in modern society. … Journalists speak of "the news" as if events select themselves. Further, they speak as if which is the "most significant" news story, and which "news angles" are most salient are divinely inspired. Yet of the millions of events which occur daily in the world, only a tiny proportion ever become visible as "potential news stories": and of this proportion, only a small fraction are actually produced as the day's news in the news media. We appear to be dealing, then, with a "deep structure" whose function as a selective device is un-transparent even to those who professionally most know how to operate it. (Hall, 1973: 181)

Robert McChesney gives the example of journalists' emphasis on individual events and news hooks (or pegs) meaning that "long-term public issues, like racism or suburban sprawl, tend to fall by the wayside, and there is little emphasis on providing the historical and ideological context necessary to bring public issues to life for readers" (McChesney, 2000: 49–50). Furthermore, news values tend to privilege individualism, regarding it as "natural", whereas civic or collective values are marginalised (McChesney,

Government documents uncovered during a man's search for his lost father have revealed how thousands of Chinese servicemen who served Britain in the Second World War were forcibly repatriated in a climate of anti-oriental racism. (SON'S HUNT FOR FATHER EXPOSES BETRAYAL OF WAR HEROES, *Independent*, February 1 2002)

The new element is the "peg" on which the story is hung, but news pegs are not always as robust as they could be. Witness the flurry of news stories in August 2001 about the fatal floods that occurred 49 years earlier in Devon, the flimsy peg being that a radio documentary on the topic was about to be broadcast (RAF RAINMAKERS BLAMED FOR 1952 FLOOD, *Guardian*, August 30 2001); the surprise is that the documentary was not delayed for a year to make it a nice round 50th anniversary.

Most news is much newer than that, of course. But many stories appearing in the national media are already a week or two old, having been passed up the journalistic food chain from the local weekly to a regional daily newspaper, possibly taking in a website or regional broadcasting and then, maybe via a freelance news agency, on to the national stage – where the "when" of the five Ws will be buried somewhere near the bottom in the hope that any whiff of staleness will be overlooked. The majority of local stories will not make the national media, never mind the international media, without some additional element to grab attention – stories such as the opening of a new school, the death of a child in a simple road accident, or a fire in a warehouse. That does not mean they are not news; it means that news values are relative.

The advent of 24-hour broadcast news channels and constantly updated news websites has also impacted upon news values in that they have so much more time and space to fill; and, on many days, *fill* is exactly what journalists have to do, as one admits: "The amount of air-time that they have to fill with analysing stuff, that 10–15 years ago you wouldn't have even thought

> ❝ There is no news tonight. ❞
>
> – BBC announcer on Good Friday, 1930.

2000: 110). This is what is meant when critical commentators argue that, far from being neutral, news values provide journalists with ideologically loaded "maps of meaning" used to make sense of the world for an audience (Hall et al., 1978: 54).

For Staab, news reporting contributes to the "stabilisation of the political and economic structures of a nation", which is essentially an ideological function (Staab, 1990: 427). Lee et al. (2006) believe that traditional news values, which they argue privilege the reporting of conflict, represent an obstacle to forms of journalism that might seek to explore the causes of and alternatives to such conflict. However, the mere existence of a conflict is not sufficient to ensure media coverage; a study of foreign news in 38 different countries found that news values provided an insufficient explanation for disparities of coverage, with factors such as economic interest, the availability of information, and the cost of production also influencing news selection (Wu, 2000).

The news values inherent in mainstream journalism have been critiqued in theory by media commentators and academics and in practice by those citizens who have set up their own forms of alternative media (Harcup, 2005; 2007: 49–66). Such critical thinking has also informed a set of alternative news guidelines drawn up by a group of European charitable and non-governmental organisations to encourage less ideologically loaded coverage of developing countries (see *Box 3.2*).

As part of their classic study, Galtung and Ruge (1965: 84–85) themselves suggested that journalists should be encouraged to counteract prevailing news values by reporting more on long-term issues and less on events, by including more background and contextualising information, by not shying away from complex and ambiguous issues, and by increasing coverage of non-elite people and nations.

Construction

As we saw in Chapter 1, Walter Lippmann argued that facts must be given a shape if they are to become news, and this is what academics mean when they refer to the *construction* or even the *manufacture* of news. It is not that facts are invented by journalists (except in rare cases), but that the process of identifying,

Box 3.1

News values

Research suggests that potential items must generally fall into one or more of these categories to be selected as news stories (Harcup and O'Neill, 2001: 279):

- **The power elite**
  Stories concerning powerful individuals, organisations or institutions.
- **Celebrity**
  Stories concerning people who are already famous.
- **Entertainment**
  Stories concerning sex, showbusiness, human interest, animals, an unfolding drama, or offering opportunities for humorous treatment, entertaining photographs or witty headlines.
- **Surprise**
  Stories with an element of surprise and/or contrast.
- **Bad news**
  Stories with negative overtones such as conflict or tragedy.
- **Good news**
  Stories with positive overtones such as rescues and cures.
- **Magnitude**
  Stories perceived as sufficiently significant either in the numbers of people involved or in potential impact.
- **Relevance**
  Stories about issues, groups and nations perceived to be relevant to the audience.
- **Follow-ups**
  Stories about subjects already in the news.
- **Media agenda**
  Stories that set or fit the news organisation's own agenda.

Box 3.2

Alternative news values

A set of alternative news guidelines drawn up by a group of European charitable and non-governmental organisations (NGO-EC Liaison Committee, 1989):

- Avoid catastrophic images in favour of describing political, structural and natural root causes and contexts.
- Preserve human dignity by providing sufficient background information on people's social, cultural, economic and environmental contexts; highlight what people are doing for themselves.
- Provide accounts by the people concerned rather than interpretations by a third party.
- Provide more frequent and more positive images of women.
- Avoid all forms of generalisation, stereotyping and discrimination.

about … has led to a change in what defines news, what is newsworthy and where hype begins and real news judgement ends" (quoted in Sugden and Tomlinson, 2007: 51).

A good story

So, if news isn't necessarily new, and if it isn't a mere reflection of reality, what exactly is it? News may be about animals, places or the weather, but it is mostly about *people*. People *doing* things. Things such as: fighting, saving, killing, curing, crashing, burning, looting, robbing, rioting, stealing, stalking, kidnapping, rescuing, giving, marrying, divorcing, striking, sacking, employing, resigning, conning, suing, investigating, arresting, quizzing, freeing, loving, hating, kissing, bonking, hunting, chasing, escaping, fleeing, creating, destroying, invading, deserting, voting, leading, following, reporting, negotiating, accepting, rejecting, changing, celebrating, commemorating, inventing, making, breaking, selling, buying, treating, operating, comforting, mourning, leaving, arriving, delivering, succeeding, failing, winning, losing, searching, finding, giving birth, surviving, dying, burying.

> ❝ News is anything that makes a reader say "Gee whiz!" ❞
>
> – Arthur MacEwen, editor of the San Francisco Examiner.

As well as doing, news can be about people *saying* things, whether in the form of speeches, announcements, publications, accusations, or replies to journalists' questions. News can also be about somebody being *set to* do something, *set to* say something, or even – surely the most postmodern of conditions – being *set to* react to somebody else being *set to* say something. Any of the verbs listed above *may* become news if the raw ingredients have the makings of a good story for your audience. It will depend on who is doing or saying something, where, when, and in what circumstances. It will also be influenced by what other stories are around to compete for limited time, space, or resources.

"News stories are what people talk about in the pub, or wherever they gather," says Brian Whittle.

selecting and presenting facts in a news story is a form of construction that is necessarily viewed through a "cultural prism" (Watson, 1998: 107). And, according to Nkosi Ndlela, the selection and construction of news represents and simplifies the world rather than reflects it (Ndlela, 2005: 3). Maggie Wykes argues that "the construction of news simultaneously constructs for audiences a framework of interpretation as it presents the 'facts'" (Wykes, 2001: 187). Studies suggest that journalists frequently construct news stories within the framework of earlier stories or even through the retelling of enduring myths (Lule, 2001) or "collective narratives" (Phillips, 2007: 8–14).

However, a focus on how events and facts are constructed into news items offers only a partial explanation of the processes at work. The concept of "pseudo-events", introduced in Chapter 2, suggests that "many items of news are not 'events' at all, that is in the sense of occurrences in the real world which take place independently of the media" (Curran and Seaton, 1997: 277). Some commentators go even further in divorcing the news from real life:

> News is not out there, journalists do not report news, they produce news. They construct it, they construct facts, they construct statements and they construct a context in which these facts make sense. They reconstruct "a" reality. (Vasterman, 1995)

For Jorgen Westerstahl and Folke Johansson (1994: 71), the journalistic processes of news selection and construction are "probably as important or perhaps sometimes more important than what 'really happens'". Similarly, Joachim Friedrich Staab argues:

> [E]vents do not exist *per se* but are the result of subjective perceptions and definitions. … Most events do not exist in isolation, they are interrelated and annexed to larger sequences. Employing different definitions of an event and placing it in a different context, news stories in different media dealing with the same event are likely to cover different aspects of the event and therefore put emphasis on different news factors. (Staab, 1990: 439)

News frames

Within journalism studies the phrase "news frames" is used to mean that journalists tend to simplify events

He should know. As the editor of a large regional news agency, his income depends on spotting stories that his customers – the regional, national and international media – will pay for. He continues:

> Six people killed in a bus crash on the M56, that's hard news. You can't get any bigger hard news story than what happened in America [the attack on the World Trade Centre on September 11 2001]. But a lot of other stories are a result of lateral thinking. When a story's been around for a few days, you're looking for where the next development will be – so good instinct will result in a good story.

Evidence of his instinct for a good story can be seen in the framed front-page splashes adorning the office walls of his news agency: CATWOMAN 'SEDUCED' BOY OF 15... PAEDOPHILE WALKS FREE ... 18,000 POLICE TO FAIL DRIVING TESTS... BOY, 9, WRECKS TEACHER'S LIFE... MCCARTNEY'S £5,000 BABY HUSH MONEY ... and so on, all stories likely to pass the test of being mentioned by people chatting in the pub or next to the water cooler.

Somebody else who knows a thing or two about telling stories is the writer Michael Frayn, whose career has combined journalism with success as a novelist and playwright. He says: "Very deep in both journalism and fiction and life in general is the concept of a *story*. Why are some things a story and others just a sequence of events? All journalists recognise a story, and that's why they begin to tell it, but it's very difficult to say what a story is" (quoted in Armitstead, 2002, my emphasis).

In his first novel, *The Tin Men*, Frayn included the morbid results of market research into what the news audience wanted:

> The crash survey showed that people were not interested in reading about road crashes unless there were at least ten dead. A road crash with ten dead, the majority felt, was slightly less interesting than a rail crash

to fit in with ways of thinking and talking that are instantly recognisable to an audience (Niblock and Machin, 2007: 196). The frame might be familiar to members of an audience not so much from personal experience as from their previous consumption of news, as Franklin (2005: 85) observes: "When people have little direct knowledge of events, they become increasingly reliant on news media for information, but also an understanding or interpretation, of those events." Arguably, alternative forms of media can play a role in challenging the most familiar frames, just as avant-garde artists might refuse to be constrained by a frame or even a gallery.

Market-driven news

Increasing commercial pressures, combined with the development of online news and 24-hour broadcast news channels, means that there is now "a strong drive to produce news feed that is less for a public, but rather that fits particular demographics, which can be used to locate the world of news events in the lives of particular market-segmented groups", according to the authors of a study of Independent Radio News in the UK (Niblock and Machin, 2007: 191). They found that news stories were selected as much on the basis of their perceived appeal to radio stations' target audiences – as measured by factors such as age, gender, lifestyle – as on any inherent newsworthiness, meaning that news was being driven by market factors which had tended to be overlooked by Galtung and Ruge and other similar studies (Niblock and Machin, 2007: 188).

> ❛ One European is worth twenty eight Chinese, or perhaps two Welsh miners worth one thousand Pakistanis. ❜
> – McLurg's 'law of public interest'.

Gatekeepers

The concept of gatekeeping is associated with a David Manning White study of how a wire editor at a US morning newspaper selected stories for inclusion during one week in 1949. White concluded that the choices were "highly subjective" and based on the editor's own "set of experiences, attitudes and expectations" (White, 1950: 72). The gatekeeping approach has since been challenged for assuming that there is a given reality out there in the "real world" which

with one dead, unless it had piquant details – the ten dead turning out to be five still virginal honeymoon couples, for example, or pedestrians mown down by the local JP on his way home from a hunt ball. A rail crash was always entertaining, with or without children's toys still lying pathetically among the wreckage. Even a rail crash on the Continent made the grade provided there were at least five dead. If it was in the United States the minimum number of dead rose to 20; in South America 100; in Africa 200; in China 500. (Frayn, [1965] 1995: 69)

It may have been a spoof but it was informed by the author's first-hand knowledge of the ways in which the **construction** of stories, and the placing of events within **news frames**, can render news predictable. As predictable as the annual stories about A-levels getting easier or the pictures of female tennis players showing their knickers at Wimbledon every summer.

Formulaic and predictable some news may be but, unlike in Frayn's novel, we have not lost the connection between real journalists and real events featuring real people. Contrary to popular belief, journalists who totally invent stories – as featured in the film *Shattered Glass*, for example – are very much the exception rather than the rule. Most news stories are not invented but they are constructed; that is, the raw material has to be observed, selected and processed into something recognisable to audience and colleagues alike as news. Perhaps that is why seasoned news junkies find so many stories so familiar; like the mythical punters in *The Tin Men*, we have heard most stories before with just the names and places changed.

"Man bites dog" stories

"Dog bites man isn't news. Man bites dog is." So goes an adage probably as old as journalism itself. Like many such sayings, it conceals as much as it reveals. True, it tells us something about the value of novelty in news stories. In the opinion of Harold Evans

newsgatherers will choose either to admit or exclude (McQuail, 2000: 279). A study by Walter Gieber suggested that the personal attitudes of individual journalists or gatekeepers was less significant than the mechanical and bureaucratic processes involved in producing and editing copy (Gieber, 1964: 219). For Gieber:

> News does not have an independent existence; news is a product of men [*sic*] who are members of a newsgathering (or a news-originating) bureaucracy. … [The] reporter's individuality is strongly tempered by extrapersonal factors. (Gieber, 1964: 223)

As Jackie Harrison (2006: 13) puts it, news is that which "is judged to be newsworthy by journalists, who exercise their news sense *within the constraints* of the news organisations within which they operate" (my emphasis).

The gatekeeping model has subsequently been developed by Pamela Shoemaker to take account of multiple levels of decision-making and wider factors:

> The individual gatekeeper has likes and dislikes, ideas about the nature of his or her job, ways of thinking about a problem, preferred decision-making strategies, and values that impinge on the decision to reject or select (and shape) a message. But the gatekeeper is not totally free to follow a personal whim; he or she must operate within the constraints of communication routines to do things this way or that. All of this also must occur within the framework of the communication organisation, which has its own priorities but also is continuously buffeted by influential forces from outside the organisation. And, of course, none of these actors – the individual, the routine, the organisation, or the social institution – can escape the fact that it is tied to and draws its sustenance from the social system. (Shoemaker, 1991: 75–76)

Individual gatekeepers may display a degree of agency but they do not operate totally autonomously, which may go some way towards explaining why studies suggest that decisions about news selection show little difference whether the editorial gatekeepers are male or female (Lavie and Lehman-Wilzig, 2003).

The very concept of gatekeeping is under threat from the erosion of distinctions between producer and audience brought about by the internet, which holds out the possibility that "the roles that journalism assigned to itself in the mid-nineteenth century … as gatekeeper, agenda-setter and news filter, are all placed at risk when its primary sources become readily available to its audiences" (Hall, 2001: 53).

(2000: 215), man bites dog is "not merely a good story. It is also a good headline, in its own right". But that is only part of the story when it comes to news, which is the lifeblood of journalism.

Man bites dog stories may be unusual but they are not quite as rare as hens' teeth. Take this intro from a newspaper report of a court case: "A drunken teenager who was said to have 'growled like an animal' as he sank his teeth into a police dog's neck has been put on probation for two years" (*Yorkshire Evening Post*, November 4 2000). Or this unlikely headline: WOMAN BITES DOG IN SAVAGE PIT BULL ATTACK (*Independent on Sunday*, June 17 2001). Replace the dog with a more exotic creature and a story can travel the world, as in this example: "Gu Gu the panda was bitten by a visitor to Beijing Zoo after attacking the drunken man for attempting to hug him" (MAN BITES PANDA, *Guardian*, September 21 2006).

For a variation on a theme, see this intro from the website *Ananova*: "A pensioner ended up in hospital in Zurich after being bitten by a dog … owner. The 74-year-old woman was attacked by another female pensioner in a row about the dog's attitude" (July 4 2001, ellipsis in original). And, to show that a bark can sometimes be as newsworthy as a bite, take this account of an unusual court case that made the nationals:

> A teenager who was arrested for barking at two dogs has cleared his name in court in a case that cost the taxpayer £8,000. … Magistrates fined him £50 with £150 costs in January but the conviction has been quashed by a judge, who remarked: "The law is not an ass." (MAN WHO BARKED AT DOGS IS CLEARED IN £8,000 CASE, *Daily Telegraph*, April 28 2007)

It is the (relative) rarity of such stories – the element of surprise – that makes them newsworthy.

However, there are times when "dog bites man" stories are also deemed newsworthy enough for selection, usually because there are additional factors involved. Maybe there is an element of the macabre, as in this newspaper account of a man's death – STARVING PET STARTS TO DEVOUR PENSIONER

(*Rhondda Leader*, January 15 2004) – that was criticised by the Press Complaints Commission for including "gratuitous" detail (*Press Gazette*, 2004). Perhaps it is the horrific death of a child, as in this example, which became a lead item for much of the national media: "The distraught mum of the baby ripped to death by two crazed rottweilers last night told of her grief over the shocking tragedy" (MY GRIEF BY KILLER DOGS MUM, *Daily Mirror*, September 26 2006). Alternatively, there could be the drama of a local child surviving an attack, as in these examples: BULL TERRIER BITES OPEN FACE OF BOY (*Yorkshire Evening Post*, June 27 2006) and ANGER OVER BOY SAVAGED BY DOG (*Belfast Newsletter*, April 4 2008). Maybe it is the unusual nature of the injuries, as in: DOG RIPS OFF BOY'S EAR (*Sheffield Star*, March 6 2007) or even: DOG BITES OFF MAN'S GENITALS (*Guardian*, September 2 2000). There could be legal action over a ruined career – GOLFER BITTEN ON FINGER BY DOG SUES OWNER FOR £1M (*Independent*, December 3 2002) – or there might be "fury" over a compensation award, as in the following story:

> A yob has been awarded £42,500 after being bitten by a police dog while taking part in a knife fight. The compensation and costs, thought to be Britain's largest payout for a dog bite, were condemned by the Police Federation as 'perverse'. (YOB GETS £42K FOR DOG BITE: FURY AT COP ALSATIAN COMPO, *Sun*, May 11 2007)

And it could be the sheer number of dog biting incidents that makes a story, as when National Health Service figures revealed that 3,787 people in England needed emergency hospital treatment after being attacked by dogs during 2007 (RISE IN A&E CASES AFTER DOG ATTACKS, *Guardian*, February 28 2008).

By examining the additional elements that can turn a dog bite story into news, we can begin to detect the existence of what are called news values. Further clues about the operation of such news values are offered by the following headlines: DEATH THREATS TO DOG THAT WAS LEFT £6m IN WILL (*Daily Telegraph*, December 4 2007); DOG SHOOTS MAN DURING HUNTING EXPEDITION (*Guardian*, October 31 2007); and possibly my favourite: TILL DEATH US DO BARK – MAN WEDS DOG (*Daily Mirror*, November 14 2007).

News values

If news isn't necessarily new, and if "dog bites man" stories can occasionally make the headlines alongside more unusual tales, such as dog shoots man or man weds dog, then coming up with a foolproof definition of news is clearly easier said than done. News values have been deconstructed by academics but rather fewer journalists have either the time or the inclination to stand back and subject the selection process to such critical scrutiny. Veteran TV reporter John Sergeant says: "It is often distressing to argue about news stories, because usually journalists rely on instinct rather than logic" (Sergeant, 2001: 226).

Recruits to journalism tend to pick up a sense of newsworthiness and develop their "nose" for a story by consuming news and by picking up prevailing news values from more experienced colleagues. It can be a fairly subjective process. The *Guardian*'s Martin Wainwright says he measures a potential story against whether it interests him or "increasingly as I get older, would it interest my children?" These days journalists can get a clearer idea of what interests the public – well, a section of the public – because figures are available on which online stories are the most read. For example, at 10.10am one day early in 2008, the top five most read news stories on the BBC's main news website were the following:

> ❝ News is what a chap who doesn't care much about anything wants to read. And it's only news until he's read it. After that it's dead. ❞
>
> – *Evelyn Waugh.*

1. Overstaying students "can remain".
2. Bag restrictions eased at airports.
3. Britons "richer than Americans".
4. Medway luckiest for lottery wins.
5. Low-energy bulb disposal warning (Most popular stories now, January 7 2008, http://news.bbc.co.uk).

At exactly the same time the top five most read stories on the *Sky News* website were:

1. Boy beats toddler to death with bat.
2. Who would Becks trust with naked wife?
3. Marines' silent mission in Afghanistan.
4. Toddler facing up to rare bone disorder.
5. Iraq soldiers kill US troops (Most read stories, January 7 2008, http://news.sky.com/sky news/home).

Trying to make sense of such charts can be a bewildering process, partly because they can change by the minute and partly because it is not always clear which aspects of particular stories have led to their popularity. Also, clicking on a story is not the same as reading it. In any event, the most popular stories only represent a tiny fraction of the daily output from the BBC, Sky and other news organisations.

Newsworthiness may be hard to define, but we can get a fairly good idea about how news values work by examining those stories that do make it into the news. A major study of the UK national press suggests that, although there are exceptions to every rule, potential news items must generally satisfy one or (ideally) more of the requirements listed in *Box 3.1* to be selected as news stories (Harcup and O'Neill, 2001).

Although the news values listed in *Box 3.1* are based on a study of the UK national press, similar considerations come into play when journalists select stories for broadcast, online and local or regional media. Let's see how they operate in practice:

The power elite: stories concerning powerful individuals, organisations or institutions

Virtually every action of the Prime Minister seems to be considered newsworthy, from cabinet reshuffles at one end of the spectrum to the width of their grin at the other. This is less so for the Prime Minister's senior colleagues and so on down the pecking order of government and opposition, through the back-benches, in diminishing order of newsworthiness. Whereas the Prime Minister's choice of clothing or holiday plans are usually enough to generate a news story, cabinet colleagues might have to make a policy announcement or a blunder to grab the headlines, while a lowly constituency MP will be of interest to the national media only if they are embroiled in some kind of scandal, row, rebellion or defection. Locally, even the most somnolent constituency MP will be considered one of the power elite, as will the leader of the council and/or a directly elected mayor, and many of their comments and actions will be reported in the local media. As with individuals, some institutions or organisations are deemed to be newsworthy because of their positions of power and/or influence – examples include Nato, the Vatican, the European Commission, the Bank of England, Oxbridge universities and Eton.

Celebrity: stories concerning people who are already famous

Celebrities are newsworthy and it has ever been thus, long before anyone had ever heard of Paris Hilton or the paparazzi. The evidence is the fading sign still adorning the wall of the old *Harrogate Advertiser* building in which I once worked – "List of visitors Wednesday" – which dates back to when the local paper began as little more than a weekly list of the rich and famous who came to stay in the North Yorkshire spa town over 150 years ago. However, today's journalists are often heard complaining that good stories are squeezed out by an increasing media obsession with celebs on the A, B, C, D and Z-lists. Brian Whittle dismisses many news editors as "daleks who only rate a story if it features a third-rate celebrity". He recalls one of his former news editors defining a good news story as "ordinary people doing extraordinary things", before adding with a hint of sadness: "I think some of that's been lost." If you come up with a story about somebody who is famous, you will have a better chance of having it used than if the same story concerns an "ordinary" person (aka civilians or muggles).

Entertainment: stories concerning sex, showbusiness, human interest, animals, an unfolding drama, or offering opportunities for humorous treatment, entertaining photographs or witty headlines

Editors look favourably on stories and pictures with the capacity to entertain or amuse an audience. Indeed, some stories have little else going for them. Why else, for example, would the *Daily Express* devote almost the whole of one of its prime news pages to a woman saying that a tree-trunk resembled the face of her dead pet dog (BARK THAT SAYS ZOE WILL ALWAYS BE HERE, *Daily Express*, November 6 2001)? See also the overweight pet stories that appear with alarming frequency, such as CHARLIE THE FLABRADOR (*Daily Mail*, October 25 2001) or KING OF THE FAT CATS (*Daily Mirror*, October 31 2001). A sex angle is also popular with editors, and court cases or employment tribunals involving sex have a greater chance of being covered than those without. Other reliable entertainment stories likely to trigger a response are those based on lists, be they the 1,000 best records, the 100 greatest films, the top 50 songs ever written, or comparisons of who is "out" and who is "in". But hard news, even tragic news, may also be judged on whether it is entertaining – not in the sense of being amusing but of offering an unfolding drama, with plot twists featuring characters we come to know. For example, there is little suspense or drama about the dozens of children killed on our roads each year, and they receive relatively little media coverage. But there is huge coverage of the intense drama attached to a police hunt for a missing child: the smiling picture, the plotting of the last movements, the release of CCTV footage, the emotional appeals, the discovery of a body, the placing of flowers with heart-felt messages, the arrest of a suspect, the howling mob outside court. Journalism as entertainment is discussed further in Chapter 7.

> ❝ Names and faces, that's what sells. ❞
>
> – *Pat McArt, editor of the Derry Journal.*

Surprise: stories with an element of surprise and/or contrast

This is where the stories of people biting or even marrying dogs come in along with other surprising, shocking or unusual events ranging from the 12-year-old who becomes a mum to the one-legged man who skywalks on the wing of an aeroplane. There is also a great value placed on contrast, as in the vicar who runs off with somebody else's wife, the police child protection officer who is arrested for downloading child porn, or stories such as the following account of an Automobile Association (AA) call-out that went wrong:

> The AA is supposed to help when your car breaks down – but that was not the case when one of its vans destroyed a couple's car, garden wall and garage. A bungling patrolman parked at the top of a quiet street but forgot to pull on the handbrake when he got out. His van rolled down the hill and smashed into a 15-year-old Ford Orion and wrecked a garage. (HE'S A VERY SILLY MAN, A VERY, VERY SILLY MAN, *Metro*, January 22 2007)

Bad news: stories with negative overtones such as conflict or tragedy

Death, tragedy, job losses, factory closures, and falls from grace are all examples of somebody's bad news being good news for journalists. Sometimes journalists might almost *create* bad news by seeking hostile reaction to an incident or comment in the hope of starting – and reporting – a "row". Or, if they are really lucky, a "war of words" – with or without a community being "up in arms".

Good news: stories with positive overtones such as rescues and cures

Positive stories are far more prevalent than is suggested by the cynical claim that the only good news is bad news. Somebody somewhere always seems to be winning a dream prize, going on the trip of a lifetime, or achieving straight As with accompanying hugs when they get their exam results. Neighbours are frequently hailed as heroes for leaping into action to rescue people from burning houses. Miracle cures are also more common than their name suggests, as in the following front-page lead: BACK FROM THE BRINK: COMA GIRL JENNIFER MAKES A MIRACULOUS RECOVERY (*Yorkshire Evening Post*, February 2 2002). Another miracle is described in a national front-page splash: OUR MIRACLE: MUM TELLS OF ESCAPE AS 100mph GALES BATTER UK: 'A mum told how her two children narrowly escaped death when a tree uprooted by storm-force winds crashed on to their gran's car' (*Daily Mirror*, January 29 2002). Even foreign miracles can make the news in the UK, as in the following tale from California: MIRACLE IN THE DESERT – CRASH GIRL, FIVE, SURVIVES TEN DAYS NEXT TO HER MOTHER'S BODY ON SPORTS DRINK AND DRY NOODLES (*Daily Mail*, April 15 2004). Such "miraculous" escapes are a recurrent theme in news stories. A classic of the genre took up a whole news page of the *Daily Mail* – LUCKIEST BOY ALIVE: THE TODDLER WHO CLIMBED THROUGH A WINDOW AND FELL 25FT … STRAIGHT INTO THE ARMS OF A PASSING DOCTOR (June 27 2001) – duly illustrated with photographs of the boy, his relieved mother, and the window in question. Animals too can have miracle escapes, as in: DOWN BOY! PUP SURVIVES 120FT PLUNGE INTO THE SEA (*Daily Mirror*, March 7 2008). As David Helliwell explains: "Hard news is often bad news so we want to break up the court stuff, the police stuff, industry or whatever with something a little bit lighter – a bit more light and shade among the death and destruction."

Magnitude: stories perceived as sufficiently significant either in the numbers of people involved or in potential impact _____

Magnitude comes into play when a journalist rejects a potential story with the words: "Not enough dead" (quoted in Harrison, 2000: 136). Martin Wainwright recalls how he decided to go to the scene of a rail accident at Selby:

> I heard about that on the news early in the morning and went out there when I knew that there were going to be more than just a couple of people killed. *It's got to be that level.*

But magnitude is relative, as can be seen from the fact that the following headline appeared over a brief news item: CYCLONE DEATH TOLL HITS 1,700 (*Mail on Sunday*, November 18 2007). That deadly cyclone was in Bangladesh, which goes some way towards explaining why the story was deemed worthy only of inclusion on page 51. Similarly, television news may lead on seven deaths in UK storms and treat 500 people feared dead after an explosion at a Nigerian arms depot as a brief item fourth in the running order (*Channel 5 News*, 9pm, January 28 2002). Had the figures been reversed, seven deaths in Nigeria would probably not have been of sufficient magnitude to warrant inclusion at all – unless they were Brits (see *Relevance*, below) – while 500 deaths in the UK would have cleared the schedules for rolling news broadcasts from the scene for days on end.

Relevance: stories about issues, groups and nations perceived to be relevant to the audience _____

"News lives on a weird globe, distorted so that the local is magnified, and the distant compressed," observes Andrew Marr (2005: 61). As we have just seen, 500 deaths in Nigeria are perceived as being of less interest to a UK audience than a fraction of that number in the UK or of Britons abroad. "It's a question of the impact on people,"

says a BBC news editor, explaining why a coach crash in India did not make the news despite the fact that 60 people had drowned (quoted in Schlesinger, 1987: 117). In the gallows humour typical of newsrooms, this is sometimes referred to as McLurg's Law, after a legendary editor who ranked events by how far away they occurred (Schlesinger, 1987: 117). But it is not simply a question of geographical distance. In the UK we get more stories about the USA than, say, Belgium because, although the latter is nearer and a partner in the European Union, we share more linguistic and cultural reference points with the former. Away from international news, the concept of relevance affects selection about topics. That's why bulletins on BBC Radio One, aimed at young people, have so many news items about drugs or the entertainment industry; why the *Guardian*, which is read by many teachers (and students), has so many stories about education; and why the *Daily Mail*, aimed at middle-class and "aspirational" working-class readers, features so many stories about mortgages and property prices. Relevance works at a micro-level as well as the national and international level, so a local newspaper in a seaside town might have lots of stories about the menace of seagulls whereas an equivalent publication in a rural area inland will be more concerned with the price of sheep, and a big city newspaper wouldn't touch either. Selecting news stories on the basis that they are likely to appeal to a certain type of audience, who in turn might appeal to a certain type of advertiser, is a form of commercial or *market-driven news*.

Follow-ups: stories about subjects already in the news _____

"News is not news until someone else reports it," is how Phillip Knightley (1998: 197) sums up the attitude of too many editors. And so broadcast journalists scan newspapers and magazines for stories, print journalists monitor broadcast bulletins, all of them constantly check news websites and news agency feeds – and vice versa. However, journalists remain concerned to "move the story on", that is, to discover new information or introduce new angles. Follow-ups have a number of advantages for journalists, including the fact that background material is readily available, that contacts have already been identified, and that certain developments may be able to be predicted and therefore planned for.

Media agenda: stories that set or fit the news organisation's own agenda

Sometimes news stories seem to be selected less for any intrinsic newsworthiness than because they fit the agenda of the news organisation, whether to promote certain commercial or political interests or to engender a sense of audience loyalty and identification. Examples of the former were discussed in Chapter 2, while examples of the latter range from a local paper running a campaign to encourage readers to carry organ donor cards to the *News Of The World's* controversial campaign to "name and shame" paedophiles. When the *Daily Mail* published a series of news stories attacking the BBC's coverage of the Queen Mother's death in 2002, it seemed to have more to do with promoting the paper's agenda of moral outrage than with reporting a row with any existence outside the confines of its pages. The *Mail's* political attitudes are frequently visible in its news stories as well as its comment pages, as memorably satirised in this spoof splash:

Middle-class newspaper readers might as well top themselves at once, according to a series of reports published every day in the *Daily Mail*. The only reason to stay alive, according to experts, is to see whether the *Mail* runs an even more depressing report the next day, suggesting that it is only a matter of time before economic ruin strikes every man, woman and child in Britain, reducing them to eating their pets and begging for loose change from asylum seekers who (cont. p94). (*Private Eye*, June 28 2002)

The news values listed above interact with each other, and the more buttons pressed by an event the more likely it is to become news. But even events that satisfy several of the above criteria do not become by themselves. First, they must be noticed, weighed up, selected and constructed.

Selection

This role in selecting the news has led to journalists in general, and those working on newsdesks in particular, being described as **gatekeepers**. In this sense, the gatekeeper allows some events to pass through to become news while the gate is shut on other events. Since the emergence of the internet, it has frequently been claimed that journalists are no longer gatekeepers because more and more people have access to a wider range of information sources. Yet most of the major providers of online news were already big players in other forms of media. Websites such as that of *BBC Online* and the *Guardian* may have been jazzed up with all manner of blogs, interactive features and user-generated content, but the news services they provide clearly still operate by selecting, filtering and processing information, or gatekeeping; arguably, that is precisely why they have proved so popular.

Changes to the organisation, production and distribution of journalists' work can impact upon the selection of news because, unlike traditional media, online news has no set deadline and is never "full". Trevor Gibbons describes life as an online journalist for the BBC:

There's more pressure to get something up immediately. Coming into a story a couple of hours after somebody else has done it is almost so late as to be no use. Writing for a newspaper, you pick one moment in time whereas we sometimes have an evolving story and we might go into a story four or five times in a day. And it's far easier to put background material *around* the story that you're doing. An internet site is never full and you never put it to bed. At any one time some bits are going out-of-date and need to be taken off.

But this is still recognisably a journalistic process, and Gibbons believes that selection remains key: "What makes a good story makes a good story online, in a newspaper or on the radio."

The internet has certainly made it easier for those with the inclination to find alternative sources of information, but for most people, most of the time, "the news" remains something that has been selected and filtered by journalists. From a newsdesk perspective, David Helliwell explains what he looks for when a reporter brings in a story:

For a front page story you definitely need some sort of drama, some action or excitement, and you need something that's going to draw the reader in. Preferably you would be looking at something that is people-led. If you were looking at a robbery, for example, we would only consider it a good front-page robbery if we had some detail, some colour, so you got to know who was involved, who the victims might be. Not just a flat police statement that "two masked men sped off in a westerly direction with an undisclosed sum". Whatever it is – be it crime, industry, business, whatever – we would always try to make it as human as possible.

Take this splash about two 18-year-olds jailed for seven years for robbing an elderly woman – YOUNG THUGS CAGED: TERROR ATTACK ON PENSIONER (*Yorkshire Evening Post*, October 6 2001) – illustrated with photographs of the two robbers. Helliwell says the pictures helped elevate the story to page one:

Getting the pictures from the police, always a tricky business, definitely lifts it. People love to see who you're talking about. Even if we didn't have the pictures it

would have been a strong page lead early on in the paper. It's the viciousness of what they did, the things they said to her, the judge's comments, and the seven years each, which are pretty heavy sentences. Even in this day and age these things are fairly rare.

However, just as most crimes reported to the police are not covered by the media, most court cases also pass unreported. This is for logistical reasons as well as ideas of newsworthiness, because newspapers have cut back on court reporters while broadcasting and online media cover only the most high-profile cases. Most coverage of the courts relies on news agency reporters ducking and diving in and out of cases looking for one with an interesting line or two, as Jane Merrick explains:

> ❛ **Isn't it amazing that the amount of news that happens in the world every day always just exactly fits the newspaper?** ❜
> – *Guardian advert.*

A murder trial wasn't enough, it had to have two or three different angles. The agency was geared to the tabloids, because they were the ones who would buy most of our stuff, so it was very much human interest. One of the first court cases I did was a woman who had killed her lover's wife, but that wasn't enough to make a good story for the papers. I think she was in the chorus line and the victim was the lead singer in this amateur play, so that was the extra line.

Even at a local level, except in the smallest of towns, the bulk of court cases do not get covered by the media at all. Helliwell again:

We have someone covering Crown Court full-time and on many days there are two people there, covering 12 courts. Like many other papers, the days of covering magistrates courts are virtually gone. We go up for things we know about but not on spec. I'm sure there are cracking stories that we miss, but so much gets adjourned that in terms of producing copy it's just not worth it. Similarly with employment tribunals. We look out for the sexual discrimination cases because a lot of the others are just too dull or too technical. A dispute over procedure isn't going to make a good lead for us. We check out sexual discrimination, unfair dismissal, or if it is a big local employer. Every now and then there will be a race equality organisation accused of discrimination. People love that. It's human nature that people love the hypocrisy of it.

Reading such an item on screen, he may find himself tutting or shaking his head, a sure sign that a reporter has delivered a good story. As with court cases or tribunals, so with the selection of other news. Yes, even hard-bitten hacks can respond to stories with feelings of shock, surprise, outrage, sadness, joy or amazement at the human condition. "That's the big test if you're on newsdesk," Helliwell explains. "If it moves something in you then it will move somebody else, and that's what you want."

That's news. In the next chapter we will find out where it comes from.

■ ■ Summary ■ ■

News is a selective version of world events with a focus on that which is new and/or unusual. However, not all news is new; much of it is predictable, and some does not concern "events" at all. Journalists identify, select and produce news items according to occupational norms, including the concept of what will interest a particular audience. Implicitly or explicitly, journalists measure potential news items against a range of criteria that have become known as news values. Academics have produced lists of such news values based on studies of journalistic output. Other theoretical models associated with the study of news include news as a social construct; journalists as gatekeepers admitting or excluding events; and news values being imbued with the dominant ideology of society. It has been claimed that the development of the internet has undermined the role of the journalist as gatekeeper and blurred the boundary between producer and audience.

■ Questions ■

Where do news values come from?

Do news values change over time?

Who are the gatekeepers now?

In what ways is the news predictable?

If news is manufactured, does it mean it is not true?

■ ■ Further reading ■ ■

The Ethical Journalist (Harcup, 2007) has a chapter discussing a range of ethical issues that arise from the ways in which news is selected, constructed and presented. Both Randall (2007) and Boyd (2001) have practical chapters discussing news from the point of view of an experienced print and broadcasting journalist respectively. Harrison (2000) includes a study of TV news values, while Harcup and O'Neill (2001) present the results of a content analysis of news values at work in the UK national press; also see O'Neill and Harcup (2009). Harrison's (2006) *News* is a readable explanation of academic analysis of the news process, while extracts from many studies – including Galtung and Ruge, Schlesinger, Shoemaker, and Gans – are reprinted and introduced in Tumber (1999). Stuart Hall's classic analysis of news values as ideology is also extracted in Tumber, but it is worth seeking out the full version from the original, Chapters 3 and 4 of Hall et al. (1978). For a critique of news values from the perspective of alternative media, see Whitaker (1981).

Sources for soundbites

The Day Today, BBC Worldwide DVD 2004; Tatum, quoted in Salas, 2007; BBC, quoted in Allan, 1997: 325n; MacEwen, quoted in Boorstin, 1963: 20; McLurg's Law, quoted in Schlesinger, 1987: 117; Waugh, 1943: 66; McArt, quoted in Greenslade, 2003b; *Guardian*, June 8 2001.

four

where does news come from?

"Have you seen those awful Harvey Nichols posters?" asked Jane, a friend who had been offended by adverts for the opening of a Harvey Nichols shop in Leeds. I hadn't. She described the huge hoardings featuring a black woman wearing a dog-lead and collar, accompanied by the weak pun: "Harvey Nichols Leeds (not follows)". Jane felt it was a degrading image of women in general, and black women in particular, made worse by the juxtaposition with unrelated posters promoting a local "zero tolerance" campaign to combat violence against women.

"I don't know if you might be able to make it into a story," she added. The answer was yes, it could be a story if somebody complained. So she duly fired off an angry letter to the Advertising Standards Authority (ASA). It turned out that the model in the dog-lead was not black at all but Jodie Kidd in heavy make-up. However, it was a newsworthy story because the complaint meant there was a row involving a high-profile, upmarket store popular with celebs including the Princess of Wales. It might not have been the kind of thing to impress journalist David Randall, who dismisses "row" stories as "the great contagion and con-trick of journalism" (Randall, 2000: 41), but it reflected genuine anger.

Having gathered some more outraged comments from locals and councillors, along with a dismissive response from the store's PR people, I filed copy to the national and local papers. Many gave it a good show the next day, accompanied by pictures and obligatory puns such as: HOT UNDER THE COLLAR (*Daily Express*), HARVEY NICKS 'DOG GIRLS' UNLEASH A ROW (*Daily Mail*), TOP STORE IN THE DOGHOUSE AS 'RACIST AND SEXIST' POSTER UNLEASHES PROTESTS UP NORTH (*Guardian*), and STORE FAILS TO FINDS FOLLOWING AMONG LEEDS LADIES WHO LUNCH (*Daily Telegraph*;

Sources

Sources are central to the practice of journalism. Sources are the people, places or organisations from whom potential news stories originate; and the people, places or organisations to whom journalists turn when checking potential stories. Allan Bell argues that "the ideal news source is also a news actor, someone whose own words make news" (Bell, 1991: 193–194). He lists the following news actors as the major sources: political figures, officials, celebrities, sportspeople, professionals, criminals, human interest figures, and participants such as victims or witnesses (Bell, 1991: 194). Journalists may like to say that sources are everywhere but most of the time they opt to use a narrow range of sources, argues Bell. He points to a series of research studies suggesting that, to a very large extent, "news is what an authoritative source tells a journalist"; alternative sources, including minorities and the socially disadvantaged, "tend to be ignored" (Bell, 1991: 191–192). Recent research suggests that a vast number of stories originate from some kind of public relations activity: "even in a sample based on the UK's most prestigious news outlets, journalists are heavily reliant on pre-packaged information, either from the PR industry or other media," according to Lewis et al. (2008a: 14). The consequence of this information subsidy is that "corporate and governmental voices speak loudly while public opinion is worryingly mute" (Lewis et al., 2008b: 30).

When assessing sources, a journalist's overriding consideration is *efficiency*, according to Herbert Gans: "Reporters who have only a short time to gather information must therefore attempt to obtain the most suitable news from the fewest number of sources as quickly and easily as possible" (Gans, 1980: 128). He has identified six interrelated "source considerations" used by journalists to evaluate sources of news. They may be summarised as follows:

Past suitability: sources whose information has led to stories in the past are likely to be chosen again and to

all October 10 1996). In the way of these things, the story was followed-up by the broadcasting media before finally becoming the property of columnists, who contributed their philosophical twopence-worth based on a pile of cuttings.

Then it was forgotten, except by me. As every freelance knows, where there is a story there is a potential follow-up. Three months later, when the ASA declared the ads to be harmless fun, I dusted off the original story and bashed out fresh copy that was used in brief by several papers. Had the verdict gone against Harvey Nichols this follow-up would no doubt have been bigger news. But such is life.

Sources are everywhere

Journalists are surrounded by **sources** of potential news stories or features. A conversation with a friend, a poster on a wall, an unexpected juxtaposition – all might result in a story if you keep your eyes, ears and mind open.

Veteran *Yorkshire Evening Post* reporter Peter Lazenby is one of those journalists who seems to be able to find stories wherever he goes. Shopping in a local supermarket one weekend, he spotted a card on the community noticeboard offering a reward of several hundred pounds for the return of a lost parrot. Thinking it must have been "one hell of a parrot" to be worth so much, he called the number and discovered that it was indeed a rare breed. But it had not been lost. It had been stolen by members of an international smuggling syndicate who were abducting exotic birds to order and delivering them in a private aeroplane to wealthy collectors. Not a bad story to bring home with the groceries on what was supposed to be a day off. In this sense, a good journalist is never off-duty.

As news agency editor Brian Whittle explains: "Sources of news are everywhere." Some sources will be routine points of contact for journalists

become regular sources (although journalists could eventually become bored of them).

Productivity: sources will be favoured if they are able to supply a lot of information with minimum effort by the journalist.

Reliability: journalists want reliable sources whose information requires the least amount of checking.

Trustworthiness: journalists evaluate sources' trustworthiness over time and look favourably on those who are honest and do not limit themselves to self-serving information.

Authoritativeness: everything else being equal, a journalist will prefer a source in an official position of authority.

Articulateness: sources capable of expressing themselves in articulate, concise and dramatic sound-bites or quotes will be favoured when journalists need somebody to be interviewed. (Gans, 1980: 129–131)

For Gans, this process means that "journalists are repeatedly brought into contact with a limited number of the same types of sources" (Gans, 1980: 144). This apparent homogeneity of sources is reinforced by the fact that journalists use other journalists and other media as one of their main sources of ideas and validation. Pierre Bourdieu refers to this as the "circular circulation of information", arguing that journalists *consume* so much news because "to know what to say, you have to know what everyone else has said". For Bourdieu, this results in "mental closure" (Bourdieu, 1998: 23–24).

Are journalists' sources really drawn from as narrow a range as suggested above? If journalism *does* tend to privilege a narrow range of "resource-rich institutions" (Cottle, 2000: 433), then it does not *have* to do so. Studies of the alternative press suggest that it may not be the routines of news production themselves that determine the choice of sources but the ethos of the organisation, thus allowing for the alternative press to select "a different cast" of sources and voices (Cottle, 2000: 434–435; see also Harcup, 2003).

News access

The question of who gets on the news is important to considerations of the public sphere, and journalists'

while others may be one-offs. Some will be proactive, approaching journalists because they want *news access* for their views or information, while other sources may not even be aware that they *are* sources. A good journalist will look for leads from a range of sources and will certainly not rely on being spoon fed by the PR industry. Some of the most common sources of news are listed in *Box 4.1*.

> ❝ **Sources of news are everywhere.** ❞
>
> – Brian Whittle.

Contacts books

The sources listed in *Box 4.1* will form the backbone of any journalist's contacts book. Contacts books come in many shapes and sizes – electronic or paper – but what they have in common is that they can be the difference between meeting the deadline and missing the boat.

A contacts book will normally list organisations on an alphabetical basis, adding names, titles, main switchboard telephone numbers, direct lines, mobile numbers, fax numbers, email addresses, and home numbers where possible. Mobile and out-of-hours numbers are particularly important, as you may be working on stories early in the morning or late in the evening when most work numbers are useless. Cross-referencing is advised, to increase your chances of finding the right name and number in a hurry. And don't rely on being able to remember who somebody is and why you have their number in your book. Even Mr Memory would struggle to remember all the people a journalist will speak to in an average year, so add titles and a brief note to aid recall.

You will also need to build up a range of individual contacts, people associated with particular interests or issues. Having such contacts listed in your book – categorised under their job, their hobby, their area of expertise – can help you find that vital comment, that missing piece of information or that fresh angle much more quickly

tendency to rely on official sources is frequently said to benefit the powerful (Cottle, 2000: 427; McChesney, 2000: 49; McQuail, 2000: 288). Unequal access to the news has damaging social effects, argues Stuart Hall:

> Some things, people, events, relationships *always* get represented: always centre-stage, always in the position to define, to set the agenda, to establish the terms of the conversation. Some others sometimes get represented – but always at the margin, always responding to a question whose terms and conditions have been defined elsewhere: never "centred". Still others are always "represented" only by their eloquent absence, their silences: or refracted through the glance or the gaze of others. If you are white, male, a businessman or politician or a professional or a celebrity, your chances of getting represented will be very high. If you are black, or a woman without social status, or poor or working class or gay or powerless because you are marginal, you will always have to fight to get heard or seen. This does not mean that no one from the latter groups will ever find their way into the media. But it *does* mean that the structure of access to the media is systematically skewed in relation to certain social categories. (Hall, 1986: 9, emphasis in original)

Such media representations do not necessarily remain unchanged over time (Schudson, 1989: 280), and black and gay voices are now heard more frequently than when Hall wrote the above words. However, notwithstanding that relationships between journalists and sources may be complex and subject to change over time – and that there will be occasions when the voices of the powerless take centre stage – there remains a *tendency* for the powerful to enjoy "routine advantages" in news access (Manning, 2001: 139). For example, Gary Younge notes that black "community leaders" tend to be regarded as authoritative sources only when rioting breaks out: "While rarely summoned to the microphone in more peaceful times, they are in great demand when it comes to condemning wayward members of their community" (Younge, 2001). News access is discussed further in Chapter 5.

Primary definers

For some cultural critics, notably Stuart Hall, the "skewing" of access to the media privileges the

---

Box 4.1

Common sources of news stories

Academic journals	Fire brigade	Pressure groups
Adverts	Government departments	Professional bodies
Airports	Government News Network	Public inquiries
Ambulance service	Health authorities	Pubs
Anniversaries	Heritage groups	Quangos
Armed forces	Hospitals	Readers/viewers/listeners/users
Arts groups	Inquests	Regeneration projects
Blogs	Lateral thinking	Regional development agencies
Campaigns	Leaks	Residents' groups
Chambers of Commerce and/or	Letters	Regulatory bodies
Trade	Libraries	Schools
Charities	Motoring organisations	Scouts, Cubs, Guides,
Churches, Mosques,	MPs and MEPs	Brownies, Woodcraft Folk
Synagogues, Temples	News agencies	Social networking sites
Colleagues	News releases	Solicitors
Community groups	Noticeboards	Sports organisations
Companies	Official reports	Support groups
Consumer groups	Online forums	Theatres
Council departments	Other media	Trade associations
Council meetings	Parish newsletters	Trade press
Council press officers	People	Trades unions
Councillors	Police	Transport companies
Court hearings	Political parties	Universities
Cuttings/diary	Post offices	Websites
Email lists	Posters	
Entertainment industry	PR companies	
Eyes and ears	Press conferences	

---

than if you have to start from scratch each time. People listed in your contacts books will vary enormously depending on the type of organisation you are working for, the geographical or specialist patch you are covering, whether you work mainly on features or news, and how you develop your own particular niche of interest or expertise.

Useful people contacts are likely to include some of the following: academics; actors; agents; alternative health practitioners; anglers; architects; artists; astrologers; astronomers; athletes; authors;

dominant forces in society by allowing them to establish the parameters of debate on social issues. Politicians, employers, the police and so-called experts become "primary definers" of events whose "primary definition sets the limit for all subsequent discussion by framing what the problem is" (Hall et al., 1978: 59). According to this analysis, journalists play the role of "secondary definers", circulating the interpretations of the powerful not because of any conspiracy but because "the hierarchy of credibility" reflects the social power structure (Manning, 2001: 138). The concept of primary and secondary definition has

barristers; biologists; bloggers; builders; business people; carers; cavers; celebrities; chefs; chemists; clairvoyants; climbers; collectors; comedians; community leaders; computer whizkids; councillors; counsellors; criminologists; cultural critics; dentists; designers; detectives; dieticians; disability campaigners; DJs; doctors; economists; engineers; environmentalists; estate agents; explorers; farmers; feminists; film directors; film stars; financial experts; footballers; gardeners; gay activists; golfers; historians; hoteliers; imams; international experts; judges; magistrates; market traders; midwives; millionaires; models; musicians; nurses; pet owners; pilots; police officers; political activists; priests; psychiatrists; psychologists; rabbis; ramblers; refugees; restaurateurs; sailors; scientists; shopkeepers; singers; social workers; sociologists; soldiers; solicitors; sports people; supporters; surgeons; teachers; transport experts; trawler captains; TV stars; undertakers; vegetarians; vets; vicars; victims; writers; zoologists. Also, don't forget to list other journalists with whom you might be able to swap favours.

A contacts book is a living thing, so if you call somebody only to be told they are dead or retired, update your book accordingly. You will also need to feed it by adding fresh contacts from stories on which you are working – even from stories on which you are not yet working, as the *Nottingham Evening Post*'s consumer affairs correspondent Kevin Peachey explains:

I get loads of people ringing me up saying, "My tumble dryer has broken down and the bloke hasn't been round for three days to fix it". And there is an art to talking to these people. Some of the time they just want to talk to somebody about it, get it out of their system and have a good rant, and that's fine. But the bottom line is they are really useful, because if you log all your calls you realise there are trends there.

One story I did as a result of that was when I got loads and loads of calls from people saying, "Something went wrong with my TV, phoneline, whatever, and it took me days to get through and complain to someone because

been criticised for neglecting the potential of media themselves to become primary definers (Critcher, 2002: 529) and for downplaying some of the complexities of journalist–source relationships (Schlesinger, 1990: 66–67; Manning, 2001: 15–17 and 137–139; Kuhn, 2002: 52–58).

Power

The journalist–source relationship has been described as resembling both a dance and a tug-of-war (Gans, 1980: 116–117). McQuail says that the growing role of PR spinning means that "it has probably become harder for the media to make any independent assessment of their own of the value of information provided to them in such volume" (McQuail, 2000: 291). Larsake Larsson's study of relationships between reporters and local politicians found an interplay based on "the exchange of information for media exposure", in which sometimes the journalist would have the upper hand and at other times the politician (Larsson, 2002: 27). However, although journalists might highlight negative news, on a day-to-day level the agenda seemed to be set not by the journalists but by their sources:

The local media obtain the bulk of their [municipal] news from matters addressed in municipal administrative and decision-making processes. Municipal news stemming from journalistic initiative is less common, since journalists' working conditions seldom permit independent inquiry and agenda building. They are forced, in a sense, to choose between the dishes offered on the municipal buffet table. Only rarely do they venture into the kitchen to see what the host may have hidden in the cupboard. … [The] media stay within the news selection frames determined by the organisations they report. (Larsson, 2002: 29)

This "framing" of media coverage may on occasions be achieved by those outside the social power structure. For example, covering farmers' protests in Brittany prompted one journalist to express ethical concerns: "After ten days we wonder if we are not being manipulated. They called us out for a photo opportunity. We got the feeling of giving backing to demonstrators. Without us, they do not exist" (quoted in Neveu, 2002: 65).

all I got was a recorded message". So I wrote all these down, we then decided that we would test out 20 companies and find out how long it would be before we could talk to a human being. A lot of the companies we chose were based on the entries I had in my book. If 10 people ring me up about the same company, then you know that's something you need to be looking at. In themselves there might not be much in it, but put them together and you can see trends.

I've literally just got a book, the same as my contacts book, and whoever they're complaining about, or the subject, I just stick in the number and a very small explanation if it's needed. Then you can always go back to them. Campaigns are another example. We don't just come up with these ideas off the tops of our heads, they're inspired by readers' letters or by reporters going out on to their patches and people saying, "What about this?"

On a quiet news day you could simply go through your contacts book and call some of the people to whom you have not spoken for a while. You never know, you might pick up a story or two. Finally, make a back-up copy. Everyone agrees this is sound advice but too few journalists get around to it until the bitter experience of losing a contacts book makes them realise what a good idea it would have been. Repeat after me: I will make a back-up copy.

> ❝ The good reporter is able to...find at least two good stories during a twopenny bus ride ❞
> – Frederick Mansfield.

> Yet it ought not to be forgotten that journalists retain the power to choose between sources, and to include or exclude certain perspectives, within the context of the constraints discussed in Chapter 2.

The calls

A reporter's first job of the day is to find out what is happening on their patch, as Brian Whittle explains:

As far as newsgathering goes, we still do the old-fashioned things. So we get up early and do the calls. By the time I come into the office I've watched the telly, read at least a couple of national papers and a couple of locals. You're immediately tuned in to what's going on and you hit the floor running.

"The calls" – regular inquiries to a range of agencies – are a staple of newsgathering. Minimum calls will be the police, the fire brigade and the ambulance service, noting down anything of interest that has happened since the last time the calls were made, including updates to ongoing stories. Weekly papers might do calls once a day; daily papers will make several rounds of calls a day; broadcast and online newsrooms, as well as news agencies, will usually do the calls hourly or even more frequently. Journalists covering coastal areas will find the coastguard and lifeboat services included in their rounds of calls, while those covering areas popular with walkers or cavers may check with the mountain rescue service. A final round of calls will be made just before deadline. When I worked Saturday shifts for a Sunday paper I even had to ring the region's prisons asking if there had been any escapes or incidents, just in case.

Time was when calls used to involve journalists gathering at the local police station when a police officer would deliver a daily briefing on the latest crimes and misdemeanours by reading from the log of incidents. It still happens like that in some places, but most calls these days are on the telephone, many to recorded voicebanks updated by press officers. Only a tiny proportion of incidents are made public by the police, as was demonstrated when freelance journalist Nigel Green (2008) used the Freedom of Information Act to find out how many incidents were dealt with by Northumbria police in a two-week period. The answer was 17,261, of which just 27 were publicised to journalists.

The system of routine calls is very much a one-way flow of information – self-evidently so in the case of voicebanks. Although journalists will occasionally find out about crimes from members of the public or personal observation, the vast majority of crime stories that make the news have been supplied by the police. It has been argued that this gives the police a privileged position as one of a number of **primary definers** able to influence how certain issues are reported and debated. This question of **power** relations between journalists and sources has been explored at length by academics, while journalists have been more concerned with the practicalities of getting the story. For journalists, making regular calls to the police and other emergency services is both a valid and a valuable way of generating copy. Calls provide a regular supply of

stories, ranging from nibs (news in brief) to leads; calls can be carried out routinely by any competent reporter even without any relevant personal knowledge or contacts; and calls provide insurance against the ignominy of missing something big happening on your patch. The calls will continue to be an important method of newsgathering.

Sources of news

Organisations contacted during the calls may be among the most prolific sources but they are only a few of the places where news comes from. Common sources, listed in *Box 4.1*, are introduced below.

Academic journals

Research by academics, particularly scientists, published in peer-reviewed journals, is a frequent source of news stories. The journalist's job is twofold: to spot a potential story among the qualifications and caveats beloved of academics, and to render the story intelligible and interesting to lay readers. There are almost daily examples, ranging from the quirky to matters of life and death.

Adverts

An advert for a high-powered job might alert you to the fact that the previous incumbent has left – maybe they resigned or were sacked. And when a state school felt the need to appeal for money in *Private Eye*'s classified ads it prompted widespread coverage about the state of the education system.

Airports

As well as being arrival and departure points for celebs galore, airports can generate stories both positive (record journey times, new routes) and negative (accidents, noise, cancellation chaos, battles over runway extensions).

Ambulance service

A routine call to the ambulance service may provide early warning of accidents, explosions, and even the occasional birth on the way to hospital.

Anniversaries

Journalists love anniversaries, especially those with a five or, even better, a zero at the end. Births, marriages, deaths, inventions, disasters, and wars starting or ending are just some of the occasions given the anniversary treatment.

Armed forces

In peacetime the armed forces can generate stories through manoeuvres, recruitment campaigns and pictures of local boys or girls overseas, plus the occasional mysterious death or case of bullying that comes to light. During times of conflict military briefings become events in their own right and military bases might become a magnet for anti-war protesters.

Arts groups

Apart from providing information about forthcoming events, arts groups can generate rows about funding or controversial subject matter.

Blogs

The term "blog" is short for weblog and covers everything from expert analysis on a particular topic to the amateurish jottings of

people who really should get out more. An example of a blog that has broken many political stories in the UK is Guido Fawkes at: www.order-order.com. Within a short space of time it became essential reading for political correspondents and editors. Many blogs are rubbish, but many contain useful tips, insights and contacts that are ignored at your peril.

Campaigns

Campaigners who want to influence public opinion on subjects ranging from animal rights to real ale are likely to come up with opinions or events that might generate news stories.

Chambers of commerce and/or trade

As spokespeople for business, such organisations can be useful sources of stories or comments about anything from interest rates to Christmas shopping.

Charities

Because charities need publicity to generate public donations, many are geared up to the needs of journalists, suggesting heartrending stories complete with photogenic victims, human or animal.

Churches, mosques, synagogues, temples

Religious organisations may make the news by holding events, by having internal rows or by attacking the views of others. But if somebody tells you that a local authority is trying to ban Christmas, it is almost certainly not true.

Colleagues

People you work with are likely to be parents, patients, residents, commuters and consumers, among other things. As such, they may come across events with the potential to become news – whether they recognise it or not.

Community groups

A good source for rows and reactions, especially of the not-in-my-backyard variety.

Companies

Behind the self-serving PR puffery, genuine business stories involve real products, real jobs and real profits or losses.

Consumer groups

Consumer stories range from the miss-selling of pensions to the discovery of a mouse in a sandwich. When groups of consumers band together they can become a valuable source.

Council departments

You will get some good exclusive stories if you manage to bypass the council press office to establish direct relationships with officers actually doing the work in departments such as housing or highways.

Council meetings

Meetings tend not to be covered in the "parliamentary gallery" style of old but they can still provide good copy as well as a chance to hang around and chat to councillors, officers and any members of the public who turn up to lobby on a particular issue. The bulky documents accompanying most agendas (now usually available online) may also have some gems buried deep within. Try to think of meetings and reports as a potential starting point for stories rather than an end.

Council press officers

Sizeable local authorities employ teams of press officers, many recruited from the newsrooms of local newspapers. They *react* to journalists' queries, coming up with information, quotes and contacts while acting as a buffer between decision-makers and journalists. And they *proactively* distribute stories in the form of well-written news releases or well-timed telephone calls. David Helliwell says that council press officers with an eye for a good story should be able to get regular coverage in local and regional media because "they know what will turn us on". He adds: "Sometimes they knock out stories *before* the meeting, which is slightly disturbing."

> ❝ The story of journalism, on a day-to-day basis, is the story of the interaction of reporters and officials. ❞
> – Michael Schudson.

Councillors

As with MPs, Euro-MPs and members of the assemblies in Scotland, Wales and Northern Ireland, councillors often have something they want to get off their chest. Many councillors have other day jobs, so work and mobile numbers are essential.

Court hearings

"You ignore the courts at your peril," explains Brian Whittle, "because you get the best human interest stories from them." Court reporters dip in and out of several courtrooms looking for cases that fit the news values discussed in Chapter 3, hence the importance of good contacts with court staff, police, solicitors, and the Crown Prosecution Service. Some reporters, especially those working for agencies, will also go after background material on defendants and "after-match quotes" from victims and relatives.

Cuttings/diary

One story often leads to another, particularly if reminders are added to the newsdesk diary. Cuttings from previous articles are a major source of background information, but beware assuming that everything in a cutting is necessarily accurate. Certain myths seem to be recycled because they were published once and other journalists have not bothered to check. The Press Complaints Commission has warned that "too many journalists now seem to act in the belief that to copy from 10 old stories is better than to write a new one with confirmation by proper fresh enquiry" (PCC, 1992: 2).

Email lists

Adding your email address to specialist lists will undoubtedly lead to lots of spam, but it might also generate some story leads.

Entertainment industry

An increasingly important source for today's media, as discussed in Chapters 3 and 7, although the line between puffery and journalism is sometimes dangerously anorexic.

Eyes and ears

Keep your eyes and ears open as you go about your life and you will be surprised at how many stories you can spot.

Fire brigade

One of the staple agencies for journalists' calls, checking with the fire brigade will provide early warning of house fires, motorway pile-ups and heroic rescues.

Forward planning services

For a subscription fee, services such as Amiplan and ForesightNews will supply constantly updated details of forthcoming events along with contact details – all searchable by geographic area or specialist interest.

Government departments

As for council departments but on a national level.

Government news network

The Government News Network (GNN) produces vast numbers of news releases on behalf of government departments and agencies on a regional and national basis. It also handles ministerial and royal visits.

Health authorities

Outbreaks of serious disease, funding crises, hospital closures and health promotion initiatives are all examples of news stories that may emanate from health authorities.

Heritage groups

Campaigns to protect everything from historic woods to old gasworks can come up with some lively stories.

Hospitals

A hospital is not going to tell you about patients left overnight on trolleys, or given inappropriate treatment – those stories will come from other sources. But hospitals are a source of "good news" stories about cures, new treatments, and general triumph-over-tragedy.

Inquests

The coroner's court provides a regular supply of tragic stories for the local media with the most high-profile or unusual making it into the nationals. A major advantage for journalists is that most inquests are relatively brief encounters compared with criminal trials. Occasionally, a large number of similar cases might indicate a story bigger than just the immediate tragedy. Inquests and coroners do not exist in Scotland, where the sheriff's court may hold a fatal accident inquiry.

Lateral thinking

Lateral thinking involves making connections and having a good memory. When Brian Whittle heard about a new report linking BSE in cows and CJD in humans – in contrast to reassurances by politicians – he remembered an earlier story about a woman who had died from suspected CJD after working in a butcher's:

> I sent a reporter and photographer to see the husband who had been left to bring up three kids on his own. They not only got a marvellous interview, he also gave them the most amazing picture. When she was dying in hospital he had taken a Polaroid picture of a nurse handing her the baby.

The picture was splashed across the front page of the *Daily Mirror* beneath the banner headline THE PROOF and a statement from the Prime Minister:

"I should make it clear that humans do not get mad cow disease" (*Daily Mirror*, March 21 1996). "It was lateral thinking, asking where there was a victim to illustrate this story, and that picture went half way round the world," adds Whittle.

Leaks

Leaks of information, whether from close contacts or anonymous whistleblowers, can lead to exclusive stories. The protection of such sources is discussed in Chapter 2, while Chapter 6 examines some stories that originated from leaks.

Letters

Letters pages and online comment spaces should not be overlooked as sources of news. They contain opinions, questions, information and allegations that might repay further investigation. Sometimes a letter or email might become a news item in its own right, as when a group of authors wrote to the *Times* to express their concern at the decision of Tesco to take legal action against critics of the superstore chain; the paper ran it on the letters page but also turned it into a major news story (AUTHORS TAKE ON TESCO 'TYRANTS', *Times*, April 29 2008).

Libraries

Hard though it is for some people to believe, not everything is available on the internet. Libraries retain a useful role in providing access to reference books, company reports, local history archives, indexes of local societies, community noticeboards and, by no means least, helpful librarians.

Motoring organisations

Organisations such as the RAC and the AA are always coming up with comments or surveys that make the news, and they are also good sources of reaction for anything to do with cars, roads or transport generally. However, given that people join for the recovery service rather than to have a mouthpiece, don't assume they speak for all motorists. The Environmental Transport Association (ETA) may provide a "greener" viewpoint.

MPs and MEPs

MPs, Euro-MPs and members of regional and national assemblies need to maintain their profile with voters so they can usually be relied upon to make sure journalists know what they are up to. This means lots of dull statements and pseudo photo opportunities among the more genuinely newsworthy items. At a national level, political correspondents spend a lot of time talking to backbench MPs, picking up gossip and gauging feeling; and don't forget that today's backbencher could be tomorrow's cabinet minister and the following day's prime minister.

> ❛ You have to be careful not to get to know them too well – it's a matter of maintaining a sound mistrust. ❜
>
> – Swedish reporter on political sources.

News agencies

News agencies are the foot soldiers of journalism at a national and international level, allowing media organisations to cover stories in areas where they have few or no staff. Brian Whittle's agency, covering the ten towns of Greater Manchester, will be called by staff reporters of the national papers every day to see what stories might be happening on their patch: "By nine o'clock in the morning we know what's going on in the region because we will have talked to the police forces, the ambulance, the fire brigade." They will also have trawled through the local media, particularly the weekly newspapers, looking for stories with the potential to be turned around for the nationals; they might also have checked churches and register offices for signs of celebrity weddings coming up. And if a London newsdesk needs somebody doorstepped at the other end of the country, it will usually be an agency reporter who gets the job, as Jane Merrick recalls:

> A lot of our work was actually finding people at the centre of the story. So, rather than just going along to a court case and reporting it, we would find the accused's husband and see if he wanted to talk. A lot of it is going through the electoral roll and finding out where people live. You have to do a lot of running around.

News releases

News releases, aka press releases, can be good, bad or indifferent. Some sections of the media are alarmingly full of scarcely rewritten news releases from councils, businesses, charities, universities and so on. Some news releases are pointers to genuine news but many are a waste of everybody's time. Even the worthwhile ones should be treated more as a beginning than an end, and there may well be a better story if you read between the lines. Also, a simple phone call may avoid the embarrassment of reporting that something has happened just because a news release said it was going to happen – when it may have been cancelled.

Noticeboards

Notices in shop windows, offices, libraries, colleges and elsewhere may tip you off about public meetings, petitions, planning applications or lost parrots.

Official reports

When confronted with an official report, don't simply rely on the executive summary. Newsworthy lines may be buried in the main text, demonstrating the value of cultivating friendly experts who will be able to help you understand such documents.

Online forums

Specialist forums might alert you to a potential story long before it is visible to more general and/or mainstream media.

Other media

All news media monitor other media, all the time, as Martin Wainwright explains:

> The pyramid of stories starts maybe with a parish magazine, then a weekly paper, say the *Wharfedale Observer*, picks it up. The *Yorkshire Evening Post* picks it up from the *Wharfedale*, then the *Yorkshire Post* picks it up, and we pick it up if it's got a national interest.

Not that the story will simply be lifted. Not always, anyway. Different outlets require different treatments. To illustrate the point, Brian Whittle spreads on his desk a copy of one of the weekly papers on his patch, the *Knutsford Guardian*. He is excited by the potential of a story about some newts that have held up work on a traffic scheme:

> That's not the story at all. The real story is, this is one of the worst accident blackspots in the country, with a couple of people killed each year or even more, and they can't put this improvement scheme in because of a pond of great crested newts. The way we'll develop that is to go and see the wife of the latest victim, who will say to us, "Who is more important, my husband or a pond of bloody newts?" And, if you do the pictures properly, you've got a page lead in one of the nationals.

It happens at a political level too, with politicians' performances on the heavyweight broadcasting programmes being monitored for signs of splits or subtle changes of direction, as well as the latest comment on the controversy of the day. Jane Merrick explains:

If they say something on TV you can use it. There are probably about four hours of political programmes on a Sunday, for example, and out of that there'll maybe be two quotes which will make a story. It's a daily cycle. If you're on the late shift you wait for the first editions of the newspapers to come in at about 10.30pm. Some newspaper will have been briefed about a story so you phone up the Home Office at 11 o'clock at night and they say yes it's all true, or no comment.

And so it goes on, with those newspapers influencing the next morning's *Today* programme (Radio Four) and the *Today* programming influencing TV news, the London *Evening Standard*, and the following morning's national newspapers – all of them influencing the major news websites, and vice versa.

Alternative and ethnic minority media can also be a fruitful source of information and story ideas.

Parish newsletters

There may be some spectacular rows lurking within their pages. Failing that, you might find stories ranging from an upcoming fête to a shortage of vicars. But you will have to put up with an awful lot of exclamation marks.

People

Potential stories can be suggested by people you meet while at work, rest and play. This can range from somebody mentioning that they have just seen a police car parked in their street to rather more substantial fare. As a student journalist on work experience, Abul Taher was researching an education story about the influence of Islam on British campuses when he came across a stronger story:

> The leader of an Islamic extremist group made a passing remark that a lot of British Muslim students had gone to fight jihad in Bosnia, Afghanistan and Kashmir for the cause of Islam. I immediately latched on to that and

he provided me with details of three students from Queen Mary and Westfield College abandoning their studies to go to *jihad*. I checked with the college, and the story made it as an exclusive in the *Guardian* and generated a lot of response from other media. This was two years before September 11th. The source was really a chat with someone.

Police

Probably the single most important source for journalists, particularly in the local and regional media, is the police. Regular calls to police voice-banks and police stations, followed up where necessary with calls to the press office or preferably the investigating officer, result in an endless stream of stories about brutal killings, bungling burglars, callous thieves and have-a-go heroes. In addition to providing this rollcall of crimes, the police will sometimes tip-off the media about operations, allowing for dramatic pictures of dawn raids and drugs busts. Police may organise press conferences with victims' relatives. Experienced crime correspondents will develop their own networks of sources within the police, bypassing the press office where possible.

Political parties

Contacts within parties can be a fruitful source of stories about rows and splits, while party spokespeople will be more keen to let you know about the selection of candidates or the launch of policy initiatives.

Post offices

A post office, particularly in a rural area, can be a focus for information and gossip on local people and events. Sadly, your chances of finding a village with its own post office seem to be diminishing

each year. But a campaign to save or even reopen a post office could make a good story too.

Posters

The Harvey Nichols story discussed in this chapter is just one example of posters prompting news stories. Another occurred when a Bradford journalist noticed that posters near his office had been covered with white paint over a picture of Anna Kournikova wearing a bra. Enquiries with locals revealed that some Muslims were behind the action because they objected to the tennis player showing too much flesh – and the story made the national media.

PR companies

Journalists and PR people love to hate – or at least poke gentle fun at – each other. But the fruits of the PR industry's labours are there for all to see in the media every day, so the reality is that PR *is* a major source for many journalists. The role of public relations as "information subsidy" to the media is discussed further in Chapter 2.

Press conferences

Away from the world of professional football clubs announcing new signings, fewer press conferences take place these days as most journalists are simply too busy to go and collect information that could be sent by email. But police press conferences, for example during murder hunts, remain an important source of news. Press conferences are also likely to be held to announce the results of official inquiries or to unveil new appointments, and they give you a chance to question senior figures who may not otherwise be available. As with news releases, it is sometimes best to read between the lines and remember that the best angle might not even be mentioned from the platform. Try to get there early and hang around at the end, talking to other journalists as well as the participants. You might pick up a useful tip.

Pressure groups

As with campaigns, except that pressure groups tend to be more long-term. Note how often the English Collective of Prostitutes is referred to in stories about prostitution, not because it necessarily represents the views of most women on the game, but because it is both quotable and easily accessible to journalists in a hurry.

Professional bodies

Stories from professional bodies, such as those covering doctors or solicitors, may include disciplinary hearings or criticism of government policy. They are also seen as authoritative sources on anything to do with their profession.

Public inquiries

Public inquiries can produce good copy, but remember to look beneath the surface. It was only by skim-reading hundreds of pages of official documents at a public inquiry into a 1990s drought that reporter Peter Lazenby discovered that a suggestion to evacuate the entire city of Bradford had been raised at a meeting between Yorkshire Water and the city's emergency planners because the water supply could not be guaranteed. It was just one line in a set of old minutes towards the bottom of a mountain of paper, but it made that night's headlines.

Pubs

Publicans and regulars can be mines of information about the community and, if you get chatting, they might tell you about anything from charity events to the death of a local character. Peter Lazenby delights in telling young journalists that more cracking news stories started out being scribbled on wet beermats than will ever be uncovered by reporters sitting at their desks. Not everyone has the personality to pick up a story in a pub, of course, and many of today's bars are not exactly conducive to chatting; but the point remains that off-diary stories come from *talking* and *listening* to people. As with post offices, pubs themselves can also be the subject of stories, from licensing rows to the decline of the traditional local.

Quangos

A quango is a "quasi-autonomous non-governmental organisation" operating at arm's length from ministers. Quangos can be sources of news by virtue of the work they do, how they spend their money, and by controversial appointments.

Readers/viewers/listeners/users

Journalism cannot exist without an audience and many members of the audience will suggest stories by emailing, telephoning, popping into the office, or by collaring a reporter at some public event. Some will tell you about personal gripes, some will describe impossibly complicated disputes, and some will tell you that government agents are using lamp-posts to beam poison rays into their bedroom at night. But others will come up with excellent stories. How you treat people will influence whether they come back to you next time.

Regeneration projects

A huge amount of public money is spent on regenerating run-down areas or former industrial sites and such projects can provide both "good news" stories and allegations of miss-spent funds.

Regional development agencies

These quangos bring together regional "stakeholders" and can come up with stories on inward-investment, planning issues, regeneration, and maybe the odd scandal about expenses.

> ❝ The responsibility for truth is left to the source, more often than not. ❞
>
> – Denis McQuail.

Regulatory bodies

Ofwat (water), Postcomm (mail), Ofgem (energy) and all the rest are regular sources of stories about customer complaints, rising prices, excess profits and directors' pay. Broadcast regulator Ofcom adjudicates on complaints from the public on matters such as taste and decency.

Residents' groups

See community groups.

Schools

Schools can provide good news stories about achievements such as productions, sporting feats and exam passes. They can also be the focus of tragic news, especially when trips go wrong.

Scouts, Cubs, Guides, Brownies, Woodcraft Folk

As organisations dependent on attracting new members, youth groups are likely to let you know about events, exchange trips and so on. They also make the news because of changes in traditional activities, songs or uniforms.

Social networking sites

Sites such as Facebook, MySpace and Bebo are now used by people for a growing number of reasons, many of which will be of interest to nosy journalists. In the old days, people upset by something or other might stage a protest on the streets; these days they are just as likely to set up a virtual protest group via Facebook. The existence of a group complaining about high food prices in university accommodation provided a student newspaper with a lively front-page splash: HUNGRY (*Sheffield Steel*, October 12 2007); and when some sixth-formers campaigned against a family being deported to Nigeria they quickly recruited 10,000 supporters by setting up a Facebook group (STUDENT PROTEST HALTS FAMILY'S DEPORTATION, *Guardian*, January 28 2008).

Journalists now routinely check the social networking profiles of people who suddenly become part of the news. When a baby was killed by a pet rottweiler in Wakefield, for example, comments about him posted on Bebo by his parents were used as the source for follow-up stories such as MOTHER OF BOY MAULED TO DEATH PRAISES SISTER (*Guardian*, December 31 2007).

Also being monitored for possible stories is Twitter, a networking system that enables users to share very brief updates via mobile phones or the web. A lot of the time it will be used just for gossip, but it may also give an early indication of something more serious happening – as when Twitterers began sending messages about the ground shaking, in what turned out to be the Chinese earthquake of 2008. Journalism professor and new technology enthusiast Jeff Jarvis (2008) says:

> Twitter is becoming the canary in the news coalmine. It stands to reason: if you've just gone through a major event, you are sure to want to update your friends about it. If enough people are chattering about an earthquake at the same time, that's an immediate indication of a major news story.

Solicitors

"Solicitors are very good sources because they represent people who have been done down," says Paul Foot. It may be in their clients' interests to gain publicity for an appeal against a miscarriage of justice, a civil action for wrongful arrest, or a compensation claim for an industrial disease. Solicitors can become valuable long-term contacts, as Jane Merrick explains:

> There are three or four solicitors in Liverpool – and it's probably the same in most other cities – who tend to deal with the big cases. So it's a question of knowing them well enough, keeping them warm so they'll speak to you and contact you about cases. They like to see their names in the paper.

Sports organisations

Apart from accounts of the winning, the losing and the taking part, you might also find stories about lack of facilities or the sale of playing fields.

Support groups

Groups set up to support people with particular conditions or diseases can come up with fascinating human interest stories.

Theatres

Events, celebs, subject matter and funding are all ways in which a theatre may prompt a news story.

Trade associations

The views of a particular industry might be newsworthy, particularly if it is calling for a change in government policy to prevent closures and job losses.

Trade press

As with academic journals, the trade and specialist press contain many stories of potential interest to the general reader, as long as you can identify and translate them. Journalists on specialist publications can also be interviewed as authoritative sources; for example, editors of railway or aviation magazines are often interviewed as experts after rail or air crashes.

Trades unions

Unions can be an excellent source of stories not just about industrial disputes but everything from pensions scandals to sexual harassment at work. The bigger unions have well-resourced research departments able to provide journalists with useful background material.

Transport companies

Cancellations, strikes, fares increases, punctuality figures, franchise bids, "journeys from hell" and crashes are all obvious news stories. Once in a blue moon you might even come across the occasional good news story from a transport company – an announcement of new investment, perhaps, or the opening of a new route.

Universities

Universities are a source of a huge range of stories, whether it is ground-breaking research, an unusual degree scheme or an ethical argument about accepting funding from a tobacco company. Universities are also where you will find experts in everything from aeronautics to the zodiac.

Websites

In addition to news from around the world there are countless potential stories lurking on the web in sites that are unusual, amusing, quirky, informative, provocative, dangerous, disgusting or just plain nasty.

From sources to stories

Although not exhaustive, the above list covers the major sources used by reporters to originate or check stories. How journalists obtain and evaluate information from sources is discussed further in Chapters 5 and 6. If you keep this list in mind as you watch the TV news, listen to a radio bulletin or read the news in print or online, you should be able to come up with a fairly good idea of where most stories are likely to have come from.

Some sources are less visible than others. There is evidence that the secret intelligence services MI5 and MI6 have attempted – and no doubt succeeded in some cases – to recruit and/or influence journalists (Keeble, 2001b: 117–119). And former Fleet Street journalist Simon Winchester recalls reporting "the troubles" in Northern Ireland and being given off-the-record briefings by military intelligence. Winchester would pass on the contents of the briefing to his audience, telling the nation that the young man shot dead by British soldiers the night before was a leading paramilitary. Only later did he realise that "most of what I gaily rebroadcast was, if not a pure figment of the imagination of some superheated British army intelligence officer, then to a very large degree, wishful thinking" (Winchester, 2001). This underlines the value to a journalist of maintaining a *questioning* attitude, no matter with whom you are dealing.

Putting unattributable briefings with spooks to one side, the strongest news stories come from journalists *talking* to people – and getting people

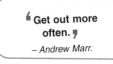

❛ **Get out more often.** ❜

– Andrew Marr.

talking to you. Even a story that originates from a news release or a cutting will be improved by talking to people. Making an extra call or knocking on that extra door might make the difference between having the same story as everyone else or coming up with a fresh angle or a new piece of information. Even though she works as an online journalist covering technology issues, and therefore spends a lot of time in front of a computer screen, Jemima Kiss emphasises the importance of journalists getting out and about to make contacts and pick up potential stories:

> Often I meet people at tech networking things, conferences or lunch, and then we'll speak later by phone about the story. And very often the stories are about US companies, so meeting in person is out. I end up leaving the office most days to meet people, but not necessarily for the stories I do that day.

> When Last.fm was acquired by CBS, I'd been in touch with the guys for a while and lots of crazy acquisition rumours and prices had been swirling around, so everyone knew there was something in the offing. But after mingling with the London tech crowd for a while and really enjoying their buzz and enthusiasm, it was great to have the story about that one, massive £140m deal to vindicate all the activity in London. It was a real good news story.

"The best slogan for a more vigorous and useful news agenda today," says Andrew Marr (2005: 116), would be, "Get out more often."

There is no substitute for speaking to the people directly involved in a story, where possible. That can sometimes require you to be tough and single-minded. But it does not excuse the behaviour witnessed by Edward Behr in newly independent Zaïre, as thousands of Belgian women and children waited to be airlifted to safety:

Into the middle of this crowd strode an unmistakably British TV reporter, leading his cameraman and sundry technicians like a platoon commander through hostile territory. At intervals he paused and shouted, in a stentorian but genteel BBC voice, "Anyone here been raped and speaks English?" (Behr, 1992: 136)

Such insensitivity might get the story, but at what cost? As journalists we have a duty to ourselves, to our sources and to our fellow citizens to pause for reflection from time to time. Without some sense of humanity and empathy, what is the point of our journalism? Lindsay Eastwood recalls one of the most satisfying stories of her career. It wasn't a big breaking news story produced in an adrenalin rush to deadline, but a television documentary about three women with post-natal depression, filmed over several months:

> I'm really proud of it. The women all wanted to do it because they thought that really serious post-natal depression, where you reject your baby, was swept under the carpet. They were really nervous about coming across as bad mothers or as fruitcakes, basically.

I didn't want to over dramatise it so it was quite tricky and I was really, really anxious that they liked the end product. It went out on air and I was really, really nervous waiting to hear from these three women. They all rang and said, "That was just great, thank you so much." I wasn't bothered about what anybody else thought, it was just the women involved, it was really important that they all liked it.

It's nice to get your teeth into something. You breeze in and out of people's lives on a daily basis and you ask them to do these things in front of camera, and do interviews and stuff, and they do it remarkably well. And you think, "I've only spent half an hour with you", so it was nice to get to know these people a bit more.

We might think of people as sources and of their lives in terms of potential stories, but a sense of humanity and a concern for ethics need not be in conflict with good journalism.

▪ ▪ Summary ▪

Journalists need sources to provide information that may be turned into news and to check information provided by other sources. Journalists are surrounded by sources of potential news stories, although many academic studies suggest that a high proportion of stories come from a relatively narrow range of sources. Information on sources is collected in contacts books, and some sources, such as the police, are contacted on a regular basis because they are major suppliers of potential news. Journalists tend to evaluate sources based on their previous experience. It has been suggested that some sources have the power to virtually guarantee access to the news and to frame debate on social issues.

 ## ▪ Questions

Why do journalists need sources?

Why do sources need journalists?

Who has more power, the journalist or the source?

Why do some people or organisations get in the news more than others?

What is the effect of journalists using other media as a source?

▪ ▪ Further reading ▪

The Ethical Journalist (Harcup, 2007) has one chapter discussing sources and another dealing with the ethics of crime reporting that considers the ways in which victims' relatives can be treated by journalists. For further practical advice on the sources of news, Randall (2007), Keeble (2006) and Frost (2002) are all worth dipping into. Manning (2001) is a good introduction to research and more theoretical frameworks on journalist–source relationships, while Tumber (1999) offers useful extracts and Hall et al. (1978) is worth reading for the concept of primary definers. The results of detailed academic research into the sources used by journalists can be found in studies by Lewis et al. (2008a and 2008b).

Sources for soundbites

Whittle, interview with the author; Mansfield, 1936: 82; Schudson, 1989: 271; Swedish reporter, cited in Larsson, 2002: 25; McQuail, 2000: 291; Marr, 2005: 116.

five

the journalist as objective reporter

"Falsehood is so easy, truth so difficult," wrote George Eliot in the novel *Adam Bede*. "Examine your words well, and you will find that even when you have no motive to be false, it is a very hard thing to say the exact truth" (Eliot, 1859: 150–151). Journalists have more reason than most to examine their words well, because they are in the **truth** business; yet the accuracy of Eliot's observation is demonstrated by the frequency with which journalists get things wrong. How wrong? Well, the *Daily Mirror* once famously proclaimed on its front page: IT'S A BOY! EXCLUSIVE: MACCA BABY A MONTH EARLY (October 30 2003), only to follow it up the following day with: ER… IT'S A GIRL! AND SHE'S CALLED BEATRICE – NOT JOSEPH. As the newspaper had the good grace to admit, "our baby scoop was half right" (*Daily Mirror*, October 31 2003). Half right in the sense that the baby of Paul McCartney and Heather Mills had actually been born, but pretty much wrong in everything else.

Journalists are not the only ones to make mistakes. On the day that Jean Charles de Menezes was killed by police officers at Stockwell tube station in London – July 22 2005 – I watched the rolling news broadcasts on television. Witness after witness said what they had seen, which was essentially an Asian man in a bulky coat – maybe wearing a baseball cap, maybe carrying a rucksack – jump the ticket barrier, run like the wind, and be chased on to a tube train before being challenged and shot dead. There is no reason to believe they made any of this up and I am sure the journalists broadcasting these accounts did so in good faith, especially as this version of events seemed to tally with indications already being given by police sources. The next day's

Truth

Truth has become an increasingly slippery notion in recent decades as the apparent certainties of modernity have come under challenge. Yet for many journalists the truth is still out there in the shape of "facts that are verified and explained" (Seib, 2002: 4). Either you can get to this truth or you can't; and if you can't, it's probably because somebody is trying to stop you. Such "general truth claims" have been replaced in much cultural analysis by a foregrounding of more subjective experience (Dovey, 2000: 25) or by a wider claim that the concept of there being *a* truth is merely a monologic *version* of truth produced from within a discourse that is white, male and elitist (Allan, 1998: 124–126). Even reporters witnessing an event for themselves may be carrying all sorts of personal or cultural baggage that can impact on what they see as true and what they recognise as facts (Keeble, 1998: 182).

Despite such claims, truth is not that difficult a concept to grasp, argues Matthew Kieran:

> In journalism, as distinct from fiction, there is a truth of the matter and this is what objectivity in journalism aims at. … Where reporting turns away from the goal of truth and journalists treat events as open to many interpretations, according to their prejudices, assumptions, news agenda or the commercial drive toward entertainment, the justification and self-confessed rationale of journalism threatens to disappear. (Kieran, 1998: 34–35)

Objectivity

Objectivity hinges on separating independently verifiable facts from subjective values (Schudson, 1978: 293). The concept is associated with the Enlightenment project of rationality and the pursuit of scientific knowledge. Such grand thinking has been challenged in recent years, with some postmodernist theorists dismissing as naïve empiricism the idea that there is a

newspapers carried the same sort of material with the *Times*, for example, informing its readers: "The suspect, described as being of Asian appearance and wearing a thick, bulky jacket, vaulted over a ticket barrier when challenged by police and ran down the escalator and along the platform of the Northern Line" (Fresco et al., 2005).

Well, no he did not, as was revealed within days (Honigsbaum, 2005). The *Times* pointed out in a subsequent leader column:

> At the time of the shooting, Scotland Yard said that Mr de Menezes' clothing and his behaviour at the station were suspicious. This claim was buttressed by witnesses who claimed that he was wearing a bulky jacket on a hot day and that he leapt over the ticket barrier at Stockwell station. Now, it turns out that he was wearing only a light denim jacket at the time of his death: perfectly appropriate garb for the time of year. Nor was he carrying a bag or rucksack. There is apparently CCTV footage that shows him walking normally into the station, picking up a free newspaper and using his Oyster card to pass through the barrier. He allegedly began to run only when he saw a train pulling into the station, after which he boarded it and sat down in an ordinary fashion. (*Times*, 2005)

❝ Fact into doubt won't go. ❞
– The Day Today slogan.

So, although the witnesses who spoke to journalists may have seen what they saw, they may not have seen what they *thought* they saw. It turns out that a man did vault the ticket barrier and run at high speed towards the train, for example; it was not Mr de Menezes, but a police officer.

Objective reporting

It is perhaps understandable that people who witness a traumatic event might put two and two together in an attempt to make sense of it, and that in the process they might make some assumptions that are wrong. As Eliot said, it can be

truth that exists "out there" in the world, independent of discourse, just waiting to be discovered.

A commitment to objectivity in journalism can be defined as meaning that "a person's statements about the world can be trusted if they are submitted to established rules deemed legitimate by a professional community" (Schudson, 1978: 294). Michael Schudson further explains:

> The objectivity norm guides journalists to separate facts from values and to report only the facts. Objective reporting is supposed to be cool, rather than emotional, in tone. Objective reporting takes pains to represent fairly each leading side in a political controversy. According to the objectivity norm, the journalist's job consists of reporting something called "news" without commenting on it, slanting it, or shaping its formulation in any way. (Schudson, 2001: 150)

But journalism was not always expected to be objective, and the above norm was not a constituent part of those 18th-century publications such as the *Craftsman* and the *Gentleman's Magazine* that helped establish the press as "a genuinely critical organ of a public engaged in critical political debate: as the fourth estate" (Habermas, 1992: 60). Before the 1830s newspapers were expected to be partisan and "objectivity was not an issue" (Schudson, 1978: 291). The emergence of the US "penny press", with many papers being politically neutral or indifferent, brought a new range of news values privileging factual coverage of human interest stories over analysis or opinion (Allan, 1997: 304–305). The gradual adoption of objectivity as a normative standard of news reporting may have been encouraged by the development of wire services such as Associated Press (AP) from 1848. AP had a market imperative to concentrate on the bare facts, compressed into the intro, so that it could sell the same stories to newspapers with widely divergent politics. This strategy of unadorned reportage helped AP staff overcome the unreliable nature of the new technology and placed a premium on brevity (Allan, 1997: 306).

But Schudson says the journalist's commitment to separating facts from values may have had more to do with the rising status of reporters in relation to their employers in the late 19th and early 20th centuries, and with a professional debate about objectivity in the years after the First World War.

very hard to say the exact truth. Yet the truth – sometimes referred to as the "objective truth" – is what journalists are aiming at; something that can be backed up with evidence, verified, and demonstrated to be the case.

Because of the constraints discussed in Chapter 2, and because of reasons outlined above, it is probably more accurate to say that journalists strive to give the most truthful version of events that can be obtained at any one time. This is what is meant by **objectivity** or objective reporting, which has been defined as:

- balance and even-handedness in presenting different sides of an issue
- accuracy and realism in reporting
- presenting all main relevant points
- separating facts from opinion, but treating opinion as relevant
- minimising the influence of the writer's own attitude, opinion or involvement
- avoiding slant, rancour or devious purposes (Boyer 1981, cited in Watson, 1998: 98).

Furthermore, broadcast journalists in the UK have a statutory requirement to be impartial. According to the BBC, **impartiality** entails "a mixture of accuracy, balance, context, distance, evenhandedness, fairness, objectivity, open-mindedness, rigour, self-awareness, transparency and truth". Phew, is that all? Not quite, because impartiality also requires "breadth of view and completeness" (BBC Trust, 2007a: 5–6). A survey of 2,000 people in the UK found 84 per cent of them agreeing – half of them "strongly" – with the statement "impartiality is difficult to achieve, but broadcasters must try very hard to do so"; only three per cent disagreed. However, this view is itself a partial one, because there was noticeably less support for impartiality among younger people, black

Therefore, "a self-conscious, articulate ideology of objectivity can be dated to the 1920s" (Schudson, 2001: 159–160). In the UK, as Chris Frost notes, the move towards a less partisan style of reporting gathered momentum only during the early part of the 20th century, culminating in the imposition of a statutory obligation to be impartial on the fledgling broadcasting industry (Frost, 2000: 159).

Impartiality

The words "impartiality" and "objectivity" are sometimes used interchangeably, but impartial reporting is normally defined as being neutral, while objective reporting is taken to be the reporting of verifiable facts. According to McQuail, impartiality means "balance in the choice and use of sources, so as to reflect different points of view, and also neutrality in the presentation of news – separating facts from opinion, avoiding value judgements or emotive language or pictures" (McQuail, 2000: 321). For Frost, impartial reporting means that a journalist is *aiming* at the truth, whereas true objectivity would require giving the *whole* picture – a task as impossible for the journalist as it is (in an analogy borrowed from Hartley) for the cartographer (Frost, 2000: 38). That is because, like a map, a news report is still a selective and *mediated* representation of reality, rather than the reality itself.

Balance and neutrality have themselves been problematised by some journalists who advocate their abandonment in situations where to be impartial would mean standing "neutrally between good and evil, right and wrong, the victim and the oppressor" (Bell, 1998: 16). This raises inevitable questions about *who* defines good and evil and whether journalists who *do* take sides automatically abandon any claims to be able to report events *objectively*. It could be argued, for example, that journalism unencumbered by neutrality might actually be *more* objective because the audience knows where the journalist is coming from. Viewed this way, *Socialist Worker* or *Indymedia* would be more objective than *BBC News* or *Sky News* because the

> ❝ The more one is aware of political bias, the more one can be independent of it, and the more one claims to be impartial, the more one is biased. ❞
>
> —*George Orwell.*

people, and working-class people (BBC Trust, 2007a: 19).

Unlike broadcasting organisations, newspapers have no statutory requirement to be impartial, whether between the commercial interests of rival proprietors or between rival political policies or parties. General elections would not be the same without *agenda setting* headlines such as LABOUR'S TAX LIES EXPOSED (*Daily Express*, March 23 1992) and a labour government will lead to higher mortgage payments (*Daily Mail*, April 7 1992). Despite the fact that broadcasting organisations are required by law to be impartial, TV and radio journalists' election coverage can still be influenced by a press agenda focusing on certain issues (tax, crime, Europe) to the exclusion of others (homelessness, poverty, jobs). And a clockwatching "balance" between the Labour and Conservative parties also tends to result in the marginalisation of the Liberal Democrats and other smaller parties.

> ❝ Between elections, if you're relevant and intelligent and know how to popularise an issue, you can help set the agenda. ❞
> – Rupert Murdoch.

Wot, no objectivity?

If objective reporting of elections is problematic – the country being divided – then what of objective reporting of warfare, when a country is supposedly united against a common enemy? That truth is the first casualty of war has become a truism, but objective reporting has repeatedly gone to the wall in the name of national unity. British Prime Minister Lloyd George alluded to this in 1917, during a private conversation about the battlefield horrors of the First World War: "If people really knew, the war would be stopped tomorrow. But of course they don't know and can't know. The correspondents don't write and the censorship would not pass the truth" (quoted in Knightley, 2000: 116–117).

political and cultural assumptions of the first two are made explicit – and can therefore be taken into account by audiences – whereas the political and cultural assumptions of the last two remain implicit or hidden.

Agenda setting

The term "agenda setting" was coined by Maxwell McCombs and Donald Shaw in their study of media coverage and voter attitudes in the 1968 US presidential election campaign. They found that the media exerted a considerable impact on voters' judgements of what were the salient issues of the campaign (McCombs and Shaw, 1972: 323–324). On the basis of this and similar studies, it is argued that, although the media might not be able to tell us what to *think*, they have an influence on what we think *about*. But agenda setting has since been dismissed as "at best a hackneyed half-truth" on the grounds that it downplays the existence of multiple agendas by media organisations and voters alike (Wilson, 1996: 30).

McQuail notes that the direction of flow in the agenda-setting model could be reversed, raising the possibility that, rather than *setting* the agenda, the media merely *reflect* the attitudes of voters. For him, agenda setting remains a "plausible but unproven idea" (McQuail, 2000: 456). Much the same could perhaps be said about other theories of media effects and about the postmodern tendency to shift attention away from media production and on to media consumption, thereby privileging "the instability of meaning and the interpretative horizons of the audience" (Stevenson, 2002: 29).

Subjectivity

Reflexivity and the foregrounding of subjective experience may have become increasingly fashionable in the mainstream media (Dovey, 2000) as well as the blogosphere, but for the most part news journalism remains a bastion of the authoritative-sounding "objective" approach. This is a deeply undesirable state of affairs for cultural theorist John Fiske, who argues that journalists would better

Are we any better informed today? Research suggests that tabloid headlines such as GO GET HIM BOYS (*Daily Star*, January 16 1991) and the obsession of TV news with "smart bombs" and "Star Wars" technology painted a very partial picture of the 1991 Gulf war, rendering invisible some of the salient issues (including oil supplies), not to mention Iraqi civilian casualties (Philo and McLaughlin, 1993: 146–155). Reflecting shortly after that war, BBC reporter John Simpson identified a gap in UK television's saturation coverage of the conflict: "As for the human casualties, tens of thousands of them, or the brutal effect the war had on millions of others … we didn't see so much of that" (quoted in Philo and McLaughlin, 1993: 155). Nor did we hear very much about the "undeclared war" waged against Iraq in the decade that followed. Figures released quietly by the Ministry of Defence in November 2000 showed that 84 tonnes of bombs had been dropped on southern Iraq by British aircraft over the previous two years (Norton-Taylor, 2000). This silent bombing campaign passed almost unnoticed by the UK media, which awoke only to cheer on occasional spectaculars with headlines such as US LAUNCHES AIR STRIKES ON BAGHDAD (*Daily Telegraph*, February 17 2001) and WE BOMB BAGHDAD (*Sun*, February 17 2001). Note the use of "we" in the latter example – a tiny word with huge meanings.

"The way wars are reported in the western media follows a depressingly predictable pattern," wrote Phillip Knightley as US and UK forces geared up to attack Afghanistan in 2001, following the September 11 attacks in the USA: "Stage one, the crisis; stage two, the demonisation of the enemy's leader; stage three, the demonisation of the enemy as individuals; and stage four, … the atrocity story" (Knightley, 2001). Such coverage prepares the public for battle "by showing that the enemy is evil, mad and a danger to the civilised world" (Knightley, 2002). Stephen Dorril traced the leaking of intelligence containing truths,

reflect reality if they became more like the writers of TV soaps:

> Objectivity is authority in disguise: "objective" facts always support particular points of view and their "objectivity" can exist only as part of the play of power. But, more important, objective facts cannot be challenged: objectivity discourages audience activity and participation. Rather than being "objective", therefore, TV news should present *multiple perspectives* that, like those of soap opera, have as unclear a hierarchy as possible. ... [The] reporters should be less concerned about telling the final truth of what has happened, and should present, instead, *different ways of understanding* it and the different points of view inscribed in those different ways. So, too, they should not disguise their processes of selection and editing, but should open them up to reveal news as a production, not as transparent reportage. (Fiske, 1989: 194, my emphasis)

It is not easy to imagine what such a form of journalism would look like in practice. But we might find out sooner rather than later if Stuart Allan is right when he says that there is no reason to expect objectivity – as a historically specific concept – to continue to be one of journalism's guiding principles (Allan, 1997: 319).

Moral panics

A moral panic could be described as the periodic response of "right-thinking people" to someone or something perceived as "other". Stanley Cohen researched the Mods and Rockers youth subcultures of the 1960s, and summarised moral panics thus:

> A condition, episode, person or group of persons emerges to become defined as a threat to societal values and interests; its nature is presented in a stylised and stereotypical fashion by the mass media; the moral barricades are manned by editors, bishops, politicians and other right-thinking people; socially accredited experts pronounce their diagnoses and solutions; ways of coping are evolved or (more often) resorted to; the condition then disappears, submerges or deteriorates and becomes more visible. Sometimes the object of the panic is quite novel and at other times it is something which has been in existence long enough, but suddenly appears in the limelight. Sometimes the panic passes over and is forgotten, except in folklore and collective memory; at other times it has more serious and long-lasting repercussions and might produce such changes as those in legal and social policy or even in the way society conceives itself. (Cohen, 1972: 9)

half-truths and untruths about Iraq to "trusted journalists" (Dorril, 2002a). "If the history of the media teaches us anything," he concluded, "it is that the 'war on terrorism' is a ripe opportunity for disinformation and the creation of provocative incidents which the press reports with casual disregard for the truth" (Dorril, 2002b).

What Paul Foot called "war fever" seemed to infect many – but not all – UK newsrooms before and during the US-led invasion of Iraq in 2003. When the *Sun* reported the start of the Iraq war with the headline SHOW THEM NO PITY ... THEY HAVE STAINS ON THEIR SOULS (*Sun*, March 20 2003), staff journalist Katy Weitz promptly resigned from the paper because, as she explained, "I want to be proud of the work I help to produce, not shudder in shame at its front-page blood lust" (Weitz, 2003).

Some journalists became "embedded" with the military: living with them, travelling with them, coming under their protection, and reporting under military restrictions. Unsurprisingly, perhaps, they tended to adopt the perspective of their hosts and protectors, as US journalist Gordon Dillow later admitted: "I found myself falling in love with my subject. I fell in love with 'my' Marines. ... The point wasn't that I wasn't reporting the truth; the point was that I was reporting the Marine grunt truth ... which had also become my truth" (quoted in Brandenburg, 2007: 957).

But it is not only those who move in military circles or who support their own government's war efforts who sometimes discard the cloak of objectivity. Reflecting on his role in reporting conflicts around the world, veteran journalist James Cameron wrote:

> [O]bjectivity in some circumstances is both meaningless and impossible. I still do not see how a reporter attempting to define a situation involving some sort of ethical conflict can do it with sufficient demonstrable neutrality to fulfil some arbitrary concept of "objectivity". It never occurred to me, in such a situation, to be other than subjective, and as obviously as I could manage to be. (Cameron, 1968: 72)

In a classic study of the phenomenon of mugging in the 1970s, Stuart Hall and colleagues concluded that a moral panic about what was perceived as a race-specific crime was created by a mutually reinforcing circle between powerful "primary definers" (police, judges, politicians and so on) and the media to effect "an ideological closure of the topic" (Hall et al., 1978: 75). This shorthand equation of black youths with mugging in the 1970s was echoed three decades on in the media's readiness to associate Muslims with terrorism (Richardson, 2001: 229; Karim, 2002: 102; Seib, 2002: 114). However, as with agenda setting, it is possible that media coverage of a "moral panic" *reflects* rather than *creates* a public demonisation of a particular social grouping at a particular time. Or is it a more circular process of mutual reinforcement of popular views – a form of "common sense"?

Strategic ritual

It may be that Tuchman's strategic ritual of objectivity is more concerned with ritual than with objectivity, becaus the journalist retains the power to select who to quote and what evidence to include. Just as, when writing this book, *I* have chosen who to interview, which publications to cite, and what issues to address. But I have not acted in a vacuum and, just as journalists act under the influence of constraints discussed in Chapter 2, so I have made my editorial choices within a wider context.

In the Harvey Nichols story discussed in this book, it could be argued that I followed the strategic ritual and that the story was true. It could also be argued that the story had little independent objective existence, because most of the opinions or actions that helped stand the story up were *solicited* by me after I received the initial tip-off. My fingerprints were all over the story that appeared in the next day's papers, yet they could not be detected with the naked eye.

The formula of presenting conflicting versions in a story means that journalists – rarely experts in a particular subject – do not normally have to decide between competing truth claims. As Keeble notes, reporters use sources to distance themselves from stories (Keeble, 2001a: 44). Sometimes journalists *do* privilege one source, or truth claim, over another. For example, in this chapter I have quoted ACPO as giving "the facts" about crime and asylum seekers. But

He felt that *subjectivity* could be important; that a journalist's attitude should be up front and open to scrutiny or counter-argument. Similarly, George Orwell argued that the reader could be freed of the influence of a journalist's "bias" only if the reader were made *aware* of it (cited in Pilger, 1998: 525). Certainly there is no mistaking the attitude of John Pilger, writing in the *Daily Mirror* about the bombing of Afghanistan under the headline THIS WAR OF LIES GOES ON:

> There was, and still is, no "war on terrorism". Instead, we have watched a variation of the great imperial game of swapping "bad" terrorists for "good" terrorists, while untold numbers of innocent people have paid with their lives: most of one village, whole families, a hospital, as well as teenage conscripts suitably dehumanised by the word "Taliban". (Pilger, 2001)

Some journalists who reject Pilger's campaigning style nonetheless question the professional commitment to objectivity when covering bloody conflicts. After ITN reporter Michael Nicholson adopted an orphaned girl he met while covering the Bosnian war, he said: "No, I don't believe in this so-called objectivity. You can still report the facts. You can still be as close to the truth as any person can be and still show a commitment, an emotional anguish. I don't see them to be contradictory" (quoted in McLaughlin, 2002b: 154).

Former BBC correspondent Martin Bell has urged what he calls "a journalism of attachment". While accepting that facts are sacred, Bell wants journalists covering conflicts to accept the "moral responsibility" that they also have the power to *affect* the events on which they are reporting (quoted in McLaughlin, 2002b: 178). Christiane Amanpour of CNN argues along similar lines without necessarily rejecting the concept of objectivity itself:

> I have come to believe that objectivity means giving all sides a fair hearing, but not treating all sides equally. Once you treat all sides the same in a case such as

is their account more objectively true than are lurid press headlines? Yes, in the sense that the ACPO version is based on crime statistics. But can such figures be regarded as objective when they are based only on *reported* rather than *actual* crime? By following the strategic ritual and stating from where information comes, and when it is disputed, journalists can absolve themselves from the responsibility of deciding who is right and who is wrong on such issues. As one journalist put it: "We don't deal in facts but in attributed opinions" (quoted in Gans, 1980: 246).

Common sense

Journalists use their common sense to assess whether something has the ring of truth about it. But common sense itself can be seen as socially, culturally and historically constructed, rendering it highly questionable as any sort of "objective" test. Useful here is the concept of hegemony, the way in which a dominant class is said not merely to rule a society but also to exert moral and intellectual leadership, albeit contested (Gramsci, 1971: 57). Hegemony goes beyond mere manipulation of opinion to saturate society and become regarded as "common sense" (Williams, 1980: 37–38). This does not mean that common sense contains *no* truths; rather, that common sense is "an ambiguous, contradictory and multiform concept, and *to refer to common sense as a confirmation of truth is a nonsense*" (Gramsci, 1971: 423, my emphasis).

> ❛ The truth is rarely pure and never simple. ❜
> – Oscar Wilde.

Bosnia, you are drawing a moral equivalence between victim and aggressor. And from there it is a short step toward being neutral. And from there it's an even shorter step to becoming an accessory to all manners of evil; in Bosnia's case, genocide. So objectivity must go hand in hand with morality. (Quoted in Seib, 2002: 53)

Taking such arguments a stage further are the few journalists who step aside from their reporting role and appear as witnesses at international war crimes tribunals. BBC correspondent Jacky Rowland was cross-examined by former Yugoslav president Slobodan Milosevic when she testified at the Hague in 2002 about events in Kosovo three years earlier. Afterwards, she explained why she defied fellow journalists' arguments that she had compromised her impartiality and posed a threat to future war correspondents:

> I believe that journalists are essentially witnesses to the events they report on. My testimony to the Hague tribunal was an extension of this. … When I met the witness who was due to take the stand after me – a woman who had lost eight members of her family in an alleged massacre by Serbian police – I felt that a journalist's arguments for not testifying looked rather weak. (Rowland, 2002)

Adhering to traditional journalistic objectivity while remaining true to a sense of moral responsibility can be a difficult ethical balancing act. Philip Seib points to another tribunal at which a reporter's notebooks – containing sensitive information on confidential sources – were scrutinised in public. Risking "burning" a source in this way may dissuade other sources from speaking to journalists in the future: "That is a substantial price, but some journalists may judge it to be reasonable given the substance of a war crimes trial" (Seib, 2002: 86).

> ❛ To journalists, like social scientists, the term "objectivity" stands as a bulwark between themselves and critics. ❜
> – Gaye Tuchman.

From enemies without to "the enemy within", which was how Prime Minister Margaret Thatcher characterised the coalminers who staged a year-long strike against pit closures in 1984/5. Much media coverage of the miners' strike was framed by a few key themes, with three phrases being repeated throughout the dispute: uneconomic pits, picket line violence, the drift back to work (Hollingsworth, 1986: 242–285; Philo, 1991: 37–42; Williams, 2009). In contrast, a decade later another group of workers found their battle largely ignored. More than 300 Liverpool dockers were sacked for refusing to cross a picket line in 1995, and for two years their campaign for reinstatement won support and considerable media coverage in other countries, but remarkably few headlines in their own country's media. At the time, one docker told me matter-of-factly that the UK government had imposed a "news blackout" on the story – it was the only explanation he could come up with for the dearth of coverage. But most editors do not need to be *told* to ignore "boring" industrial disputes in favour of celebrity gossip, as John Pilger notes:

> Because the myths of the "market" have become received wisdom throughout the media, with millions of trade unionists dismissed as "dinosaurs", the dockers' story has been seen as a flickering curiosity of a bygone era. That their struggle represented more than half of all working people caught up in the iniquities of casual or part-time labour, making Britain the sweatshop of Europe, was not considered *real news*. (Pilger, 1998: 354, my emphasis)

Objectivity, then, is not simply concerned with *how* a particular story is covered, but also with *what* is selected as a potential story – and what is ignored. It sometimes seems as if issues come from nowhere to dominate headlines for a few weeks before disappearing again; mugging, "devil dogs", a mysterious flesh-eating bug, video nasties, juvenile crime, paedophiles, "happy slapping", and asylum seekers are just some examples of what have become known as **moral panics**, during which professionals with expert knowledge of a field are often appalled by the media's apparent lack of objectivity or regard to the facts. For example, in February 2001 – after more than a year of hostile press coverage claiming that asylum seekers had brought a crime wave to parts of Kent – the Association of Chief Police Officers (ACPO) noted:

> In Dover, continual interest from the media, locally and nationally, has been focused on the 'apparent' *increase* in crime since asylum seekers have been in the town. In line with general trends in Kent, the local commander was able to report an actual *reduction* in all aspects of reported crime over a three year period. This generally resulted in the national media not reporting anything as this was not what they had been told by some locals and was *not what their editors wanted*. (ACPO, 2001, my emphasis)

We heard in Chapter 2 how headlines about asylum seekers in the *Express* caused disquiet among some of the paper's own journalists. Even a brief item about the publication of a new dictionary was headlined NOW ASYLUM SEEKERS INVADE OUR DICTIONARY (*Daily Express*, September 26 2002). Similar themes are to be found in the *Daily Mail*: ASYLUM: YES, BRITAIN IS A SOFT TOUCH! (February 1 2001) and PATIENTS LOSE GP'S SURGERY TO ASYLUM SEEKERS (September 5 2002) being just two of many similar examples.

The *Mail* has an agenda of moral outrage and has long been accused of abandoning notions of objectivity in favour of peddling a particular "Middle England" world view, exemplified by its ideal of aspirational, property-owning Conservative voters who believe in family values. In the words of a former *Daily Mail* journalist: "You kind of know what the obsessions are, and you very much know

you've got to do a story in a specific way" (quoted in Beckett, 2001).

Objectivity as a 'strategic ritual'

The above examples might suggest that objective reporting is honoured more in the breach than in the actuality. But this does not mean the concept of objective reporting has no resonance for working journalists. In my experience, *most* journalists, *most* of the time, *do* attempt to be objective; albeit their objectivity can be very different depending on the culture, market and ownership of the news organisation they work for.

According to Gaye Tuchman, objectivity can be seen as a **strategic ritual** that journalists use as a defence mechanism. She identified four routine procedures that allow journalists to claim objectivity for their work:

> ❝ Opinions are like assholes. Everybody has one. ❞
> – *Clint Eastwood as Dirty Harry.*

- The presentation of conflicting possibilities.
- The presentation of supporting evidence.
- The judicious use of quotation marks.
- The structuring of information in an appropriate sequence (Tuchman, 1972: 299–301).

Journalists might see themselves as satisfying their professional commitment to objectivity by taking the following steps before publishing:

- Looking at both sides of a story.
- Assessing conflicting claims.
- Assessing the credibility of sources.
- Looking for evidence.
- Not publishing anything believed to be untrue.
- In short, seeing if the story stands up.

In the light of this formula, let's revisit the Harvey Nichols story discussed in Chapter 4. The initial source was known to me as someone reliable, so

I immediately took her call seriously. My experience told me it was a potentially newsworthy story because of the high-profile nature of the Harvey Nichols store. After looking at the offending posters to confirm what I had been told, I suggested to my source that there might be a story if someone actually complained. From her I obtained copies of several letters of complaint sent to the company and the Advertising Standards Agency. I also spoke to Harvey Nichols' PR people to get their side of the story and consulted cuttings for background on the firm. I approached a senior councillor on the local authority women's committee to ask whether she would be proposing that the council itself made a formal complaint. She gave some strong quotes and said that she would indeed be proposing such a course of action. So I had some complainants, meaning the Advertising Standards Authority would have to investigate the issue; I had opinion from someone in a position of some authority; I had background information on the company involved; and I had a comment from the company, disputing claims that the posters were offensive. The story stood up.

> ‘ Comment is free, but facts are sacred. ’
> – CP Scott, editor of the Manchester Guardian, 1921.

If a story stands up it will be written with the journalist taking care to give both sides. The journalist will make it clear when claims are disputed, will attribute information and opinion to external sources, and will not mix what appear to be facts with the journalist's own comments. At least, that is what *usually* happens. Things are not always quite that simple. For a start, aren't there often more than *two* sides to a story?

Even looking at "both sides" is not always strictly adhered to. One of my first assignments on one local paper was to report on residents' complaints about a group of Gypsies – the usual allegations of theft, defecation and general lowering of the value of property. Eyebrows were raised in the newsroom when I said I was going to ask the Gypsies themselves for their version of events. It seemed that a comment from the police or local authority was thought to be sufficient to balance the story. I persisted and not only got a better story – the Gypsies threatening to move their caravans on to hallowed town-centre grassland if they continued to be hounded from pillar to post – but also found out that many of them were actually "locals", having been born in the area (*Harrogate Advertiser*, September 23 1989). It was nothing special, it was just journalism. But it remains unusual to see Gypsies or asylum seekers quoted in response to allegations against them. Given social prejudices against such groups, is it not *more* rather than *less* important for journalists to get their side of the story?

Checking the facts

Journalists routinely assess conflicting claims, weigh the credibility of sources, and check the facts by looking for evidence. Sources, however, are not equal. If the police say that three people have been killed in a road accident, then journalists will report that "fact" without first feeling the need to drive to the scene, count the bodies and feel for a pulse. But if a motorist calls the newsroom with the same story, then a reporter will check it out – by calling the police – before reporting it. Checking the facts of a story begins with comparing what we have been told with what we "know" of the world; with our knowledge and experience; asking whether, at a **common sense** level, it has the ring of truth about it? If it doesn't, a potential story might be dropped as not worth further effort.

If a potential story survives this first test, we might check the facts further by looking at published sources, by observing at first hand, by talking to people involved, and/or by talking to independent observers or experts. If the story involves a suggestion of some kind of wrongdoing, it becomes even more important to look for independent verification. During their epic Watergate investigation into undemocratic and illegal activities carried out by supporters of US President Richard Nixon, reporters Carl Bernstein and Bob Woodward had a secret source – Deep Throat – who would give them information on condition of anonymity. They did not publish what the source told them unless they could verify it elsewhere. "Gradually, an unwritten rule was evolving," they later wrote. "Unless two sources *confirmed* a charge involving activity likely to be considered criminal, the specific allegation was not used in the paper" (Bernstein and Woodward, [1974] 2005: 79, my emphasis). This is referred to as the three-source guideline, whereby a serious allegation should normally be corroborated with two additional and reliable sources of information (Brennen, 2003: 123).

However, despite a desire to check facts, journalists frequently publish things that turn out to be untrue. Inaccuracies might appear because sources do not (yet) know the full story. Initial reports after the attack on the World Trade Centre on September 11 2001 suggested that 10,000 people had been killed (*Sun*, September 12 2001; *Daily Mail*, September 13 2001). For weeks journalists were still reporting that up to 7,000 people had died, but by November 2001 New York police put the death toll at 3,702 (Lipton, 2001). A year after the attacks the official death toll had been reduced to 2,801 (Lipton, 2002) and in 2003 this was reduced further to 2,752 (BBC, 2003). By the fifth anniversary of the attacks the official number of dead had been reduced to 2,749, although there may also have been an unknown number of undocumented "illegal" workers killed (Tutek, 2006).

Inaccuracies might appear in stories because a journalist has made an assumption and not

bothered to check, because an inaccurate cutting has been relied on, and because of a shortage of time to check. Foreign correspondents complain that they are under such time pressure, filing reports for different news outlets, that they barely have time to go outside and see for themselves what is happening; they end up simply regurgitating information fed back to them from London (Harcup, 1996). Inaccuracies might appear because a journalist has misused or misunderstood statistics, or has failed to question such misuse by a source. And inaccuracies might appear because a source lies, as when 13 art students claimed to have spent their £1,000-plus exhibition grant partying on Spanish beaches (STUDENTS USE GRANT FOR HOLIDAY, *Daily Express*, May 19 1998), only to reveal that they hadn't spent a penny, had faked the holiday snaps in Yorkshire, and that the resulting media spectacle had been "a talking point about what is art" (STUDENTS' WORK OF ART WAS CHEAP FORGERY, *Times*, May 20 1998). How about the shark fever in the summer of 2007, when it was widely reported that a deadly great white shark had been spotted – and photographed – off the coast of Cornwall? It turned out that the picture had been taken during a trip to South Africa by Cornish bouncer Kevin Keeble, who sent it to his local newspaper "as a joke" (Morris, 2007).

And, when Gretna football club sent out a spoof press release (dated on April Fool's Day) about one of their players starring in a TV soap opera, the story was splashed all over the *Carlisle News and Star*. Richard Eccles, deputy editor of the hoaxed newspaper, commented afterwards: "You could say there is a genuine lesson for us all about following up press releases" (quoted in Lagan, 2007). Indeed you could.

There is an old tabloid saying that, "It's all right flying a kite, but remember to keep hold of the string". Yet there are occasions when the kite soars into the sky with the journalist still trying

> ❛ Who you gonna believe, me or your own eyes? ❜
> – Chico Marx.

to cling on. This is particularly the case when a reporter comes under pressure to *make* a story stand up. I once came across a tabloid hack trying desperately to find non-existent irate white parents to condemn their local authority serving curry for school dinner, just because his editor had already thought up a possible headline: WE'LL HAVE NAAN OF THAT! Mercifully, I don't think that particular story ever appeared; it had just been an editor's passing fancy at morning conference, later overtaken by the day's events. Pure invention remains the exception in journalism, although Abul Taher warns: "There is a lot of cutting corners, dishonesty about sources and interviews. A lot of people end up doctoring the truth for a good story. It's a job that is a daily ritual of moral and intellectual compromise."

A compromise it may be but, however imperfectly, most reporters seem to retain some sense of objectivity in their everyday routines. Jane Merrick gives a not untypical journalist's response when asked about objective reporting:

When I sit down to write a story I never think, "Is this objective?" But I'm always aware of being fair and balanced and having both sides of a story. I'm not sure you *can* be objective. I've never really thought about it, to be honest.

The key thing is to be *fair*, argues Jon Snow of *Channel 4 News*:

I don't think there's such a thing as a neutral journalist. Human beings are moved by what they see, either against it or for it, admiringly or despairingly, or whatever it is. And I think those qualities are essential, otherwise what the journalist reports becomes an unnatural event. ... I'm against neutrality. But I'm for fairness at the same time. Complete fairness. You've got to recognise what your dispositions are, and balance them by allowing other points of view. (Quoted in Roy, 2002: 38)

For Martin Wainwright, objectivity means approaching stories with an open mind, giving all sides their say, including as much contextual information as possible, and trying to show what underlies people's actions. This leads him to be critical of the more heart-on-sleeve style of journalism associated with the likes of James Cameron and John Pilger:

All my experience as a journalist teaches me that situations are always complicated, and there very seldom is *one* source of evil. Very emotional journalism has some limited use in waking people up to a bad situation, but when it comes to actually telling people what's going on and why it's happened I do think you need to be as dispassionate as possible. The less of the journalist the better, I think. Some people say it's more dangerous to pretend to be objective and actually not be, and they say nobody is objective because you can't be. That's all true. But *you can have a very good shot at being objective*, I'm sure you can. It's a counsel of despair to say we've all got to be subjective.

One of the ways of guarding against inaccurate reporting is to acknowledge how easy it is to make errors, as Anna McKane (2006: 86) suggests: "Probably a general assumption that you have got it wrong, rather than a general assumption that you have got it right, would help. So develop the habit of checking everything three times." That is advice that would have appealed to George "examine your words well" Eliot, whose real name was Mary Ann Evans ... until she changed the Mary Ann to Marian (Drabble and Stringer, 1990: 176). One of the very first things that journalists must learn is to get people's names right; the fact that one person might have several different names only emphasises how tricky such a seemingly simple task can be.

> ❛ Don't believe anyone, not even us. ❜
> – Radio B92 slogan.

▆ ▆ Summary ▆

Objective reporting is commonly understood to involve separating verifiable facts from subjective feelings. Journalists' use of objectivity has been described as a "strategic ritual" to distance themselves from stories; a defence against charges of bias and lack of professionalism. This formula involves presenting conflicting possibilities and supporting evidence, with attributed opinion and information, in an appropriate sequence. The objectivity norm and the related concept of impartiality have been challenged for being impossible to achieve; for ignoring the existence of multiple perspectives; and for being undesirable in conflicts between right and wrong. Nonetheless, most journalists appear to retain some sense of objectivity when assessing sources and checking facts to establish whether a story stands up.

▆ Questions

Is there a distinction between objectivity and impartiality?

How would impartiality change our newspapers?

If objectivity is impossible to achieve, does it make any sense to aim for it?

Which gets closer to the truth, subjective or objective journalism?

How might journalists feature different narratives and multiple perspectives?

▆ ▆ Further reading ▆

Handy hints on reporting accurately on – and questioning – anything to do with numbers, statistics and averages can be found in the entertaining book *The Tiger That Isn't* by Blastland and Dilnot (2007); Randall (2007) and McKane (2006) also have useful chapters on the subject, while Frost (2002) provides a brief practical account of the basics of reporting and fact-checking. Edited collections with readable and illuminating contributions covering objectivity include Kieran (1998), Bromley and O'Malley (1997), and Tumber (1999). John Pilger's (1998) eloquent if holier-than-thou critique of the world amounts to a sustained challenge to most of what passes for objective journalism in the mainstream media; Nick Davies (2008) offers a similarly bleak view of how most members of the fourth estate fulfil their function. McLaughlin (2002b) has an interesting discussion of objectivity, conflict and the "journalism of attachment", based in part on interviews with war correspondents. For a more theoretical perspective, Stevenson (2002) explores various Marxist explanations of the media – touching on objectivity, hegemony and moral panics – as well as the postmodernist challenge to the concept of the truth. Critcher (2002) subjects the concepts of moral panic and agenda setting to critical scrutiny within the context of the *News of the World*'s "name and shame" campaign on paedophilia.

Sources for soundbites

The Day Today, BBC Worldwide DVD, 2004; Orwell, quoted in Pilger, 1998: 525; Murdoch, Channel 4, 1998; Wilde, *Importance of Being Earnest*, Act 1; Tuchman, 1972: 297; Eastwood in *The Dead Pool*, quoted in Hudson and Rowlands, 2007: 271; Scott, quoted in O'Malley and Soley, 2000: 23; Marx, *Duck Soup*; B92, quoted in Seib, 2002: 99.

six

the journalist as
investigator

When freedom of information legislation came into force in 2005 I wanted to use it to shine a bit of light into one of the dark corners of the UK: quangoland, a place that is populated by the great and the good who sit on each others' boards and spend well over £100 billion of taxpayers' money every year without the hindrance of elections or democratic accountability. I used the new Freedom of Information (FOI) Act to ask a publicly funded regional development agency, Yorkshire Forward, how much it spent on corporate hospitality – wining, dining, boxes at big sporting events, that kind of thing – and for the names of the recipients. In response to my FOI request I was told that people's names were exempt information under data protection laws; and that, even if it wasn't exempt, accessing such information would simply be too expensive.

To cut a long story short, I persevered with an internal appeal, followed by a referral to the Information Commissioner, and finally with an appeal to the Information Tribunal. Three years later, after exchanges of correspondence and evidence amounting to well over 300 pages, I won a victory of sorts when the tribunal dismissed as "absurd" the argument of Yorkshire Forward and the Information Commissioner that individuals' names were significant personal information, and therefore exempt from release. But, although I won on principle, the tribunal ruled that the information need not actually be released because collating it would cost the quango more than the £450 limit set by the Act.

Undeterred, I put in a couple of fresh FOI requests: one, to get the names of those wined and dined over a shorter (and therefore cheaper) period of time; two, to discover how much had been spent on legal fees to resist my original request. This time

Investigative journalism

The concept of investigative journalism is a problematic one, as Mark Hanna notes: "The term 'investigative journalist' smacks of pretension, and has few ardent adherents among practitioners. But it helps denote the self-motivation, the experience and knowledge, the methodology and the set of skills which sustain a journalist through a complex, lengthy assignment" (Hanna in Franklin et al., 2005: 122–123). The term retains some currency among both practitioners and academics as denoting a particular type of journalistic inquiry, as defined by John Ullmann and Steve Honeyman:

> It is the reporting, through one's own work product and initiative, matters of importance which some persons or organisations wish to keep secret. The three basic elements are that the investigation be the work of the reporter, not a report of an investigation made by someone else; that the subject of the story involves something of reasonable importance to the reader or viewer; and that others are attempting to hide these matters from the public. (Quoted in Northmore, 2001: 188–189)

Such a definition is not without its own problems, particularly its reliance on the formulation "something of reasonable importance to the reader or viewer", which can be taken to mean anything from an obscure arms deal (for *Panorama* viewers, at least until it was forced to become a more populist programme) to the recreational drug-use of a Z-list celebrity (for *News of the World* readers).

For Stephen Dorril, the methodology of investigative journalism "is characterised by in-depth and near-obsessional research, dogged determination, accumulated knowledge, team-effort (though some of our best ... have been loners), the crucial support of editors and the space to pursue stories not because of notions of the truth but because it might turn out to be interesting" (Dorril, 2000). The extent to which investigative skills are, in essence, the

I got the names I wanted within 20 working days and I also got the answer that Yorkshire Forward had paid £19,641 of public money to lawyers to argue that it would have cost too much public money to tell the public how our money is being spent. Three years is not a realistic timescale for most journalistic inquiries, although the absurdity of the whole business allowed me to get a couple of stories out of it: QUANGO SPENDING IS A WELL-KEPT SECRET (*Guardian*, February 20 2008) and PUBLIC PRICED OUT OF GETTING THE FACTS (*Guardian*, March 5 2008). However, not all FOI requests take so long and some organisations have been much quicker to hand over information to me as well as to other journalists and indeed other citizens.

"There's something in this"

At a national, regional and local level FOI has been used to make public otherwise private information, ranging from the number of police officers arrested to the expenses claims of MPs. One journalist who has used it to great effect is Deborah Wain of the *Doncaster Free Press*, who revealed how one of the UK's biggest education projects in a poor part of the country had spent vast sums of public money on luxury travel, hospitality, consultants' bills, a huge salary hike for the chief executive, and even a personalised number plate for a subsidised BMW X5 car. In the process, she demonstrated that investigative journalism does not have to be restricted to specialists or to journalists working in big-budget newsrooms; she is a general reporter on a weekly paper within the Johnston Press empire, and she only works three days a week.

> ❝ Never believe anything until it is officially denied. ❞
> – Claud Cockburn.

"I don't think I really saw it as an investigation as such at the start, I saw it as a story and follow-ups," she says when I ask her to talk me through her probe into Doncaster Education City, a £100 million partnership between a council and a further education college. Over an 18-month

same as those used by "ordinary" journalists – but with added scepticism – varies according to which practitioner is consulted. However, it should also be considered that elements of investigation can come into otherwise simple reportage and that many journalists who conduct investigations also find themselves working on relatively straightforward news stories; investigative journalists and ordinary journalists not only inhabit the same universe, they may actually be the same people.

Constraints

Deborah Chambers wrote as recently as 2000 that investigative journalism in the UK had been "flourishing in the last three decades of the twentieth century" (Chambers, 2000: 89), prompting Dorril to retort that investigative journalism had enjoyed "a brief bloom in the sixties, flowered for a short period in the seventies, badly wilted in the eighties and is now effectively dead" (Dorril, 2000). Not dead but clearly in decline, according to Hanna, who blames structural changes within the media since the 1970s for "shrivelling" investigative journalism at its roots; changes such as relentless cost-cutting, under-staffing, speed-up and, on television, a ruthless drive for ratings (Hanna, 2000: 2–7).

Working in such conditions effectively undermines the "relative autonomy" enjoyed by journalists (Manning, 2001: 105), an autonomy necessary if the time and space are to be made available for investigations. After all, investigative journalists might be seen as mavericks even by their colleagues, never mind their employers. As Tom Bowyer notes, investigations can frequently be unproductive, and "even the rarity of success earns the investigative reporter only the irksome epithet of being obsessional or dangerous" (quoted in Spark, 1999: 17). It is claimed that today's recruits to journalism are "quickly schooled into understanding that investigative journalism is basically a myth and that their success is strongly related to their accuracy and skill in applying journalistic techniques and formulas" (Harrison, 2000: 113). Constraints, including the law, are discussed in more detail in Chapter 2.

period Wain wrote between 20 and 30 stories, gradually uncovering the reality that lay behind the scheme's big budgets and grandiose promises. She ended up collecting one of the best awards that a journalist can win; but more of that later. Where did the story come from?

> We had an anonymous letter from an insider at the college, pages and pages of allegations. I was quite shocked by it. The temptation is to file it away in a desk somewhere, but I was also hearing snippets of information from other sources that made me think, "There's something in this". It was just a question of where to start.

> I got wind of the fact there was a report by the Learning and Skills Council into the deficit at the college, and that was the tangible thing I was looking for. So I used FOI to request that report, which confirmed that the college had gone from being very robust financially into being significantly in the red, and the purpose of the report was to look into financial problems.

Having got hold of official confirmation that questions were being asked about the project's finances, Wain's story was now up and running. One thing led to another:

> The thing about the investigation is that there were so many different strands to it. After the initial couple of stories were published people came to me from the inside, again with lots of extreme allegations. You can't always use what your sources are giving you because the information is too specific and you might betray the source. But the same things kept coming up.

> FOI is the key; I probably put in half a dozen requests to the council, the college and the Learning and Skills Council. I managed to firm up most of the stuff from official sources through FOI, getting the facts and figures.

Parallel with this, she was also speaking off-the-record to employees and on-the-record to their trade union officials, who were usually more willing to speak out publicly about staff unrest. That was not all:

> I also spent quite a lot of time going through the college board's papers in the college library. The papers are

Facts

Investigative reporting typically abandons the journalistic convention of allegation-and-denial, or attributed opinions, in favour of an attempt "to establish facts which, if possible, decide the issue one way or the other" (Spark, 1999: 1). However, facts themselves are far from unproblematic. There does not exist some universally accepted bundle of facts, just waiting to be gathered, that will decide most issues. Facts may be disputed all the way to the High Court or the prison cell. Even when the facts are accepted, their relevance – or the inter-pretation placed upon them – may not be. Investigative journalists may therefore find themselves piling fact upon fact on what turn out to be shifting sands. Even so, the very pursuit of the facts, and the reporter's willingness to adopt the role of accuser, challenges the notions of formal balance and impartiality so important to much conventional reporting (Manning, 2001: 70). Facts and truth are discussed further in Chapter 5.

Democracy

For Hugo de Burgh, the investigative journalist plays a vital democratic role as "the tribune of the commoner, exerting on her or his behalf the right to know, to examine and to criticise" (de Burgh, 2000: 315). It is a tempting image, particularly for those of us who have tried our hands at such stories. But how democratic is it really? Quite apart from legal and economic constraints, there are other limitations on the democratic claims of inves-tigative journalism. *Who* decides what is worthy of investigation, and on what basis? Some stories are undoubtedly seen as more sexy than others, and if there is the possibility of good pictures, film or audio material, then so much the better. Similarly, some people are seen as more deserv-ing of sympathy – again it helps if they are photo-genic – and others are easier to paint as villains.

Of course, investigative journalism can achieve results such as the jailing of Jonathan Aitken, but could that not be seen as perpetuating a myth that society is divided into a large number of fundamentally good people and a smaller number

available but nobody ever goes. They had to hunt them out for me and I got a frosty reception. I had to sit in the basement, it was the middle of summer and I was sweltering, and at one point I thought I was going to be locked in overnight, I thought they might forget I was down there.

How did she manage to find the time, given that she works in a small newsroom where she is a general reporter as well as a specialist health reporter, and also writes features and reviews?

On Wednesday afternoons when the paper had been put to bed I would go and do my research. I'm quite used to multi-tasking and juggling numerous stories, and fitting in research as and when, really. I think as you get more experienced you can bash out quite a few stories on a day-to-day basis and create time for stuff that you are particularly interested in.

A supportive news editor with an interest in the workings of local government clearly helped, but Wain was also motivated by discovering a lack of public accountability as well as by her love of a good story:

The thing that struck me was these huge sums of money. I think the college's spending was quite unaccounted for. There are people within the council and the college who have pooh-poohed the work that I've done because they don't get it. They don't get why people are asking questions, because they are so used to talking about these huge sums of money, £10 million here, £1 million there.

I like to come at a story from all angles. I found it really fascinating once I got into it, it became a challenge to try and peel back the layers. I think you have to be really tenacious and thorough, and just not give up. I enjoy storytelling so I really wanted to get to the story. I still do really, because I think there's still more to come.

There may indeed be more to come, but she had already done enough to be declared the joint winner of the 2007 Paul Foot Award for investigative journalism, an award named after the veteran journalist who died in 2004.

of fundamentally bad people? Where is the investigative journalism into *structural* forces in society? Largely notable for its absence. Instead, particularly on television, we tend to have personalised stories of goodies, baddies and heroic reporters. Hanna challenges us to consider whether, rather than exemplifying a democratic spirit, even the heyday of UK investigative journalism in reality offered an "elitist and pompous" form of journalism (Hanna, 2000: 16).

The realities of investigating

As a quietly spoken woman who works part-time on a local weekly paper, Deborah Wain does not fit the stereotype of the pushy investigative journalist as portrayed in movies such as *All the President's Men*, *Defence of the Realm* and *The Insider*. As it happens, Paul Foot had watched *The Insider* the night before I turned up at his home to interview him for the first edition of this book. That film's portrayal of the intense relationship between journalist and source clearly struck a chord. "That's the key to all this, the source," he told me almost as soon as I walked through the door.

The Insider tells the true story of how journalist Lowell Bergman (played by Al Pacino) persuaded tobacco scientist Jeffrey Wigand (Russell Crowe) to defy a confidentiality agreement and blow the whistle on his former employers. As they battle against corporate lawyers and frightened TV executives, the pair go through all the emotions of trust, mistrust, and trust again before finally getting to tell the story. At one point the tormented Wigand tells the journalist: "I'm just a commodity to you, aren't I? I could be anything worth putting on between the commercials." Bergman promises not to leave his source "hanging out to dry" (Roth and Mann, 1999). It is a telling exchange, raising ethical issues of motivation and responsibility.

Investigative journalists in movies are often unshaven characters – usually men – who meet mysterious whistleblowers in dark corners. They tend to be chain-smoking obsessives who won't take no for an answer; unorthodox loners who risk life and limb to establish the truth. The reality is often rather more mundane. Most **investigative journalism** would not make for dramatic footage – the meticulous cross-referencing of information strands, the days phoning people with similar names and trawling Facebook or FriendsReunited to track somebody down, and the hours poring over obscure documents or computer databases until your eyes scream for mercy. Compared with other forms of reporting, investigative journalism may involve more time, more money, more risk (Palast, 2002: 9). There is the occasional threat or even act of violence, of course. But, in the UK at least, legal or commercial *constraints* – not forgetting under-staffing and a shortage of time – are more likely obstacles than an invitation to sleep with the fishes.

> ❛ All journalism should be investigative, from football to cookery. ❜
> – *John Pilger*

Although investigative journalism remains an integral part of journalism's image and sense of self-worth and professional standing, in reality it is a minority pursuit. Whenever the topic of investigative journalism is discussed, somebody can be relied upon to say that *all* journalism is supposed to be investigative. But much journalism, as it is practised, is reportage. It is descriptive. It is attribution. It is based on a reporter seeing or being told something and then passing that on to an audience in the form of a story, as Martin Wainwright explains:

> I'm not like a detective, I'm more of a describer. Somebody rang me up the other day and said he had a scandal which involved everybody from the Prime Minister downwards, and you think, "Oh God..." It's terribly difficult and you don't have very much time.

The head of news in one regional television newsroom described her brief as the production of human interest stories for ultra-busy people, adding: "Our role is not to be investigative" (quoted in Ursell, 2001: 191).

The public interest

Investigative journalism goes beyond description. For David Randall, investigative reporting differs substantially from other reporting because it involves *original* research into *wrong-doing*, because someone is trying to keep the information *secret*, and because the *stakes* tend to be higher (Randall, 2000: 99–100). Although some investigations – many of those in the Sunday tabloids for example – expose nothing more than the personal predilections of some celeb many of us have never actually heard of, the credo of investigative journalism is uncovering information that it is in the *public interest* to know.

But what *is* the public interest? The answer, according to the Press Complaints Commission, is: detecting or exposing crime or a serious misdemeanour; protecting public health and safety; and preventing the public from being misled by some statement or action of an individual or organisation (www.pcc.org.uk). The National Union of Journalists has added the exposure of corruption, conflicts of interest, corporate greed or hypocritical behaviour by those in power (see Appendix). The government-appointed Nolan Committee on Standards in Public Life declared in 1995 that "a free press using fair techniques of investigative journalism is an indispensable asset to our democracy", contributing to "the preservation of standards in public life" (quoted in Doig, 1997: 210).

From a high point in the 1970s, investigative journalism in the UK is often said to be on the wane (Doig, 1997: 189; Northmore, 2001: 183). However, as with all discussions about journalism, there is a long-established tendency to bestow "golden age" status on earlier periods; the breadth of entries to the annual Paul Foot award demonstrates that reports of the death of investigative journalism are greatly exaggerated.

Before moving on to consider some more examples of investigative reporting it is worth recording a cautionary note sounded by Martin Wainwright, who believes that investigative journalists may sometimes be tempted to ignore shades of grey: "I'm always a bit suspicious of them, because often if you go into a story carefully you find there's another side to it, and it's not quite what it seems."

Methods of investigation

Consumer affairs correspondent Kevin Peachey frequently finds himself investigating dodgy companies. How does he set about checking out a story?

> First you look in the files, the archives, because the same issues crop up sometimes. Then the internet, to see if somebody else has written about them. Then it's contacts. Consumer stories are no different from any other specialism – if you've got good contacts that's half the battle. I've got enough people now who I can ring up and they can tell me whether there's something in it or not. I can see if there's a news angle in something, but as far as the law is concerned you need someone to explain it to you. So my most important contacts are in the trading standards service, in the same way as a crime reporter's best contacts are in the police.

David Spark offers the following advice for fledgling investigators:

- Get to the **facts** at the heart of an issue – don't be content with spokesmen's comments.
- Explain difficult concepts – don't write around them.
- Don't just echo the views of your main source – find other sources with other views.
- Speak to as many relevant people as possible.
- Ask the simple and obvious questions which open out the subject.
- Don't take everything and everyone at their face value.
- Remember that everyone, every organisation and every event has a history which may have a bearing on what is happening now. (Spark, 1999: xii)

It sounds simple. That is the point. There is no need for the mystique that too often surrounds the subject. Paul Foot insisted there were dangers in treating investigative journalism as a separate genre carried out by "grand" journalists:

It's a complete fraud, the idea that there is a race apart called investigative journalists. An ordinary reporter doing a perfectly ordinary story carries out these functions, the difference would be the enthusiasm and the scepticism with which you approach something.

Another difference might be the *time* you have available. Reporters required to produce up to a dozen stories a day will simply find it impossible if they question everything. On the other hand, journalists who invest their own time in working on their own stories can become known in the trade as "self-starters"; if they are both lucky and skilled, they may be able to earn themselves the rare luxury of being employed on a specifically investigative brief. That was how Paul Foot was able to spend so much time at both the *Daily Mirror* and *Private Eye* "piling fact on fact to present a picture of cock-up or conspiracy" (Foot, 1999: 82).

Foot talked me through one of his most celebrated investigations, concerning the case of four men wrongly jailed for the murder of newspaper delivery boy Carl Bridgewater:

> I started writing about it in 1980. Ann Whelan, whose son was convicted, wrote to me at the *Mirror* a very moving letter. My initial feeling was, "What mother wouldn't say that her son was innocent?" So it was some time before I went up there. But I went up to Birmingham and met her and her family. I wasn't convinced to begin with because it was a horrible murder and there was *some* evidence against them, there was a confession. It took quite a lot of time before I became in any way convinced, but I did become absolutely convinced, and as I did so I wrote with more and more certainty.
>
> Ann found witnesses who said, "I told a pack of lies, I didn't realise how important it was". But mostly it was just going over the evidence that had been presented in court against them, reading depositions, the judge's summing up and so on, talking to everyone involved. There were things showing they were somewhere else at the time, that somebody else had done the murder, it just went on and on. I must have written at least 30 articles in the *Mirror.* Eventually the men were released in 1997.

Apart from his forensic skill and the willingness to immerse himself in countless legal documents,

what is immediately apparent from Foot's account is the *repetition* of stories over a long period of time:

> The *Mirror* subs would joke, "Here comes the man who supports the murder of newspaper boys", and occasionally the editor would say, "Oh Christ, you're not doing this again are you?" But the repetition is absolutely crucial because it encourages other sources to come forward.

> **❝ The main point is to be curious and sceptical … all the time. ❞**
> – Paul Foot.

Another experienced investigator, TV reporter Christopher Hird, describes his *modus operandi* as:

- Get everything we can anywhere in the public domain (libraries, Companies House and so on).
- Establish a chronology of events. We often see connections not seen before.
- Relentlessly look up everybody who might know something. (Quoted in Spark, 1999: 53)

These activities will often overlap. Checking the details of a company under investigation might give you some more names to contact; contacting those people might give you some more companies to check out; doing that might throw up other connections; and so on. That's why Randall advises "throw nothing away", because you never know when it might be useful (Randall, 2000: 108). During the Watergate investigation, Woodward and Bernstein filled several filing cabinets with all their notes, memos and early drafts of stories; periodically they would review their files and make lists of previously unexplored angles (Bernstein and Woodward, [1974] 2005: 50 and 330).

A different form of investigative journalism is the sending of a reporter undercover. This is when a journalist pretends to be somebody other than a journalist, with a view to discovering the truth behind a public façade. Kevin Peachey once went undercover – as a duck. He didn't have to dress up, he just bought products with a credit card and instead of signing his real name he signed it "Donald Duck", thereby illustrating how rarely card signatures were checked. He also exposed the trade in bogus qualifications by buying a fake degree on the internet. "You can have some fun with investigations," he says.

> ❛ Remember, *All the President's Men* was so unusual they had to make a movie out of it. ❜
>
> – Greg Palast.

But going undercover can be a tricky, even dangerous thing to do. It can also be immensely satisfying when it comes off, especially when the story is then picked up by other media. At the *Sunday Times*, Abul Taher recalls going undercover in France as one of his most rewarding assignments:

> The story came from a simple idea that we should look at the migrant situation in Calais again, as there were reports that the situation was worsening. I went there posing as an illegal immigrant from Bangladesh, trying to get to the UK. It was a good exercise in information and intelligence gathering, which I did over a period of two weeks. I spoke to fellow illegal immigrants, charity workers and actual people smugglers – in the guise of an illegal immigrant – and managed to put together a good picture of the migrant problem in Calais, as well as giving a picture of the routes the migrants took from Asia to get to Calais.
>
> The story line we got from it – that the French were building a new Sangatte refugee camp in Calais – caused a political uproar, with the Home Secretary making comments on it. Nicolas Sarkozy, by then president-elect of France, also condemned the plan. The story ran in the national papers for about a month.

In addition to the various techniques discussed above, journalists may keep unregistered mobile phones for talking to sensitive sources, and avoid leaving paper trails by ensuring they pay cash for meals and so on. Some use the so-called "dark arts" of investigation, which mostly involves paying informants, private investigators or bent coppers for information. Quite apart from any ethical considerations involved in paying for information or going undercover, such activities are not dealt with in

detail here because they are not jobs for novice journalists.

The phrase "computer-assisted reporting" has entered some journalists' vocabularies in recent years, imported from the USA. It involves the collection and manipulation of data from existing or specially created databases or spreadsheets, looking for patterns, trends, mistakes or missing information that might make stories. "They have been there all the time, sitting in the data," observes Mike Ward. "It's just needed a journalist to ask the right questions, run the right sequence of numbers" (Ward, 2002: 69). Getting hold of such information should be easier thanks to FOI legislation, but it still requires time and skill in analysing it.

As with all journalism, it needs to be borne in mind that apparent connections may be as much coincidental as causal, and that networks are not necessarily conspiracies. Despite the thrill of the chase, therefore, it remains important to question your *own* expectations and assumptions during any investigation. Then, once you have gathered your material from a range of sources, you must decide if the story still has potential. If it does not stand up, either forget it or file it. But if it has substance, sooner or later you must confront your "target" with the allegations. "There are two sides to the story and everybody has a right of reply," explains Peachey:

> If they choose not to reply then that's fair enough, but we make every effort we can. In some cases we give them a 10 bullet-point letter through their door if we know where they are, saying, "We're thinking of writing a story, these are some of the issues that have been raised, we want your reply". Give them sufficient time, a couple of days generally. Log your phone calls too, so that you know when you've left messages. A couple of times I've spoken to people who've given me some abuse down the phone – that always makes an interesting line in the story.

During her investigation in Doncaster, Deborah Wain repeatedly contacted the troubled college and its chief executive. "I gave him numerous opportunities to respond but he never did," she says. But the material she had gathered – official documents plus interviews with other sources, written in shorthand notebooks, dated and filed just in case – was strong enough for publication. In larger newsrooms such stories would probably have been "legalled" by a lawyer beforehand, but Wain relied on her own knowledge of the legal system gained during her NCTJ training: "As a local paper, everything has got to be legally sound, you're not going to take the same risks as the nationals. Knowing the law, knowing what you can publish, is really key – and the stories were all strong enough."

When considering whether something can be published, reporters and their editors can be guided by what is known as the "Reynolds defence" (see *Box 6.1*). Arising from a House of Lords legal ruling in 1999, the defence – so named because it stemmed from a libel case between the *Sunday Times* and former Irish prime minister Albert Reynolds – consists of 10 points that judges might take into consideration when deciding whether publication of potentially defamatory material might be in the public interest.

"We've developed experience at working with the new world of the Reynolds defence," explains David Leigh who, along with colleague Rob Evans, shared the 2007 Paul Foot Award – with the aforementioned Deborah Wain – for the *Guardian* duo's massive investigation into allegations of bribery and corruption involving Britain's biggest arms manufacturer, BAE Systems. "The result is that the BAE lawyers haven't laid a glove on us" (quoted in Smith, 2007).

Although the list of points is neither exhaustive nor foolproof, and its interpretation relies on the thinking of judges, the Reynolds defence is used as a checklist for many journalists investigating allegations against powerful individuals or organisations. Because case law is still being developed, journalists need to keep up to speed with the latest interpretations and guidance; check the

most up-to-date edition of *McNae's Essential Law for Journalists*.

Following a hunch

Let's now consider a story I investigated on the basis of a hunch. I'd like to say it was *my* hunch, but it wasn't. I was working a freelance shift on *Yorkshire on Sunday* when editor Mike Glover handed me a brief cutting he had taken from that morning's *Yorkshire Post*. It was a nothing story about a private health company going into liquidation after failing to pay a printing bill for publicity material. Mike's suspicions were aroused by the odd spacing of the paragraphs, suggesting to him that something might have been removed from the story at the last minute – possibly on legal advice. He asked me to dig around to see what I could find.

The result was a front-page exclusive – CLINIC HIT BY SCANDAL CLAIMS – and two full news pages inside – RIDDLE OF CLINIC BOSS: PATIENT'S THREE DAYS OF AGONY IN PRIVATE HOSPITAL (*Yorkshire on Sunday*, February 19 1995). More stories followed, MPs demanded action, and finally the government reviewed its inspection procedures for private clinics. How did a hunch turn into a successful piece of investigative journalism? As Hird says, by getting hold of everything we could in the public domain, by tracing connections, and by tracking down as many as possible of those involved.

It meant repeated visits to Companies House, which now has a website that is a vital source of information for journalists, holding records on more than 1.8 million companies, including details of directors, major shareholders and company accounts. It was there I discovered that the company in liquidation was one of 49 businesses established by the same man. Most were involved in the private health industry,

Box 6.1

The 10 points of the Reynolds defence, as outlined by Lord Nicholls in a House of Lords ruling in 1999

Circumstances that a judge should consider when deciding whether media might have a public interest defence to an allegation of defamation:

1. The seriousness of the allegation. The more serious the charge, the more the public is misinformed and the individual harmed, if the allegation is not true.
2. The nature of the information, and the extent to which the subject matter is a matter of public concern.
3. The source of the information. Some informants have no direct knowledge of the events. Some have their own axes to grind, or are being paid for their stories.
4. The steps taken to verify the information.
5. The status of the information. The allegations may have already been the subject of an investigation which commands respect.
6. The urgency of the matter. News is often a perishable commodity.
7. Whether comment was sought from the claimant. He may have information others do not possess or have not disclosed. An approach to the claimant will not always be necessary.
8. Whether the article contained the gist of the claimant's side of the story.
9. The tone of the article. A newspaper can raise queries or call for an investigation. It need not adopt allegations as statements of fact.
10. The circumstances of the publication, including timing.

Source: Welsh et al., 2005: 250-251.

including pregnancy advisory operations, private abortion clinics and cosmetic surgery clinics. I found that, at the same time as one company was apparently unable to pay its printing bills, the firm running an abortion clinic made hundreds of thousands of pounds in profit. And I obtained addresses for the businessman and his wife, who was a fellow-director of some of the businesses.

With the names of several companies to go on, I searched local newspaper cuttings for related stories and found an account of an employment tribunal concerning the abortion clinic. That gave me the names of ex-employees to follow-up, which in turn led to more names. As the story concerned abortion we contacted "pro-choice" and "pro-life" campaign groups who, from diametrically opposing standpoints, questioned the ethics of the same individuals running both a pregnancy "advisory" service and the profitable abortion clinic that patients were referred to. One of the groups also referred to an earlier radio programme that had mentioned allegations of botched surgery by a related company. Following this up, and talking to local solicitors, led to further cases. The solicitors were happy to pass on detailed information that raised serious concerns about procedures at the clinic. Further inquiries revealed that the local health authority – responsible for inspecting and licensing the clinic – had privately been alerted to staff concerns about standards.

All these leads gave me many individuals to contact by the usual methods of telephone books, directory enquiries, medical directories and the electoral register – hours and hours on the telephone, in the reference library, going back to Companies House, and driving around Yorkshire turning up unannounced on people's doorsteps. Some had moved home, meaning I had just a few seconds in which to persuade the new occupant why they should give a total stranger the forwarding address for the person who used to live in their house. The best advice I can offer for such occasions is to act confident but friendly, as if nothing in the world could be more normal than for them to offer the address to a total stranger. When I found the right people, some were happy to tell their side of the story, some wanted to forget about it all, and others had to be assured of their anonymity before they would speak. There is no great trick in getting such people to talk, but a sympathetic and non-threatening tone generally helps.

Putting together what I was told on the doorstep and telephone with information already in the public domain, plus the concerns of solicitors and others involved, meant there was sufficient evidence to put to the businessman at the centre of the story. We tried telephoning, we tried doorstepping, and we tried writing, all to no avail. No matter on this occasion. We had enough to go on. We obtained comments from the health authority, the General Medical Council, and an independent consultant gynaecologist – and we ran the story. That prompted other people to come forward, resulting in several follow-ups. We sent the published stories to politicians, whose reactions resulted in further articles and a government review. All from a hunch.

> ❝ **Get off your asses and knock on doors.** ❞
> – *LA Times newsroom sign.*

Legwork and lateral thinking

As the above accounts show, information already in the public domain can be vital if you know what you are looking for; so begin with the assumption that someone somewhere has *already* sourced the information you need (Northmore, 2001: 192). One online investigator, who relies largely on public records for his probes into the rich and powerful, told me:

> I've built up quite a good relationship with people in the local reference library. They can be really helpful, I think it makes their lives more interesting. You're getting annual reports, company accounts, all that kind of stuff, and spending weeks and weeks reading it, looking for connections. Also Companies House and other publicly available records like birth and marriage certificates. Then visiting buildings, going round talking to people, or trying to. I like to *go* to places to see them just to get a feel. It's not a mystery, it's just diligence and hard work.

Targeted use of FOI has now added to the investigator's armoury, but that does not mean there is no need to get out on the streets. A combination of "legwork" and "lateral thinking" allowed Brian Whittle's freelance agency to break a number of stories about serial killer Dr Harold Shipman. After Shipman's trial, the agency's reporters revisited the small town in which he had embarked on his murderous medical career a quarter-of-a-century previously. They investigated deaths for which Shipman had not been charged, as Whittle explains:

> Before anybody else thought of it we obtained all the death certificates for the 22 people he'd signed while he was practising in Todmorden. Just looking at the death certificates told you that three people died in one day. We then went round all the addresses. A third of the

houses no longer existed, and in another third the people had moved away and weren't contactable. But we did find relatives of the three people who died in one day, and we found relatives of the first male victim.

This is old-fashioned reporting, it's knocking on doors, it's talking to people. If you turn up on the doorstep people will talk to you, if you ring them up it gives them the chance to put the phone down. If you want to find out about somebody you don't just knock on *their* door and the *next* door, you do the entire street. You do *both sides* of the street – two of you – and you do it again in the evening because people may be out in the daytime. Go to *every* address and ask, "What do you know about this person who lived here 25 years ago?"

You don't know who you're going to find, maybe it's a son or whatever. Out of the 22, six or seven came out with absolutely key stuff. We were totally vindicated when the police started an investigation about a month later and sent various cases to the Crown Prosecution Service.

As well as uncovering new information about the UK's biggest mass murderer, the agency reporters' repeated visits also led them to a series of photographs of "Dr Death" partying with his wife – all smiles and silly hats. The pictures probably didn't add much to the sum of human knowledge but, thanks to an exclusive deal with the *Sunday Mirror* in January 2001, they turned out to be lucrative for the agency as well as the owner of the photos. This technique of hitting the doorsteps early and often will be familiar to anyone who has worked as an agency reporter on the frontline of domestic news; most would probably not call themselves investigative journalists, but that is (part of) what they are doing.

> ❝ Never forget that they lie, they lie, they lie. ❞
> – *Nicholas Tomalin.*

But what's it all for?

What is achieved by journalists taking on the role of investigators? For a start, journalists exposing

miscarriages of justice such as the Bridgewater Four, the Birmingham Six and the Guildford Four all resulted in innocent people walking free from prison, eventually. Sometimes journalists are more concerned with sending guilty people *to* prison than getting innocent people *out*, and Michael Crick's determined pursuit of Jeffrey Archer helped ensure that his Lordship ended up behind bars rather than as Mayor of London (Tench, 2001). The *Guardian's* dogged investigations into Jonathan Aitken in the 1990s resulted in the government minister being jailed for perjury, albeit only because the paper's team discovered a crucial piece of evidence at the very last minute of the court case (Spark, 1999: 99).

Apart from the occasional release of an innocent prisoner or jailing of a guilty politician, what is it all *for*? Is investigative journalism really a force for **democracy** or merely a relatively minor subdivision of showbusiness (de Burgh, 2000: 315; Northmore, 2001: 185)? One of the most often-cited successes of investigative journalism is the *Sunday Times'* coverage of the Thalidomide babies in the 1970s. It was a success story in that it resulted in compensation for victims of the drug. But some of the journalists involved have since questioned what was actually achieved:

> It has taken me twenty years to face up to the fact that the *Sunday Times* Thalidomide campaign was not the great success it was made out to be. … [When] some of us get together and look back at the fight on behalf of the children we end up discussing two crucial questions: Did we do it right? Would it have been better to have kept out of the whole affair? … To start with, some of the parents found the exposure in the press a painful experience. … Next, there was discontent over the way the compensation was paid. … Disturbing stories of greed and envy began to emerge. (Knightley, 1998: 155–178)

Paul Foot recalls that, at the time, it felt like few people noticed his early investigations in *Private Eye*, including those concerning the corrupt local government empire of John Poulson: "Again and again real revelations sank like a stone"

(Foot, 1999: 82). Yet he is in no doubt that it is a socially worthwhile occupation:

> Apart from getting people out of prison who shouldn't be there, there are things like the cancer drugs that were killing people quicker. The publication in *Private Eye* of four or five of those articles and the whole project was exposed. And Frank Wheeler, the busman up in Scotland who kept asking why the government had stolen the pensions surplus of the National Bus Company when it was privatised. That was £300 million. He says the whole thing changed when I went up here and spent a couple of days with him and his wife and wrote a piece for the *Guardian*, and then several things for the *Eye*. That set of articles made a difference to those people in that they got their money back.

And Deborah Wain found that tens of millions of pounds of public money were being spent in Doncaster apparently without any effective accountability. The only public accountability was provided by the press reporting what was going on and informing its readers – the town's citizens and voters.

Investigative journalism is as much about approach as it is about subject matter. It is more of an attitude than it is a genre. And just as journalists working on investigations will use many of the techniques they would use on "ordinary" stories – only more so – a more inquiring and investigative approach can also inform otherwise mundane reporting. Increasingly, for example, journalists are routinely putting in FOI requests to find information on all sorts of subjects; not just those that would previously have been thought the preserve of investigative specialists. If a public authority is likely to hold information on something – from hygiene inspections of local takeaways to government files on reported UFO sightings – then an FOI request might be worth considering for a journalist working on virtually any story.

Be curious and sceptical

How does Foot sum up the attributes necessary for a journalist to be an effective investigator?

There are certain skills that you learn from experience, but the main point is to be curious and sceptical. You can't be an investigative journalist unless you are both curious and sceptical *all the time*. That, and the ability to ring people up and talk to them all the time, the ability to believe the most absurd things that people tell you – even when perhaps nine times out of 10 they're talking absolute bollocks.

David Hencke stresses the value of a bit of humility as you learn the basics of reporting:

> You can't come in as a high-flying reporter, you have to start with the parish fêtes, the youth club and the magistrates court. I still make mistakes, but it's better to make the bog standard mistakes at a level where you can't cause too much damage. (Quoted in C. Adams, 2001)

He also feels that journalists should guard against the trend prevalent in television investigations of relying on secret filming and/or of presenting the reporter as heroic, whereby: "By the end, as with a John Wayne movie, we can safely go to our beds, knowing that all the villains have had their just deserts and that our hero has fought his way through, against the odds, and emerged victorious" (Hencke, 2001).

For Foot, it all boils down to the relationship between journalist and source: "The source is more important than the story. The whistleblowers who break cover and say, 'I'm not going to continue with this because I'm doing something wrong' – they are the goldmine. You do not sell them out." The source may be more important than the story, but the story should be more important than the journalist, believes Wain, who told me:

> You talk in your chapter [in the first edition of this book] about the notion of the investigative reporter as hero, and I have found that there has been a lot more media interest in the story of me getting that award – people *like* the story of the reporter on the *small* paper – than there ever was in the original story of what was going on in Doncaster with all that money. I think they should have been a bit more interested in that at the time.

▇ ▇ Summary ▇

Investigative journalism goes beyond description and attributed opinion to uncover information, typically about powerful individuals or organisations. Many investigative skills will
be used by journalists every day. Stories are typically investigated by combining information already in the public domain with leaked information and/or by talking to as many as
possible of the people involved. There are claims that investigative journalism has been in
decline since its heyday in the 1970s, and that many investigations – on television in
particular – are now more concerned with entertainment than information. Investigative
reporting has been explained variously as an essential element of democracy, as a subdivision of showbusiness, as favouring a narrative of "good versus evil" at the expense of
questioning structural forces, as an elitist form of journalism of little interest to the public,
and as the tribune of the common people.

▇ Questions

How does investigative journalism differ from other journalism?

What are the main obstacles confronting journalists as investigators?

Is investigative journalism really in decline?

Is investigative journalism essential to democracy?

Do investigative reporters create a myth of good versus evil?

▇ ▇ Further reading ▇

For practical advice on using freedom of information legislation, see Heather
Brooke's (2007) extremely helpful book *Your Right to Know* and her website of the
same name – www.yrtk.org – which includes blow-by-blow accounts of some of her
own FOI successes, including a three-year battle to reveal the expenses of MPs. But
anybody interested in reading more about journalists as investigators should really
start with *All the President's Men* by Bernstein and Woodward ([1974] 2005), which
is at least as much about the journalistic process as it is about the scandals of the
Nixon presidency.

A personal account of investigative reporting is given in brief but typically
entertaining fashion in Foot (1999), while Palast (2002) includes several of his own
investigative reports as well as details of the processes involved. Spark (1999) offers
an illuminating introduction to some of the main techniques, based on a series of
interviews with practitioners; his account of the downfall of Jonathan Aitken is
instructive, although the book contains little analysis. Some online methods of

research are introduced in a useful chapter in Ward (2002). Contributors to de Burgh (2000; 2008) attempt, with varying degrees of success, to place investigative journalism within a wider social and academic context. The concept of the public interest is discussed in depth in Harcup (2007), which also includes an interview with the reporter who spent two months undercover in Buckingham Palace, working as a footman to the Queen.

Sources for soundbites

Cockburn, quoted in Foot, 1999: 82; Pilger, quoted in C. Adams, 2001; Foot, interviewed by the author; Palast, 2002: 8; *LA Times*, quoted in Brennen, 2003: 126; Tomalin, quoted in Hastings, 2004.

seven

the journalist as entertainer

Anyone who has seen the film *Bridget Jones's Diary* is likely to remember the scene in which intrepid reporter Bridget concludes a piece-to-camera in a fire station by sliding down the pole – bum-first on to the camera. Regional television reporter Lindsay Eastwood recalled the scene when she was sent out to produce an "And finally…" piece about the apparent growth in popularity of pole dancing:

> Pole dancing is now regarded as a form of exercise rather than a seedy lap-dancing thing. There were all these very attractive women, and I'm not exactly the best example of a pole dancing babe, but I thought I'm going to have to be in this to make it funny, and to poke fun at myself. So I did a Bridget Jones style slide down the pole on to the lens of the camera, which did the trick really. It was just lucky that I had trousers on.

Such light and fluffy stories have long been a part of journalism. I recall working on a newspaper during a heatwave when some bright spark had the idea of testing the legend about it being "hot enough to fry an egg on the pavement". A posse was gathered and we rushed from the newsroom to put the theory to the test – but the egg steadfastly refused to fry. After half-an-hour we conceded defeat, scraped up the mess, and beat a retreat to the sound of jeers from drinkers who were enjoying the sun and the spectacle outside the pub next door.

It was not the best piece of investigative journalism I had ever been involved with. It was just a bit of fun – entertainment. Some stories are entertaining by virtue of their subject matter. Others can be rendered entertaining by being well written, by holding the attention of the audience,

Dumbing down

Debate about so-called "dumbing down" extends far beyond journalism to include education, the arts and society in general. Of direct relevance to journalism is the claim that news is being transformed into "newszak"; that is, "news as a product designed and 'processed' for a particular market and delivered in increasingly homogenous 'snippets' which make only modest demands on the audience" (Franklin, 1997: 5). Supporters of the dumbing down thesis bemoan the fact that news is being "converted into entertainment" (Franklin, 1997: 5). Chris Frost writes that journalists are facing increasing pressure to become entertainers by "finding stories and features that will delight the audience rather than inform, titillate rather than educate" (Frost, 2002: 5). For Pierre Bourdieu, this results in journalists being so terrified of being seen as boring that they increasingly favour:

- confrontation rather than debate
- polemics or polarised views over rigorous argument
- promotion of conflict
- confrontation of individuals rather than their arguments
- discussion of political tactics rather than the substance of policies
- dehistoricised and fragmented versions of events (Bourdieu, 1998: 3–7).

There is nothing new about the "perennial" complaint that "journalism just recently got worse", observes Samuel Winch. He argues that the boundary between news and entertainment is "socially constructed" and therefore to an extent arbitrary (Winch, 1997: 6 and 13). Back in the 1960s, the cultural theorist Stuart Hall observed – with little attempt at hiding his disdain – the apparent obsession of some UK newspapers with the private lives of celebrities:

by the use of anecdotes or asides, or by injecting humour. One colleague used to speak of "sprinkling topspin and stardust" on to a news story, brightening it up with that extra bit of colour or drama to make it more entertaining. After all, we call news items stories because we adopt many of the conventions of the storyteller.

Entertaining is not a new role for journalists, as this 19th century verse demonstrates:

Tickle the public, make 'em grin,
The more you tickle, the more you'll win;
Teach the public, you'll never get rich,
You'll live like a beggar and die in a ditch. (Quoted in Engel, 1997: 17)

Even if we *do* want to teach the public, we won't get very far if nobody reads, watches or listens to our work because we have made the stories too dull. Without an audience there can be no journalism, and we are not likely to gather much of an audience if we do not seek, at least in part, to entertain as well as inform. Difficulties can arise when the distinction appears to be forgotten, as documentary maker Eddie Mirzoeff felt was the case when he asked for his name to be removed from a serious BBC2 series that had been "MTV-ised, with music" to make it more zappy. A statement from the BBC said the documentaries had simply been "reversioned", whatever that is supposed to mean (Brown, 2003). Richard Klein, one of the key figures in charge of BBC television documentaries, later suggested that popular celebrities, such as Lisa Tarbuck, should be used to front factual programmes, adding: "The premium is to find brighter, more entertaining documentary programming. Documentaries can be seen as a rather painful dose of medicine, and I believe we are there to entertain people" (quoted in Brown, 2005).

As with documentaries, so with current affairs broadcasting, where investigative journalism has shifted towards individual reporters, such as Donal MacIntyre and Paul Kenyon, becoming stars in

> ❝ We are in the entertainment business. ❞
> – *Rupert Murdoch.*

The marriages, engagements and divorces of celebrities *may* be of real public interest, and, in a general sense, they can help to give a very rough idea of how people other than those with whom most of us are acquainted live. But on the whole they contribute little to the kind of news we need to know to make sense of modern life: they become a species of "tittle-tattle", the instinct on the journalist's part for "getting the story" slipping away in the direction of gossip, scandal and irrelevant social-voyeurism. (Hall, 1967: 111, emphasis in original)

Such disdain for the popular dates back much further than the 1960s, as media historian Martin Conboy notes:

The suspicion of popular taste goes right the way back to the start of print technology – almanacs, chap-books and printed ballads had been predominantly aimed at the lower end of the market – as soon, in fact, as print allows forms of expression which have escaped from the authorisation, approval and sense of good taste of the elite classes to have large circulation. (Conboy, 2002: 31)

Popular forms of journalism today can be seen as drawing on the 19th-century "new journalism" that was "marked by a definitive shift towards entertainment, a deliberate policy of appealing to the masses as part of a cultural and commercial proposition rather than as the more sedate organ of enlightenment and instruction" (Conboy, 2002: 94).

Not that entertainment and enlightenment need be seen as opposites. Journalism professor Mick Temple has gone so far as to argue that "dumbing down is good for you". According to his academic paper of that title:

[T]he so called "dumbing down" of political coverage, referring largely to the simplification and sensationalism of "serious" news by journalists, is an essential part of the process of engaging people in debates about the distribution of resources in modern democratic societies. ... Arguably, news has become more democratic, reflecting the concerns of a wider population rather than the views of a cultural elite. (Temple, 2006: 257 and 262)

In other words, many of the concerns of journalistic and academic critics voiced in this chapter are a form of elitism and a harking back to a largely mythical golden age of journalism (Temple, 2006: 260).

their own right, being part of the story. There are also recurrent complaints about the lines between journalism and entertainment being blurred, resulting in a concentration on ratings-friendly subject matter such as sex, drugs, crime and anything-from-hell. Rather than well-informed talking heads given the time to talk at length, there is a growing reliance on brief soundbites, fast cuts, odd camera angles, secret filming and often gratuitous reconstructions (usually, but not always, labelled as such). Dramatic mood music now almost always accompanies current affairs journalism on TV, including reconstructions of serious crime, and musical clips are becoming far more common in radio packages. Sometimes all this can make for gripping, engaging and informative journalism delivered in a style that is popular yet serious, innovative yet appropriate. Sometimes.

Criminals, celebs and miracle cures

Many journalists feel that the balance has tilted too far in the direction of entertainment, in news as well as current affairs. One such critic is former BBC war correspondent Martin Bell, whose friendly fire against the BBC reinforces criticism by insiders that BBC news has become "more Madonna than Macedonia" (Wells, 2001b). But his biggest guns are reserved for commercial television news:

> I can think of no time in my life when we needed to be better informed about the world beyond our shores, and no time when we have, in fact, been worse informed. … The Palme d'Or for the dumbing-down of British television goes to ITN, which was once a proud name in journalism. … In hock to the advertisers, ITN set the trend by its decision, early in the 1990s, to promote an agenda of crime, celebrity and miracle cures – and to downgrade foreign news to a couple of slots a week on Tuesdays and Thursdays, unless anything more sellable happened closer to home. The judgements were not editorial, but commercial. (Bell, 2002)

Authority

Journalism and other media output increasingly emphasise – or foreground – the individual subjective experience at the expense of more general and authoritative "truth claims", argues Jon Dovey (2000: 25). As part of this process, it is claimed, the "we" of the bourgeois public sphere – which in any case was a rather narrow and male "we" – has now collapsed into "fragmented individualised subjectivities" (Dovey, 2000: 165). This can be translated into two contrasting ways of looking at media output (see Box 7.1).

Such considerations form part of the cultural backdrop against which so many sections of the media now seem to place greater credence on user-generated content and audience comment than on authoritative pieces of journalism researched by specialist reporters.

Elitism

Critics of the dumbing down thesis argue that it is an elitist concept, far too simplistic to do justice to the complexity of today's journalism – or journalisms. Paul Manning points out that there needs to be some entertainment value in journalism because "news audiences are unlikely to warm to a format that has the feel of a sociology seminar" (Manning, 2001: 7). For the optimistic Brian McNair, the recent proliferation of outlets and styles, along with the blurring of boundaries between elite and popular culture, mean that journalism is less deferential towards the powerful than in the past (McNair, 2000: 59–60). He explains:

> [The] distinction between "serious" and "trivial" information is no longer one which can be taken as the basis for evaluating the public sphere. … An earlier form of detached, deferential, more or less verbatim political reportage has gone from the print media…,to be replaced by styles and agendas which, if they are occasionally entertaining, are at the same time more penetrating, more critical, more revealing and demystificatory of power than the polite, status-conscious journalisms of the past. And it is precisely the commercialising influence of the market which has allowed this to happen. (McNair, 2000: 60)

Indeed, television programmes such as *Trisha* and *Richard & Judy* have been held up as examples of how a more populist approach can "capture and

Box 7.1

Traditional and popular views of media output (Dovey, 2000: 4)

TRADITIONAL	POPULAR
Authoritative	Reflexive
Film	Video
Public service	Reality TV
Observational documentary	Docu-soap
Investigation	Entertainment
Argument	Pleasure
TV news	TV chat
Working	Shopping
Elitist	Democratic
Boring	Fun

In a similar vein, *Channel 4 News* anchor Jon Snow has accused ITV news of letting down the democratic process by abandoning serious news coverage in favour of more and more lifestyle and entertainment stories (Arlidge and Cole, 2001). In an echo of their BBC counterparts, ITN reporters have complained about being urged to make news bulletins "more Geri Halliwell than Gerry Adams" (Wells, 2001a).

Research into changing trends in TV news in the last quarter of the 20th century found that there had indeed been a decline in the amount of political coverage and a shift towards a more tabloid domestic agenda, but that there was still "a healthy balance of serious, light and international coverage". However, the same researchers warned that increasing commercial pressures would pose a serious threat to this balanced approach in the 21st century (Barnett and Seymour, 2000).

Broadcast news may have taken on board elements of the tabloid agenda, but the redtops remain in a league of their own when it comes to the blurring of lines between news and entertainment through their coverage of sex, soaps and

engage an audience who will fail to respond to more conventional coverage of social and 'political' issues" (Temple, 2006: 257). Kees Brants similarly argues that a mixture of "entertainment and consciousness raising" could help to "re-establish the popular in politics", taking in not only "the discursive and decision-making domain of politics but also the vast terrain of domestic life" (Brants, 1998: 332–333).

The debate about dumbing down and tabloidisation reflects anxiety about "a slippage of control" on the part of those who have traditionally led public opinion, according to Conboy (2002: 181). For Gill Ursell, given the multiplicity of media outlets and experiences now available to potential audiences, it may well be that "exposure to *some* kind of news is arguably better than *no* exposure at all" (Ursell, 2001: 192, my emphasis).

celebs. Consider a typical page three of the *Sun*. The page lead is an "exclusive" about a pet rabbit who had scratched its owner's companions (HOP OFF! THUGS BUNNY SCARES AWAY ALL BOYFRIENDS RUTH HAS EVER HAD). There is also the traditional soft-porn photo, this one featuring a topless model in a soapy bath accompanied by two rubber ducks, in homage to the same paper's front-page splash of a few days earlier: QUEEN HAS RUBBER DUCK IN HER BATH. Of the four other items on the same page, one is a story about a TV chat show, another concerns a celeb's pregnancy, and two are nibs about funny foreigners (*Sun*, November 7 2001). Yet even the *Sun* is too serious for *Daily Star* editor Dawn Neesom, as she explains:

> ❝ It's the part of the job they don't prepare you for at journalism school – staying up till three in the morning on the phone to some agent trying to arrange an interview with someone who'd been sticking a bottle up their nether regions on TV. ❞
> – Mark Frith, editor of Heat.

> The *Daily Star* is about making people smile. Young people can get news and information from the web and 24-hour news channels. The job of a newspaper has changed. Yes, it's important people get news but it's also important that they have fun,

> ❝ We like bottoms – because bottoms are fun. ❞
> – Peter Hill, when editor of the Daily Star.

that they can open a newspaper and it makes them smile. I think the *Sun* is losing the plot. There is nothing to smile at in there. I don't want to read another campaign about paedophiles. I know they are out there and I know it's a problem but on a Monday morning I don't want to think, "Oh no, it's another week of more doom and gloom". (Quoted in Plunkett, 2003)

Such tabloid values have been crossing over into the broadsheet, and formerly broadsheet, national press for well over a decade now, according to academic commentators such as Bob Franklin (1997: 7–10). The *Times*, for example, has certainly changed since it unleashed a classical music critic on a Beatles record in the 1960s; the resulting article about the group's aeolian cadences and pan diatonic clusters baffled fans and Beatles alike. Serious newspapers now have "a fluffier feel", in the words of one *Daily Telegraph* journalist (quoted in Ponsford, 2006). Newspapers have adopted many

of the ideas and styles of magazines. But engagement with popular culture, leisure, lifestyle and entertainment does not mean that newspapers necessarily *ignore* more traditionally weighty subject matter. Editors such as Alan Rusbridger, of the *Guardian*, argue that their papers, alongside their online offerings, now have a much broader range of subject matter than in the past, incorporating the popular *alongside* the serious; the fact that they also have many more printed pages as well as websites means there has been no decline in the *quantity* of heavy news, foreign reports, political analysis or serious arts coverage (Rusbridger, 2000).

Similarly, regional media are in the entertainment business as well as the information business, according to David Helliwell:

First and foremost we're there to inform, but in this day and age you've got to do more than that because there's so much competition. There will always be pages in the paper where you are trying to be entertaining, to give people a read – features, the women's supplement, travel pages, reporters trying the latest high street fad, that sort of stuff. It's a balance, but our two big sellers are still local news and local sport.

Entertainment values

As noted in Chapter 3, editors tend to look favourably on stories with the capacity to entertain or amuse. A national survey of 25,000 adults found that, while just over a third said they relied on newspapers to keep them informed, one in five admitted to reading a daily paper more for entertainment than for news (Powell, 2001). They are unlikely to be disappointed. A study of the UK national press found that many news stories seemed to have been included not because they contained serious information for the reader but because of their entertainment value (Harcup and O'Neill, 2001: 274). Patricia Holland writes, in the context of the *Sun* but with wider resonance, that the concepts of news and entertainment are becoming more entwined:

> The relentless push towards entertainment values has meant that the definition of what makes "news" is itself constantly changing. The carefully established distinction between fact and opinion is now less easy to maintain. The need for accuracy has become dissolved into the excess of the headline, through a joke, an ironic exaggeration or an expression of outrage. (Holland, 1998: 31)

A number of components go together to form the entertainment package that influences news selection in erstwhile "serious" media as well as the more popular end of the market. These entertainment values include: humour, showbiz, sex, animals, crime, and pictures.

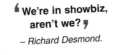

❛ We're in showbiz, aren't we? ❜
– Richard Desmond.

Humour

Humorous stories are popular with newsdesks. When council workers took an unusually long time to mend a streetlamp it became national news not because of any particular significance, but because it echoed jokes about how many people it takes to change a lightbulb: FOUR MONTHS, 16 MEN AND £1,000 TO MEND LAMP (*Sun*, September 16 2002). Sometimes the opportunity for a headline pun is enough to warrant a story's inclusion, as when Rolf Harris's accordion caught fire: FRY ME ACCORDION BROWN, SPORT (*Daily Mirror*, August 5 2002).

Showbiz

Stories about TV stars and other celebs are rife in the tabloids, but all UK national media – normally with the exception of the *Financial Times* and one or two of the BBC's more austere outputs – now carry showbiz stories. The *Independent*'s Paul Vallely believes it "muddles world views" when journalists write about fictional characters "as though they were real rather than actors" (BBC, 2002). Then there is the practice of introducing characters or plots from films and TV to enliven otherwise straight news reports. Take this intro from a hard news story: "Detectives hunting a brutal axe murderer are bringing in a *Cracker*-style psychologist to carry out a profile of the killer" (SEND FOR CRACKER, *Yorkshire Evening Post*, May 31 2001). Similarly, a story about working hours in the *Sunday Times* business section referred to northern bosses' attitudes as being "more akin to that of *Coronation Street*'s Mike Baldwin", illustrated with a picture captioned: "Northern boss: Mike Baldwin" (BOSSES WORK HARDER IN SOUTHEAST, *Sunday Times*, February 24 2002).

Sex

If there is a sex angle to a story it is regarded as more entertaining and is therefore more likely to be used, with the sex angle emphasised even if it is marginal to the events described (Harcup and O'Neill, 2001: 274). Court cases and employment tribunals with sex angles are more likely to be covered, all other things being equal, than are those without. A typical example is WREN HUMILIATED BY SUPERIOR'S SEX BANTER (*Daily Telegraph*, March 23 1999).

Animals

Animals feature in many entertaining stories about unusual behaviour. Igwig the iguana, for example, made the front page of the *Times* when he was involved in a court case because his owner threw him at a police officer after being ejected from a pub (IGUANA IS CALLED TO THE BENCH, *Times*, February 26 2002).

Crime

It is now more than 60 years since George Orwell recorded the complaints of newspaper readers that "you never seem to get a good murder nowadays" (Orwell, 1946a: 10). But crime stories continue to fascinate journalists and readers alike. During the wall-to-wall coverage of the unfolding drama in the village of Soham in August 2002, when two girls disappeared and were eventually found dead, every national tabloid newspaper increased sales throughout the UK (ABC, 2002). After Madeleine McCann disappeared on a family holiday in Portugal in 2007 the BBC sent its big-name anchorman Huw Edwards to present BBC TV news live from on the spot, despite the fact that there seemed to be no new news to report (Jenkins, 2007). The validity of crime news is compromised if journalists put entertaining their audience above reporting the facts or informed analysis, argues David J Krajicek, former crime reporter for the *New York Daily News*:

> [The] bulk of crime coverage amounts to drive-by journalism – a ton of anecdote and graphic detail about individual cases drawn from the police blotter but not an ounce of leavening context to help frame and explain crime. Too many of these reports begin and end with who did what to whom, embellished with the moans of a murder victim's mother or the sneer of an unrepentant killer in handcuffs. (Krajicek, 1998)

Pictures

Many of the above stories provide opportunities to include entertaining, amusing, dramatic, tragic or titillating photographs and/or footage. *Sunday Express* editor John Junor once remarked that "a beautiful young woman lifts even the dreariest page" (quoted in McKay, 1999: 188), and his unreconstructed views live on in much of today's media. The importance of pictures is considered further in Chapter 11.

Entertainment versus elitism?

Telling entertaining stories is part of the journalist's job, as is telling stories in entertaining ways. Lighter stories can also be enjoyable, as Lindsay Eastwood explains:

> ❛ The focus is on those things which are apt to arouse curiosity but require no analysis. ❜
> – *Pierre Bourdieu.*

I enjoy doing the "And finally…" stories because you can be creative. I've done a giant mushroom story, and a dog that was allergic to grass so they made it these special little red wellies. That was sweet. I did a lollipop man who'd won a "best lollipop man" award and he did a rap, so we got him dancing with some kids. I did a baby boom in a Hull supermarket where everybody on the checkout had had a baby. We got them to do the Marge Simpson thing with the checkout going "ping" when the baby was scanned in. And they've even taken a shot of my cleavage for National Cleavage Day.

You can have a lot of fun on TV. When you've been doing serious stories like the floods, it's nice to do the light stuff. The strangest thing I have covered recently was a live report from a naked bike ride in York by protesters trying to highlight environmental issues. On that occasion I think I had a really good excuse to defy the ITN remit of doing a reporter involvement piece-to-camera. It was a tricky job, since we are under strict guidelines not to show any genitals in our programme and yet the whole story was about naked people. I don't know how, but I managed to pull it off.

So how would she respond to anyone who said that such stories, or her Bridget Jones pole routine mentioned earlier, were too formulaic, in some way demeaning of the journalist's craft? "No, I don't think they're formulaic at all. I think news stories are formulaic. You know, you get the scene of the murder, you get eyewitnesses, you try and chase the family. That's formulaic. I think the 'And finally…'s are a real challenge."

Whenever journalists address "popular" subjects, or report in ways intended to entertain, they run the risk of being accused of ***dumbing down*** or of lacking *authority*. And when critics accuse journalists of dumbing down, they in turn tend to be accused of cultural *elitism*. Yet even the most serious news is reported in ways designed to be entertaining, to keep the audience engaged. That is why news is told in the form of stories that usually focus on individual people rather than abstract concepts; why news stories are written in language that is accessible, active and sometimes colourful; why news stories may be presented visually and creatively to attract an audience.

A journalist's job is *both* to inform and to entertain. The trick – for journalist and audience alike – is to recognise the difference between the two and to understand that if it fails to inform then it ceases to be journalism. And it is worth remembering that sometimes the facts of a story, simply told, can be the most entertaining of all.

▓ ▪ Summary ▪

Journalists have long sought to entertain as well as to inform, to attract and retain an audience. This takes the form of selecting entertaining subject matter (humour, showbiz, sex, animals, crime, pictures) and of telling stories in entertaining ways. It has been claimed that the lines between information and entertainment have become blurred in recent years as part of the process known as "dumbing down". The dumbing down thesis has in turn been criticised as elitist. As the journalist's job will continue to involve elements of entertaining as well as informing, journalist and audience should both be able to recognise the distinction between the two.

 ## ▪ Questions ▪

Can journalism be both entertaining and informative at the same time?

Why do journalists tell news as stories?

Why do audiences seem to enjoy stories about crimes?

Is the idea of authoritative news necessarily elitist?

Is *any* news better than *no* news?

▓ ▪ Further reading ▪

For an enjoyable historical account of the press as popular entertainment, see Matthew Engel's (1997) *Tickle the Public*. Conboy (2002) covers similar territory with a more analytical approach. Franklin (1997) offers an eloquent and still cogent critique of the tabloidisation of the print and broadcast media in the UK, countered in part by McNair's (2000) case that coverage of politics in particular has *not* been dumbed down and Temple's (2006) provocatively titled paper, "Dumbing down is good for you". Conboy's (2006) *Tabloid Britain* explores the peculiarities of the UK's redtop tabloid newspapers, particularly when it comes to their use of language, while Dovey (2000) examines the "carnivalesque" excesses of so-called reality TV, raising questions of authority, authorship and the public sphere. Finally, Bourdieu's (1998) consideration of journalism concludes that journalists' increasingly human interest agenda tends to depoliticise citizens.

Sources for soundbites

Murdoch, quoted in O'Neill, 1992: 30n; Frith, quoted in Hilton, 2007; Hill, quoted in *British Journalism Review*, Vol 13, No 2 (2002); Desmond, quoted in Ruddock, 2001; Bourdieu, 1998: 51, 159.

eight

interviewing

key terms	

Control; Conversation; Death knocks; Doorstepping; Interviews; Performance; Pseudo-events; Questions; Quotes; Selection; Victims

It has now passed into legend as one of the great apologies. It concerned a feature article profiling a singer who had decided to stand for election to political office. For a black woman, she had apparently revealed to her interviewer a surprising degree of sympathy for the old South African system of racial segregation and discrimination. The subsequent apology is worth quoting in its excruciating entirety:

> In an article headed BLACK AND BLUE, Page 6, G2, yesterday, we interviewed Patti Boulaye about her intention to stand for the Greater London Assembly, as a Conservative. The interview took place in Conservative Central Office. In the course of the article we quoted Ms Boulaye, a prominent black actress and singer, as saying: "This is a time to support apartheid … I mean people say, 'Why didn't you support it when it was in government?' Because it would have been the fashionable thing to do. This is a time to support apartheid because it's unfashionable." What Ms Boulaye actually said was "a party", meaning the Conservative Party. At no time during the interview was apartheid mentioned. The journalist concerned misheard Ms Boulaye's remarks but then asked no follow-up questions about what she thought she had heard. The offence was compounded by the picking out of part of these misheard remarks as a subsidiary heading in the middle of the text. The *Guardian* apologises profusely to Ms Boulaye for suggesting she made remarks which seemed to show she supported something totally abhorrent to her. (*Guardian*, March 18 1999)

Any journalist about to interview somebody would do well to keep the above story in mind. If the mishearing was unfortunate, the real error was the failure to follow it up during the interview. Such an apparently bizarre statement should have

Pseudo-events

The concept of the pseudo-event was introduced in Chapter 2. Daniel Boorstin categorises the media interview – alongside the press conference and the press release – as such a pseudo-event; that is, not so much a way of reporting the news, but of *making* the news. From the second half of the 19th century onwards, interviewing gradually became a common practice in the press, first in the USA and then in the UK (Chalaby, 1998: 127). But interviews were seen by some at the time as invasions of privacy and by others as wholly contrived events. One 19th-century editor described interviewing as "the most perfect contrivance yet devised to make journalism an offence, a thing of ill savour in all decent nostrils"; despite such hostility, the interview eventually became established as a legitimate way of gathering material for journalism (Boorstin, 1963: 26–27). Not just *gathering* material but also *creating* it:

> Nowadays a successful reporter must be the midwife – or more often the begetter – of his news. By the interview technique he incites a public figure to make statements which will sound like news. During the twentieth century this technique has grown into a devious apparatus which in skilful hands can shape national policy. (Boorstin, 1963: 34)

Before interviewing became commonplace, notes Michael Schudson, US President Lincoln often spoke with reporters informally "but no reporter ever quoted him directly" (Schudson, 2001: 156). Schudson argues that the growth of interviewing on both sides of the Atlantic helped journalists establish themselves as a separate group, brandishing notebooks and practising something called objective reporting:

> In the late 19th century and into the 20th century, leading journalists counselled against note-taking and journalists were encouraged to rely upon their own memories. But by the 1920s journalism textbooks

prompted further questions that would almost certainly have revealed the misunderstanding.

The Boulaye interview did at least take place, unlike a *Sun* interview with a widow whose husband was posthumously awarded the Victoria Cross for his actions in the Falklands war. Labelled "world exclusive", the article began: "VC's widow Marcia McKay fought back her tears last night and said: 'I'm so proud of Ian'…" In fact, she had refused to speak to the paper. So the *Sun* stitched together quotes from old cuttings and a second-hand account from the soldier's bereaved mother, and presented it as an interview with the widow. The Press Council (forerunner of the Press Complaints Commission) ruled that the paper had perpetrated "a deplorable, insensitive deception on the public" (Chippindale and Horrie, 1992: 163–165).

The *Guardian* and the *Sun* are not the only newspapers to have given readers cause to doubt the veracity of interviews. The vast majority of interviews are reported more accurately, but *all* interviews have been described as manufactured encounters or **pseudo-events**. Yet the interview – the asking of questions and the recording of answers – is the basic ingredient of both news and features. As Cedric Pulford explains:

> Interviewing is the chief tool of active journalism. Without talking to people who can give us information or opinions, by phone or face to face, we can only print what others send us or recycle what has appeared somewhere else. (Pulford, 2001: 17)

Preparation

The interview may be a brief encounter over the phone, a lengthy affair over lunch, a setpiece live broadcast, or a few questions answered via email. Whatever it is, you should have some idea *why* you are interviewing this particular person: for factual answers to one or two questions, opinions, quotes, emotions, description, scraps of colour, background, whatever.

dared to recommend "the discriminate and intelligent use of notes". The growing acceptance of note-taking suggests the acceptance and naturalization of interviewing. This is not to say the interview was no longer controversial. … There was still a sense that an "interview" was a contrived event in which the journalist, in collusion with a person seeking publicity, invented rather than reported news. As late as 1926 the Associated Press prohibited its reporters from writing interviews. But generally, reporting in the United States by that time meant interviewing. … It [fitted] effortlessly into a journalism already fact-centred and news-centred rather than devoted primarily to political commentary or preoccupied with literary aspirations. (Schudson, 2001: 157)

Control

John Sergeant's account of his encounter with Tony Benn (see p. 132) hinges on the question of *who* should have the right to control an interview. The relationship between interviewer and interviewee has been described by feature writer Fiammetta Rocco as an "ambivalent coupling" (Rocco, 1999: 49). Some of this ambivalence stems from the fact that, while today's journalistic style may be less deferential than that of half a century ago, the interviewee may be more media-literate and schooled in the arts of spin than were their predecessors.

Some celebrities try to impose tight control on interviews by setting conditions in return for (limited) access, as Gary Susman explains:

> There's always an army of publicists hovering over our shoulders, some from the studios, some employed by the stars, all making sure we don't ask anything impolite or embarrassing or anything that strays too far from the movie. The threats are never spoken but always implicitly – if you ask the star about his ex-wife, he'll walk out, and you'll have ruined the interview for yourself and your colleagues; or worse, you'll be blackballed from future junkets. (Susman, 2001)

This "increased PR interventionism" in interviews can result in "journalistic passivity and compliance in a sanitized promotional drive", argues Eamonn Forde (2001: 38). At its most extreme, it leads to editors agreeing to give 'copy approval' to PR companies acting on behalf of highly prized celebs. When the *Observer* was criticised for giving such approval to a

Having decided *why* you are interviewing someone, *how* do you go about it? Many journalists stress the importance of meticulous planning to ensure they remain in control, working to set questions or even a "script" determined by the particular angle being pursued (Aitchison, 1988: 40–42). Planning anything that resembles a script may encourage a rather stiff and inflexible approach to an interview, but thinking of *some* questions in advance is certainly a good idea. Of course, an interview may take an unexpected turn – and that might turn out to be a route you want to follow – but along the way you should make sure you cover the ground you need to.

You will often have time to conduct background research before the interview. You might spend a couple of hours searching news archives and reading cuttings about the subject, looking for basic information and useful insights, and possibly thinking of an angle nobody has yet come up with. You might Google them, but remember to read beyond the first page of results and to not rely on Wikipedia as an infallible source; in fact, don't rely on *anything* as an infallible source. You might look in specialist magazines, consult reference books, and talk to colleagues or friends who know something about the subject – or who have something they would like to ask. When Simon Hattenstone mentioned that he was going to interview film director Woody Allen, for example, one of the journalist's friends suggested: "Ask him how somebody so ugly gets off with so many beautiful women?" It turned out to be good advice because it became clear it was the very question that Allen had "obsessed over for most of his adult life" (Hattenstone, 2007).

> ❝ Sure, writing/broadcasting skills are crucial, but you won't get anywhere without being a nosy sod. ❞
> – Simon Hattenstone.

> ❝ When people ask me what my favourite interview is, I always say "the next one". ❞
> – David Frost.

The 'winning grace' of interviewing

There is plenty of often quite prescriptive advice available on interviewing techniques, but trial and

singer's PR people, the deputy editor said the paper had signed the "silly piece of paper" only because the interview was likely to be uncontroversial, adding: "[Our] advice to anybody who signs anything like that is to utterly disregard it if it gets in the way of doing the piece that you want to do, even if that means retrospectively breaking an agreement with some tinpot PR agency" (quoted in Morgan, 2002b). In that case, why sign it in the first place? Or why not at least give the article a health warning?

The relationship between journalist and source is explored in more detail in Chapters 4 and 6; control of the finished product is discussed in the section on quotes, below.

Victim

The victim is a familiar character in journalism. Most information on victims comes from interviews with victims themselves if they are still alive, or from interviews with the bereaved. Thoughtful journalists may pause from time to time to consider why reporters and, presumably, readers are so fascinated with details of victims' lives. "Being the victim of crime is to lay oneself open to having one's privacy invaded," argues Chris Frost, who adds:

> Journalists need always to remember that victims of crime are not there by choice and rarely through any fault of their own. If the report will make things worse for the victim, then the journalist should think carefully about how the report should be handled. (Frost, 2000: 146)

And yet, do those critics who flinch from the very idea of "death knocks" not want to know about the person who was found dead in their neighbourhood last night? Where do they think such information comes from if not by interviewing distressed relatives, friends, neighbours and workmates? Journalism lecturer Sallyanne Duncan told a seminar of the Association for Journalism Education in 2008 that journalism students should be encouraged to think *positively* about death knocks as one of the legitimate

error is the way most trainee journalists feel their way through their first interviews. Experiment with different approaches and see what works for you in different circumstances. Remember that it is rarely a good idea to pretend to have a completely different personality from your own. Nor is it necessarily a good idea for every fledgling hack to try to be Jeremy Paxman, who is often said to have said that he approaches every interview by asking himself, "Why is this lying bastard lying to me?" He didn't actually say that, he just quoted Louis Heren of the *Times* (Wells, 2005), but his style is certainly more suited to the interrogation of a slippery politician than asking a nice old couple about their golden wedding anniversary.

Journalists have to be comfortable speaking to all sorts of people from millionaires to the homeless. This remains as true today as when Frederick Mansfield instructed trainees back in the 1930s:

> Personality counts for much. A reporter has to meet all classes of people, who are potential sources of news; to talk to Cabinet Ministers as well as costermongers, I am tempted to say on their own level, and to inspire in all the confidence essential to successful approach. The happy medium between the "inferiority complex" and cocksure audacity, should be the aim – a reasonable self-assurance, born of a well-informed competence. The winning grace that will extract news equally from a Lord Lieutenant and a trade union secretary, is a great asset. A reporter touches life at all points and in his deportment should show respect for the feelings and opinions of others, no matter how much he may be out of sympathy with them. Journalism tends to breed cynicism and a hypercritical attitude, but good manners, and often diplomacy, forbid a display of contempt. (Mansfield, 1936: 87–88)

Experienced interviewer Martin Wainwright believes that a journalist's main assets during interviews are being *curious* about people and allowing enough *time* to let them talk:

> People can be diffident, so the interesting things sometimes come out only at the very end of an interview.

ways in which reporters can find things out and allow those directly involved in events to have their say. Lecturer Jackie Newton told the same event that journalists on death knocks should remember that the story on which they are working ultimately *belongs* not to the reporter but to the family, to whom it will always be more than just a story (Harcup, 2008).

The idea of the victim is discussed in more detail in Chapter 9.

Quotes

A good quote is highly prized. According to Allan Bell, direct quotation serves three key purposes in journalism:

> First, a quote is valued as a particularly incontrovertible fact because it is the newsmaker's own words. ... A second function is to distance and disown, to absolve journalist and news outlet from endorsement of what the source said. ... The third function of direct quotation is to add to the story the flavour of the newsmaker's own words. (Bell, 1991: 207–209)

But most of what is said in most interviews will not be quoted directly; rather, the bulk of information gleaned from sources will be used as background or turned into reported speech. Bell argues that this power to edit "puts the journalist in *control* of focusing the story, able to combine information and wordings from scattered parts of an interview" (Bell, 1991: 209, my emphasis).

Ethical concerns are raised about this role of the journalist in selecting the parts of an interview to quote, the parts to paraphrase, and the parts to discard, as Lynn Barber explains:

> The journalist has *all* the power when it comes to writing the piece: she chooses which quotes to use and which to omit, which to highlight and which to minimise. I use a lot of quotes compared with most other inter-viewers, but they probably still only amount to at most two pages out of a twenty- or thirty-page transcript. So obviously with this degree of selection, one has almost limitless opportunities for "slanting" the interview, favourably or unfavourably. All I can say is that I don't aim to do that and I hope I don't. (Barber, 1999: 202, emphasis in original)

That's true to an amazing extent. As a journalist you spend most of your life rushing, but it's still worth spending as long as you can with people. Also, people can open up more if you appear a bit naïve.

An example of somebody opening up came when the short-lived Conservative party leader Iain Duncan Smith held a lunch to get to know local journalists. A young journalist from the *Wanstead and Woodford Guardian* took the opportunity to ask him some friendly enough questions, in the course of which the Tory leader remarked that Tony Blair's children had been used "ruthlessly" to promote the Labour Prime Minister. The day after the local paper appeared, the interview was being quoted throughout the national media. Reporter Sara Dixon reflected on her scoop:

> A young Diet-Coke-drinking local reporter sitting opposite you in a Woodford restaurant is distinctly less threatening than a grilling on party policy under the glare of studio lights by Andrew Marr or Jonathan Dimbleby. But it is also a question of approach. ... [Without] the roundabout questions of how have the past six months been treating you Mr Duncan Smith, the contentious statement would never have been uttered. The comment about Blair and his children is not a thing that is extracted in pugnacious interviews, rather it *emerges out of conversations*. (Dixon, 2002, my emphasis)

Conversation is the key to good interviewing. Even the briefest interview should involve the techniques of conversation, and that means listening as well as talking. Yet the listening part is too often overlooked, according to Carl Bernstein of Watergate fame: "One of the things I've observed having been interviewed so many times is that reporters tend to be terrible listeners. They have usually decided what the story is before they do the interview, and they will choose the one which will manufacture the most controversy" (quoted in Silver, 2007). So interviewers need to listen and

engage with what is being said rather than just wait for a gap to fill with the next question on their list. In face-to-face interviews it is important to make eye contact, and in all interviews the interviewee needs to be reassured via sounds or gestures that the interviewer is still awake and, ideally, still interested.

> ❛ The only time I penetrated Tony Blair's defences over Iraq was by keeping eye contact while telling him he never seemed to be sorry. ❜
> – Andrew Marr.

On the telephone

You cannot make eye contact over the telephone, and the vast majority of non-broadcast interviews are conducted this way. Although there is an impersonality about the phone, many journalists develop chatty relationships with regular contacts whom they may never have met in the flesh.

Tone of voice is obviously important, as is the manner in which you begin the call. When somebody answers the phone, you have no idea what they were in the middle of doing when you called – or whose call they might have been hoping for – so it is not usually a good idea to launch into a fusillade of questions the second they come on the line. Speaking clearly, politely and not too fast, explain who you are and why you are ringing them. Ask for a few minutes of their time – be prepared to call back at a pre-arranged time if you are not on deadline – and try to sound bright, alert, non-threatening and friendly. It has been suggested that standing up while speaking on the phone exudes extra confidence, and that making facial and arm gestures can help inflect the voice with the appropriate tone (Keeble, 2001a: 63). I've also heard advertising reps being urged to "smile while you dial". That might be the sort of advice to make hardened hacks do the finger-down-the-throat routine, but it is endorsed by Sally Adams, who adds, "probably the most important thing is to *like* talking on the phone" (Adams with Hicks, 2001: 85, my emphasis).

Telephone interviews are almost always shorter than face-to-face ones, so you tend to get down to details pretty quickly. It is usually worth getting the interviewee talking by asking, "Could you talk me through what happened to you?", "Describe what you saw," or "What is your reaction to…?" Their replies should prompt further questions. This is all well and good when you have called somebody and your research is fresh in your mind. But it's not so easy when *they* call *you* back hours or days later, by which time you may have forgotten why you wanted to talk to them in the first place. That's one reason why many journalists prefer to keep ringing somebody rather than rely on a return call that, if it comes at all, will probably be at the least convenient moment.

A word of warning on telephone interviews. You need to be absolutely clear if the interviewee is being serious or is joking. Given that you have no visual clues you may have to ask, "Are you being serious?" Better to be thought of as lacking a sense of humour than to risk publishing a flippant or ironic remark as if it were a genuine opinion.

Email

Telephone interviews may be impersonal but trying to establish a rapport in written communication via email can be even trickier. Traditionally, email interviews – like the faxed ones that preceded them – have not been recommended except when they were the only way of getting through to somebody. That's mainly because email lacks the instantaneous to-ing and fro-ing of actual conversation. Some email interviewees will write in rather stiff, formal language, and there is a limit to how many times questions and answers can be batted backwards and forwards before one side or the other gets fed up. The result is that email encounters tend to be more brisk and businesslike than do face-to-face or telephone conversations. Often, though, it is possible to establish some kind of rapport via email so that the exchange becomes semi-conversational even though it is in written rather than spoken form. Almost all of my interviews with journalists featured in this book were conducted face to face, but a couple were carried out via email; can you tell which?

Some people are happier to be interviewed by email because it means they can answer questions at their own convenience. Email may be the most convenient way of contacting a range of academic experts all over the world, for example, because your message will be waiting for them when they log on in their different time zones. Also, if you are asking technical questions, email has the advantage that the interviewee will be putting the answers in writing for you; so your chances of misquoting the answer should be dramatically reduced.

Arguably, email has made it harder for people in positions of power to hide from journalists by resorting to the age-old device of never being available to speak to them. When Paul Foot rang people from his desk at the *Daily Mirror* they tended to take his calls because of the kudos associated with that title, but when he switched to *Private Eye* such people often seemed to be "in meetings" whenever he telephoned. That can be a frustrating experience when investigating alleged wrongdoing, because you need to put allegations to those involved, as Foot explains:

> Getting information out of the people you're accusing is absolutely crucial to the whole operation. Just as email has changed our lives, the fax changed our lives. I got in the habit of faxing questions to people. Whereas if you rang them up they would never be available, once you've got the fax through, you're home. Because if you don't get an answer you can always say "well I faxed them with these questions". With the phone you might never get even to ask the question.

If you are going to contact an interviewee via email, it is safest to assume they would prefer to be addressed formally rather than informally, with a message that is spelled and punctuated correctly. And remember that you lose control of your email the moment you press Send, meaning that anything you have written may be forwarded to anyone to whom the recipient chooses to send it.

Face-to-face

When I interviewed veteran Labour politician Tony Benn in his Chesterfield office he brought out his own tape machine to record the conversation. He recorded all his interviews partly to check later if he had been misquoted, and partly to warn journalists not to stitch him up when writing up their stories. The only other interviewee I have seen make their own recording was miners' union leader Arthur Scargill. Profile writer Lynn Barber expresses surprise that so few interview subjects make their own tapes to safeguard against being misquoted (Barber, 1999: 201).

Benn's refusal to accept that journalists should have total **control** of interviews managed to unsettle seasoned reporter John Sergeant, who recalls arriving at the MP's home to record an interview during the 1984–85 miners' strike:

> When he opened the door, I immediately noticed a small tape recorder, which he thrust forward, with its red light on, showing that it was recording. "Hello," he said; and I did not know whether to reply to him directly or speak into the tape recorder. I said hello to the machine. He then proceeded to give me a short lecture on the unfairness of the BBC's coverage of the miners' dispute. I took this in reasonably good heart, but *knowing that all my remarks were being recorded I said nothing which might be used against me.* (Sergeant, 2001: 236–237, my emphasis)

It was a rare case of the tables being turned, with the journalist rather than the interviewee having to think twice before saying anything. That particular interview ended with Benn erasing the BBC's tape with a demagnetizing device, leaving the journalist "struck dumb" (Sergeant, 2001: 238).

Happily, most encounters are less prickly affairs. Just as well because, unless you are accusing the interviewee of wrongdoing, you need to establish a *rapport* between the two of you. First impressions are important, so don't be late. Don't smell of booze or fags, unless you know that will help you fit in, and do dress appropriately – not as if you are going to a wedding or a funeral, but smartly enough so that your state of dress will not be an issue for the interviewee. Non-verbal communication is important, so show interest by making eye contact without staring, nodding but not nodding off. Give verbal reassurance that the interviewee is not speaking into a vacuum – laugh at their jokes, sympathise with their troubles, and use phrases such as "Really?", "Yes", "uhh-huhh" to demonstrate that you are engaged. But don't overdo it.

Learn to listen, interrupting their flow only if they are digressing too much and you are on deadline. Interrupting a dramatic narrative to check a minor detail – "How do you spell the name of the first boy eaten by the crocodile?" – can be irritating. Make a note and check at the end. But don't be afraid to interrupt to clarify something you don't understand or to get some specific examples. Keep your eyes as well as your ears open because you might discover a visual clue to the interviewee's character or a visual prompt for an unusual question. Clothes, hair, tattoos, piercings, pictures on the wall, books on the shelves, an unusual plant, a view from the window – all might spark off a question and lead to the discovery of a different angle.

Chat is more common at the end of an interview conducted in person than one conducted on the telephone or via email, and sometimes this can result in further information or angles to follow up. Unless you don't mind risking any future relationship with the interviewee, you might think twice before quoting something said after a formal interview has finished without asking, "Do you mind if I use that?" See discussion below of "off-the-record" comments.

Audio and broadcast interviews

Much of this chapter deals with interviews for text-based journalism, whether in print or online. Increasingly, however, journalists who were once print only are now also filing audio and even video reports for online media. The *Guardian's* Martin Wainwright, for example, now routinely records interviews using a digital recorder that he then plugs into his laptop; once he has selected the necessary information and quotes for his written news story or feature, he can pass on the audio file for uploading on to the web. "The thing I really like about it is that it allows people to speak for themselves," he says.

Interviews for audio and visual use – whether online or on radio or television – will rely on many of the same techniques as do interviews for magazines or newspapers. But there are also many differ-

> ❝ Go on, you've got another five seconds. Say something outrageous. ❞
> – Bill Grundy, to the Sex Pistols.

ences: most notably the fact that you can use the speaker's *voice* as well as their words, and that broadcast interviews often have more than an element of *performance* about them. Whereas the questioning is often invisible to the reader of a print interview, it is central to many audio-visual interviews. None more so than when Jeremy Paxman asked Home Secretary Michael Howard the *same* question 12 times without getting an answer (Wells, 2005). If that was a moral victory for the interviewer, an earlier *Newsnight* interview turned into a personal disaster for presenter Peter Snow. Miners' leader Arthur Scargill turned the tables on the experienced journalist who gave in to the fatal temptation to bluff.

Scargill:	Have you read my full speech in Moscow?
Snow:	Yes I have.
Scargill:	Have you? I don't believe you, I'm sorry... Mr Snow, have you seen the full text, because every other broadcaster has told me that they haven't? Have you seen it, truthfully?
Snow:	Can you, can you...?
Scargill:	No, I'm asking you a question then I'll answer your question. Have you seen the full text?
Snow:	I have not seen any reference...
Scargill:	I didn't ask you that. Have you seen the full text?
Snow:	I have not seen any reference...
Scargill:	Have you seen the full text?
Snow:	Would you tell me Mr Scargill, would you tell me...?
Scargill:	I'm asking you a question.
Snow:	I'm asking the questions, if I may say so.
Scargill:	Well, not this time you're not. I'm asking you, have you seen the full text?
Snow:	To be quite honest, I have not seen the full text.
Scargill:	Right...

(*Newsnight at 20*, BBC2, January 29 2000)

All this talk of victory and defeat emphasises the adversarial nature of many such interviews. But, apart from the setpiece studio slanging match or the doorstep challenge to a rogue, the aggressive approach is not usually to be recommended. You will win few prizes by exhorting the organiser of a local charity jumble sale to, "Come on, come on, answer the question!"

Asking questions

The precise nature of the questions you ask will be determined initially by the purpose of the interview and the research you have done, but it is important that you listen attentively to people's answers and adjust your line of questioning if necessary. It is usually a good idea to get the interviewee talking in an open way at the beginning, even if you intend to end up by accusing them of some skulduggery. So, unless you specifically want a yes or no answer, try to avoid asking *closed* questions such as, "Did you see the accident?" To get them talking opt for more *open* questions such as, "What did you see?" People often stop after a sentence or two, looking for reassurance that this is what you want. Give it to them by asking, "And then?" or, "What happened next?"

Whatever the topic, you are likely to want to know the answers to the five Ws of journalism introduced in Chapter 1: Who? What? Where? When? Why? And, of course, How? You may have to keep working at it because, as Fiammetta Rocco notes: "The story that a subject tells about himself is almost never the whole story. 'Why?' is the question I ask most often" (Rocco, 1999: 50). You will often have to do some lateral thinking while listening. *Who* is that person? *What* is their relationship to so-and-so? *Where* did they meet? *When* did they arrive? *Why* did they go there? *How* did they travel? The answer to any one such question might end up providing you with the most newsworthy angle to a story. But you might never know if you don't ask. Clarify any vague answers such as "recently" or "about". Getting specific examples by asking, "Such as?" can sometimes bring a dull interview to unexpected life. Do not be afraid to say: "Sorry, I'm not sure I've understood that, could you please explain it again?"

Unless you are transmitting live, it is a good idea to ask towards the end: "Is there anything else you'd like to add?" It is polite, it stops the interviewee feeling annoyed that they didn't get the chance to talk about their pet subject, and they might just say something far more important and interesting than anything that has gone before. Then, make sure you have checked spellings, especially names, and exchanged contact details. And don't forget to thank people for their help and time.

Off-the-record

An interviewee may tell a journalist that something is "off-the-record", meaning that you should not attribute the information to them. That does not mean that you cannot include the information in an unattributed form. Check exactly what information they are referring to. They may have good reason – perhaps they might lose their job for criticising their employer in public – or they may be feeling paranoid with little justification. As the interview progresses they may begin to trust you more, so you could try suggesting that something said earlier off-the-record might be restored to on-the-record. But if you break your word, having agreed to something being off-the-record, then you will have betrayed a source.

Confusion arises if somebody *assumes* that a journalist will treat something as off-the-record without making it explicit, as when a politician put his hand over a journalist's tape recorder when he passed on some gossip about the prime minister's wife during an interview about the health service. His comment was included in the subsequent article, causing outrage in Downing Street. A *Press Gazette* leader column noted at the time:

> ❛ I always tell beginner journalists: "Look, all you have to do is be punctual, be polite, and ask questions". ❜
> – Lynn Barber.

[Lord Winston's] naïvety serves to remind us that interviewees and journalists can have very different beliefs about what constitutes off-the-record. Most of the public would regard Winston's covering of the mic as placing the Cherie item out of play. Most journalists would not: *something is off-the-record only when interviewee and journalist so agree. (Press Gazette,* January 21 2000, my emphasis)

Such agreement cannot be imposed unilaterally by the interviewee, and it certainly cannot be made retrospective by adding: "Of course, everything I have said must be off-the-record." In such circumstances the journalist *may* choose to agree, but it remains a *choice*.

People may say things that, with hindsight, they wish they had kept to themselves. A journalist who combines a conversational tone with a keen news sense will sometimes be "lucky" enough to catch an interviewee in just such a mood. Jane Merrick recalls the time that, as a Press Association reporter, she made a routine telephone call to a petrol company press office at the beginning of the fuel protests that paralysed the UK in September 2000:

> It was during the protesters' first blockade of an oil refinery. In London the company's line was that petrol supplies won't be affected. When I called the PR guy in the North-West I got lucky because he was really annoyed and he said: "Don't these people realise we're going to run out of fuel by Sunday night?" I said, like, "Really?" And he said, "Yeah, and it's really peeing me off." I said, "OK, fine", put the phone down and ran the story, "Warning of fuel shortage by Sunday".

The warning became a national talking point and the panic buying of petrol increased as a result. Merrick continues:

> This guy got into so much trouble. He phoned me on the Monday and said: "It wasn't off-the-record because I didn't say it was off-the-record, but I shouldn't have said that to you because our line was that it was fine." When clearly it wasn't fine.

Doorsteps and death knocks

Some interviews are fraught with difficulties, ranging from the boredom of hanging around for hours waiting for somebody to emerge through a doorway to the possibility of a punch in the face. The "doorstep" and the "death knock" bring out differing emotions in journalists and interviewees alike.

Doorstepping is a peculiarly British tradition, argues Matthew Engel. And a peculiarly ineffective one, it seems:

> ❝ I was sick of asking: "How did you feel, Mrs Smith, when your son was knifed to death by muggers?" What is she going to say? "Oh, I never liked him much"? ❞
>
> – Terry Pratchett, on why he left journalism.

Photographers and reporters descend on the home of a person touched by scandal or tragedy … and wait, in the hope of a picture of one of the actors in the drama or, far less probably, a comment. It is a tiresome and, for the reporters, almost always a pointless chore, unless they are actually paying to buy the story. (Engel, 1997: 279)

Not so, according to Nick Davies. He has no time for reporters who bully people, camp outside their homes and peer through their windows, but he argues that arriving unannounced on people's doorsteps remains an integral part of the journalist's armoury: "That's how you get good stories. It is the most exciting and most skilful part of our job" (quoted in Stevens, 2001).

When it comes to death knocks – calling on a bereaved family to ask for information, quotes and a picture – few journalists actually enjoy the task, although some adopt a macho pose and boast of their experiences. Both the Press Complaints Commission and the National Union of Journalists advise reporters to be cautious about intruding on people's grief, and families may be actively hostile to journalists' enquiries at such a difficult time. Some people genuinely welcome the chance to talk about the death of somebody close to them, even to a stranger with a notebook, while others may answer questions to avoid inaccuracies appearing in the media, or simply because they do not think of refusing.

Deborah Wain is experienced at talking to victims' families after crimes, accidents or inquests. People usually seem to talk to her, so I asked her why:

> I try to be really straight with people when I interview them. I try to be polite and people respond really. I never give people the impression that I'm doing anything other than what I'm doing. On death knocks, be upfront. Don't try to be over-sympathetic, don't say, "I'm sorry", because you obviously didn't know that person. It's a hard one to get right, a lot of it is play it by ear. Be straight about it, say this story will go in the

paper and we want to give you, the family, the chance to say something about your son or whoever as a person. I've often rung people up and asked them if I can come and see them, rather than just turn up. Most people say yes. I'm a great believer that if people want to talk they will, or will ring you back. I know some people say don't do it over the phone or don't leave a message because they won't ring you back, but I don't think that's the case. If they want to say something they will get back in touch with you if you open that window of opportunity. I think women do better at death knocks. I know it's a bit of a cliché to send women out, but it's for good reason.

Reporter Sue White agrees on the importance of being polite and non-pushy, as she describes her own approach:

> Normally it would be quiet and I'd knock on the door. It would open a crack and someone would answer. … I'd say, "Hello, I'm Sue White from the *Birmingham Evening Mail*. We've heard from the police about the dreadful accident last night. Could I come in and have a word with you about it?" Almost everyone would say, "All right". … It's important to be very, very courteous and understanding …. I'd be taken in and sat in the lounge. It would be very quiet, they'd be stunned. I felt if I talked openly, in as friendly and sympathetic a way as possible – one person to another, making it clear I just wanted to confirm some facts – people would give me that information. I was usually right. (Quoted in Adams with Hicks, 2001: 142–143)

To the non-journalist it might sound callous, even manipulative. But when we hear there has been a murder or a terrible accident, we *expect* the media to tell us about the **victim** – their name, how old they were, and something about their character and interests. This information does not appear in the media by osmosis, not everyone is yet on Facebook (nor is everything on it necessarily accurate), and full details are rarely supplied by the police or other third parties. Such details are usually obtained by journalists knocking on the doors or ringing the telephones of

relatives, neighbours, friends, schools and workplaces.

Relatives don't have to be bereaved to be contacted by journalists at times of trauma. Jane Merrick was working for a regional news agency when news came through that the former Beatle George Harrison had been attacked, and that someone was being held by police in connection with the incident. She recalls:

> The name of the man arrested had got through the rumour mill so we contacted all the names in the book and I got to his mum first. I introduced myself as a journalist and she asked me what had happened. I said, "It's OK, I'll come out and speak to you." She said, "Tell me what's happened, is he OK?" I said, "He's absolutely fine but I need to come and see you in person". Then she got very defensive and said she would put the phone down if I didn't tell her what was going on. So I said, "There's been a bit of an incident that Michael has been involved in, but he's absolutely fine". She put two and two together and shouted to her husband, "Oh my God, Michael's stabbed a Beatle!" And then she put the phone down. In the end I had to go out there. Eventually she invited everyone in, but by then we weren't the only ones.

Reflecting on the experience, Merrick says:

> I felt terrible because you can't say straight out, "Your son has stabbed someone", and I was quite surprised that the police hadn't contacted her. It was a really difficult way to tell her, and I tried to soften it as much as possible, but you can't just be really mysterious and say, "I need to come and speak to you". With hindsight, I should just have established that she was the mother, and then turned up at the door to speak to her.

Brian Whittle favours the in person approach rather than giving anyone the opportunity of putting the phone down on you. People can, however, shut the door and tell a journalist to go away. The Press Complaints Commission tells journalists that, except in cases in the public interest, they "must not persist in questioning, telephoning, pursuing or photographing individuals once asked to desist" (PCC Code of

Practice). Such harassment still goes on, but not as much as it once did. As agency reporter Denis Cassidy says: "If you are told to leave, nowadays, then you leave" (quoted in Stevens, 2001).

Quoting

As well as being a means of obtaining information, interviews provide journalists with direct quotes. **Quotes** are a vital ingredient of journalism, adding authority, drama and powerful or colloquial expression to an account. Opinions differ on the editing of quotes, although all agree that little purpose is served by including excessive repetition of phrases such as "like", "know what I mean?", or "um" – unless you are doing it to make a point about the speaker. David Randall questions the point of quotation marks if what they contain is not "a word for word, syllable by syllable, accurate report of their actual words" (Randall, 2000: 187). But journalists frequently "tidy up" quotes. If they did not, it would be a remarkable coincidence that sources interviewed by tabloid journalists seem to speak in short, sharp sentences, while those quoted by broadsheet reporters speak in more complex sentence structures – even when they are the same people.

Whittle defends the practice of editing quotes:

> I think you can put words in people's mouths in the sense that most people are not particularly literate. That's perfectly acceptable if you know what you're doing, but only experience can tell you that. We go over people's quotes. Don't misunderstand me on this, we're pretty careful about it.

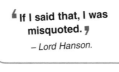

‘ If I said that, I was misquoted. ’
– *Lord Hanson.*

Merrick found contrasting policies at work when she moved from another regional news agency to the Press Association: "At the agency we could paraphrase people almost and still put it in quotes because it would be neater, whereas at PA it's the *exact* words. Now I have two dictaphones as a back-up and tape everyone as well as take shorthand notes, to cover my own back really."

Wynford Hicks and Tim Holmes urge a similar caution:

> [You] can always summarise quotes in indirect speech if tidying up causes difficulty – but you must never do the reverse: indirect speech can never be used as the raw material for a concocted quote. In subbing quotes … the key word is accuracy: the exact meaning of the original must be preserved. In condensing and clarifying a quote … you must never change the emphasis. So if somebody makes a statement that is qualified in some way, you remove the qualification at your peril. (Hicks and Holmes, 2002: 65)

The ethical line between tidying and changing can be a fine one. It can sometimes disappear entirely, especially if a reporter edits somebody's comments when making notes, then slightly strengthens them when writing up, before passing the story on to a sub who might tidy the quotes a bit more. The published result might end up being wholly unrecognisable to the interviewee, not just in words but in meaning. The golden rule when selecting or shortening quotes, and pruning out repetitions or irrelevancies, is to retain not just the interviewee's *voice* but the speaker's *sense*. Otherwise, why bother quoting at all?

▪ ▪ Summary ▪

Journalists interview sources – on the telephone, in person, by email – to obtain information, facts, opinions, analysis, description, emotion, colour, background, and direct quotes. The interview has been described as an ambivalent encounter in which the interviewee controls what information they disclose but, with the exception of live broadcasts, the interviewer retains control of how the interview is passed on to the audience. Interviews can themselves create news and in this sense can be seen as pseudo-events. Ethical issues associated with interviewing include questions of intrusion into grief, control of access, selection of material, copy approval, and the alteration of direct quotes.

▪ Questions

Why do journalists interview people?

Why do people agree to be interviewed by journalists?

How can journalists prepare for interviews?

Who has most power, the interviewer or the interviewee?

Is it ever right to edit people's quotes?

▪ ▪ Further reading ▪

Despite the rather prescriptive tone, there are many good tips and instructive anecdotes to be found in Adams with Hicks (2001); it also includes some interesting material on body language, but don't take all the pop psychology as gospel. Randall (2007), Sissons (2006), Keeble (2006), Frost (2002), and Pape and Featherstone (2005) all have sections on interviewing, while McKay (2006) includes two chapters specifically on magazine interviewing. For more detailed exploration of the various techniques and rules of broadcast interviewing, see Hudson and Rowlands (2007) or Boyd (2001); Beaman (2000) also offers a practical guide to radio interviewing. For a different perspective on the death knock, Harcup (2007) includes a chapter on crime reporting that features an interview with a victim's relative as well as a crime reporter.

Sources for soundbites

Hattenstone, 2007; Frost, quoted in Martinson, 2005; Marr, quoted in Barnicoat, 2007; Grundy, 1976: 12; Barber, 1999: 200; Pratchett, quoted in Jeffries, 2008; Hanson, quoted in Boyd, 2001: 117.

nine

writing news

Arthur was the future once. Arthur was the name given to a computer program devised in 2001 to take raw facts from the wires and rearrange them into punchy news stories. The only drawback for the scientists behind Arthur was that he lacked the human ability of being able to tell fact from fiction (Millar, 2001). Using robots to replace flesh-and-blood journalists may be a dream of the bean counters in charge of much of the media – no attitude problems, no ethical qualms, no maternity leave – but the idea isn't as fresh as it seems. Michael Frayn invented just such a news machine more than 40 years ago in his novel *The Tin Men*:

> Assistants bent over the component parts of the [Newspaper] Department's united experiment, the demonstration that in theory a digital computer could be programmed to produce a perfectly satisfactory daily newspaper with all the variety and news sense of the old hand-made article. With silent, infinite tedium, they worked their way through stacks of newspaper cuttings, identifying the pattern of stories, and analysing the stories into standard variables and invariables. At other benches other assistants copied the variables and invariables down on to cards, and sorted the cards into filing cabinets, coded so that in theory a computer could pick its way from card to card in logical order and assemble a news item from them. (Frayn, [1965] 1995: 37)

So a story such as a child being sent home from school because of unsuitable clothing would have just three variables: the particular clothing objected to, whether the child also smoked, and whether the child was humiliated in front of the whole school. The department judged such a story to be very satisfactory: "Basic plot entirely invariable. ... Frequency of publication: once every nine days" (Frayn, [1965] 1995: 38). Throw in the odd haircut, tattoo or piece

Stories

Allan Bell argues that journalists do not so much write articles as *stories*: "Journalists are professional story-tellers of our age. The fairytale starts: 'Once upon a time.' The news story begins: 'Fifteen people were injured today when a bus plunged..."' (Bell, 1991: 147). According to Dan Berkowitz, journalists develop "a mental catalogue of news story themes, including how the 'plot' will actually unravel and who the key actors are likely to be" (quoted in Cottle, 2000: 438).

Traditional stories start at the beginning and continue to some sort of resolution at the end. But news stories start with the end and often end in the middle. As Bell notes, the central action of news stories is told in a non-chronological order, "with result presented first followed by a complex recycling through various time zones" (Bell, 1991: 155). So a typical news story "moves backwards and forwards in time" (Bell, 1991: 153).

Rather than being resolved neatly, news stories tend to finish in "mid-air" (Bell, 1991: 154). This is not simply because news values and journalists' training dictate that the least important material be left to the end, but also because many stories are ongoing. The version of events given in the newspaper has always been merely a snapshot taken at deadline time; the advent of online news and 24-hour broadcasting without fixed deadlines allows stories to be constantly updated, but no update is ever sure to be the final word.

Myths

Simon Cottle argues that storytelling has long been used by society to "tell and re-tell its basic myths to itself", thereby reaffirming society as (after Anderson) an "imagined community": "Approached thus, news becomes a symbolic system in which the informational content of particular 'stories' becomes less important than the rehearsal of mythic 'truths' embodied within the story form itself" (Cottle, 2000: 438).

of body-piercing, and you've got a hardy-perennial that is as common today as when Frayn – a journalist as well as a novelist – was observing the production of such stories for real.

We have already seen, in Chapter 3, that news can be predictable and repetitive. This is partly because little happens that hasn't happened somewhere before. But it is also because much news tends to be written, or constructed, in the predictable, almost formulaic way satirised by Frayn. Journalists often say about a particular story that "it writes itself"; it is such a good story that, having established the intro or the top line, the rest flows almost effortlessly from the notebook to the finished product. An experienced journalist may be able to rush from a courtroom or a news conference and, seconds later, be dictating a perfectly constructed news story over the phone without pausing to write it out first. It looks like magic to the beginner who has to pore over every word, but it can be learned with practice and it is made possible by the fact that journalists already have potential *stories* in their heads. It is even said that many news stories are rewrites of ancient *myths* in contemporary settings.

The language of news

There are some obvious differences in the writing styles of different types of media, including differences over the amount of colour, and the number of adjectives, allowed into news copy. For example, when Jane Merrick worked for a regional agency selling mostly to the redtop tabloids, her copy would be sprinkled with words such as "brave", "pretty" and "tragic". When she switched to the Press Association she quickly learned that PA's style was to remove all such adjectives.

> ❛ Lots of facts, plainly stated and grouped with drama and maybe a dash of sentiment – no more. That's the journalistic cocktail. ❜
>
> – James Milne.

Jack Lule argues that journalists repeatedly write the news in terms of myth; that is, stories that draw on "archetypal figures and forms to offer exemplary models for human life" (Lule, 2001: 15). Not *every* news story is written in such terms, but many are. Why? Because, for Lule, stories already exist before they are written:

> Journalists approach events with stories already in mind. They employ common understandings. They borrow from shared narratives. They draw upon familiar story forms. They come to the news story *with* stories. Sometimes the story changes as the journalist gathers more information. But the story doesn't change into something completely new and never before seen. The story changes into ... another story. (Lule, 2001: 29, emphasis and ellipsis in original)

He identifies seven enduring myths that are told and retold by journalists through supposedly new news stories. They are:

- The victim – transforming death into sacrifice.
- The scapegoat – what happens to those who challenge or ignore social beliefs.
- The hero – the humble birth, the quest, the triumph and the return.
- The good mother – models of goodness.
- The trickster – crude, stupid, governed by animal instincts.
- The other world – the contrast between "our" way of life and the "other".
- The flood – the humbling power of nature (Lule, 2001: 22–25).

Consider the crime news that makes up such a large proportion of our print and broadcast news, particularly at a local and regional level. As we have seen in Chapter 4, most crime news is supplied by the police. Journalists can predict that there will be a reasonably steady supply of crime news and how many of various types of crime are likely to occur on their patch. A murder will be a shock in a rural village but almost expected to occur in an inner-city area (though it may still come as a shock to those who live in nearby streets). It does not take long for recruits to journalism to absorb how particular crimes tend to be covered.

But, although journalists working for different outlets may differ in their news values and their stylistic flourishes, they mostly share a common language – a basic grammar of journalism. Study the language of news stories in newspapers or news-based websites and you will find that most news is written in the past tense, reporting on something that has happened or been said. This contrasts with broadcast and some online news, in which the present tense is more common, although the past and even future tenses also make appearances. You will find that reporters' sentences are mostly active rather than passive, with somebody *doing* something rather than having something done *to* them. And you will find that concise writing is the norm – journalists never circumambulate the domiciles when they could simply go round the houses.

So news sentences are made up of active and concise language. They also tend to be short. They must have a subject and a verb, although the subject may be implied. Paragraphs, too, are much shorter than in other forms of writing, often just one sentence long, sometimes two or three. Journalists are taught to use short pars because when stories are set in newspaper columns long pars look like indigestible and off-putting chunks of text; stories on web "pages" may not be in such narrow columns but they still require paragraph breaks to make them appear easier to digest. Shorter pars are also thought more likely to keep the attention of readers, although some variety in longer stories is probably a good idea. Wynford Hicks (1998: 43) offers the following advice: "In news a par that goes beyond three sentences … is likely to be too long; never quote two people in the same par: always start a new one for the second quote; never tack a new subject on to the end of a par." When you are a beginner you won't go far wrong if, when in doubt, you start a new par.

> ❝ Who the hell's gonna read the *second* paragraph? ❞
> – The Front Page.

Structure: KISS and tell

Most news stories follow the "KISS and tell" formula – KISS standing either for "keep it short and simple", or "keep it simple, stupid". I have

Murder victims, for example, might be innocent (wouldn't hurt a fly), heroic (have-a-go-hero) or tainted (gunned down in a drugs turf war), and this approach helps determine how much effort is expended on painting a sympathetic picture of their lives by means of comments from family, friends and neighbours, duly illustrated by snaps from the family album.

Lule studied coverage of an American tourist who was killed when hijackers seized a cruise ship and he concluded that, "by elevating the victim into a hero through the great grief of those left behind", journalists consciously or unconsciously "give meaning to the meaningless and … explain that which cannot be explained" (Lule, 2001: 58–59). In this way the story of the victim is told again and again in the news:

> Names and places change but the story remains essentially the same: an innocent victim – guilty only of coincidence, bad timing, the unfortunate fate of being in the wrong place at the wrong time – is somehow killed in a hijacking, airline crash, fire, robbery, flood, or explosion. Then, through the words of the widow or others left behind, the news elevates and transforms the victim into a hero, a person whose life story is gathered and told, whose passing is marked and mourned. (Lule, 2001: 54)

Angela Phillips has reduced Lule's list of myths to five basic narratives that influence news stories "by selection and exclusion" and which "can overwhelm, or completely change the emphasis and interpretation of the information". Her list of narratives are: Overcoming evil; Transformation; Tragedy; Romance; and Coming of age, aka rags to riches (Phillips, 2007: 13–20).

For Lule, the telling of news stories as myth usually helps to "manufacture consent" towards the existing social order. However, such ideological power is not predetermined because news is "messy and complicated" and is "a site of personal, social, and political struggle from its conception by a reporter to its understanding by a reader". Therefore, mythic stories might potentially be used to offer alternative perspectives on society (Lule, 2001: 192). Phillips agrees:

> Myth and metaphor are not, by definition, conservative and uncritical. They can also be used to challenge the status quo and to break down conventions. Transgressive stories are often more arresting than those that operate within conventional normative boundaries. When we read sympathetic stories about people who have, conventionally, been

heard journalists on a local freesheet being told to imagine they were "writing for your granny". Complexity, abstract notions, ambiguity and unanswered questions tend to be frowned upon and subbed out of news copy. As is anything seen as personal comment by the reporter.

News stories should answer the Five Ws that, along with an H, are the starting point of most journalism: Who? What? Where? When? Why? And: How? Like this: "Lady Godiva [WHO] rode [WHAT] naked [HOW] through the streets of Coventry [WHERE] yesterday [WHEN] in a bid to cut taxes [WHY]" (Hicks et al., 1999: 15). News should be specific, not general; clear, not vague. Telling the Five Ws is one way of achieving this. In most cases you shouldn't try to answer *all* those questions in the intro – it would be too wordy and clumsy – but news intros are likely to give us the answers to two or three of the Five Ws. The others should normally follow fairly quickly afterwards.

A good news story will be important and/or be of potential interest to the audience; it will be based on evidence, with sources of information and opinion clearly attributed; and it will be written in clear, precise and active language. But how will it be structured? Traditionally, trainee journalists have been taught to think of the structure of a news story as a triangle, a pyramid or, more commonly, an ***inverted pyramid***. However it is visualised, the idea is that the most important information should be at the top, followed by elaboration and detail, ending up with the least important information at the bottom (Hicks et al., 1999: 16). If space is short, the material at the bottom can be removed by subs, and what's left should stand alone and still make sense. So a 500-word article could swiftly be transformed into a nib (news in brief), a four-par story for a website, or even a one-sentence headline for a mobile phone or Twitter message. Combined with the Five Ws, the pyramid – or inverted pyramid – is a good way of starting to think about constructing relatively simple news stories. The most striking or important information goes at the top – usually several of the Who?

> treated as pariahs, they challenge our assumptions. ... The challenge is to understand the power of myth, to know how to use it, but also how to subvert it. (Phillips, 2007: 23–24)

Inverted pyramid

Although the image of the inverted pyramid is commonly used in journalism training, it also has its critics. Don Fry of the US-based Poynter Institute, for example, argues that readers will not be able to fully comprehend a news story written according to the inverted pyramid model because "the background goes at the bottom, somewhere between 'boring' and 'dull'. Without background, readers cannot understand the story, and simply give up before they get to the information they need." He prefers the idea of a "stack of blocks" consisting of a beginning, a middle and an end, in which: "The beginning predicts the middle in form and content, and the ending cements the main points into the readers' memories" (Fry, 2004).

The concept of the inverted pyramid and the order in which more or less important information is placed also raises the question of *who* decides what is more or less important. Daniel Hallin argues that *where* information appears in a story, and *how* it is inflected, can have an ideological effect by emphasising some views or voices and by marginalising others. To illustrate the point, he suggests that reporting of the Vietnam war saw a "reverse inverted pyramid" in operation, whereby the nearer the information was to the truth, the further down the news story it would be placed (cited in Schudson, 1991: 148–149). Then again, as we have seen, the truth itself is not always a simple matter.

Attribution

One of the primary questions of journalism is, "Who says?", argues Bell, who suggests that, as so much news is based on *somebody saying something*, a pertinent question for journalists and readers is to ask what credentials the source has:

> Attribution serves an important function in the telling of news stories. It reminds the audience that this is an account which originated with certain persons and organisations. It is not an unchallengeable gospel, but one fruit of human perception and production among other conceivably alternative accounts. In theory a news story should be

What? Where? When? Why? How? – and the rest follows in diminishing order of importance.

The intro

The intro is crucial because it sets the tone for what follows. A poorly written intro might confuse, mislead or simply bore the reader; a well written intro will encourage the reader to stay with you on the strength of the information and angle you have started with. Lynette Sheridan Burns explains the importance of the intro in this way:

> We are breeding a four-par generation.
>
> – Hugh Berlyn, editor of BBC News Interactive.

News writing always starts with the most important fact. When you report on a football game, you do not start with the kick-off, you begin with the final score. So it is with news. If someone were to blow up the building across the street from where you work today, when you got home you would not start the story by saying, "Today seemed like an ordinary sort of day, little did I know how it would turn out." You would say, "Someone blew up the building across the street!" In other forms of journalism it is fine for your story to have a beginning, a middle and an end. News stories, in contrast, blurt out something and then explain themselves… (Sheridan Burns, 2002: 112)

Study news intros on any given day, and you will see a variety of techniques at work. In the literature of journalism training, these are often given fancy names, such as the "delayed drop". Here's an example of the delayed drop:

It is one of Britain's most advanced police aircraft – perfect for pursuit.

Equipped with satellite navigation, thermal imaging camera, searchlight, video equipment and loudhailer, the West Yorkshire force's helicopter can be in the sky within minutes of an alert.

So when a call came through about a crime in a park, the American-built 180mph MD902 Explorer was swiftly scrambled.

regarded as embedded under a stack of attributions, each consisting of source, time and place. (Bell, 1991: 190)

Attribution of sources is important to the notion of journalistic balance, writes Keeble:

Reporters use sources to distance themselves from the issues explored. Rather than express their views on a subject, reporters use sources to present a range of views over which they can appear to remain objective and neutral. The title or descriptive phrase accompanying the quoted person clarifies the bias. But this is the bias of the source, not the reporter. (Keeble, 2001a: 44)

But good attribution is not sufficient to produce good journalism, writes Nick Davies in his critical examination of the news industry, *Flat Earth News*. He quotes Press Association editor Jonathan Gunn as explaining: "What we do is report what people say accurately. Our role is attributable journalism – what someone has got to say. What is important is in quote marks." For Davies, this approach renders such journalists incapable of discovering the truth because: "Whether what is said is itself a truthful account of the world is simply not their business. … If the Prime Minister says there are chemical weapons in Iraq, that is what the good news agency will report" (Davies, 2008: 83).

Text

Many words have been written in recent decades analysing media texts from a perspective that says a text is not simply a collection of words and/or images, but "the meaningful outcome of the *encounter* between content and reader" (McQuail, 2000: 349, my emphasis). In other words, the work of the journalist only becomes a *text* when it is read by somebody. And, given that we bring our own knowledge, experience, expectations and prejudices into play when we read a news report, the same piece of work may have multiple meanings (be *polysemic*). Of interest here is the work of Mikhail Bakhtin, who spoke of language as *dialogic*; that is, everything we say or write is in some sense both *responding* to things that have already been said and *anticipating* future responses:

The living utterance, having taken meaning and shape at a particular historical moment in a socially specific

And soon, twin jet engines roaring, the £3.3 million machine was hovering over a lake … chasing two boys in a pedalo. (CATCH THAT PEDALO!, *Daily Mail*, September 11 2004)

Such a delayed drop, in which the point is not immediately apparent, is often used for light or faintly amusing stories such as the one above, but as we shall see it can also work for more grim subject matter. As with so much in journalism, there is no hard-and-fast rule saying that a particular kind of story should have a particular kind of intro. The familiar question, "what works?" is best answered through observation and trying it out.

Let's take a common news story: the tragedy. There is the straightforward unadorned factual style:

A yachtsman died and a fisherman was feared dead in gales yesterday. (SAILOR, 80, DIES IN GALE, *Daily Mirror*, October 21 2002)

Another example from the same day's paper:

Two strawberry pickers were crushed to death after falling into a machine, it was revealed yesterday. (TWO KILLED AT FARM, Rosa Prince, *Daily Mirror*, October 21 2002)

Neither intro gets bogged down in too much detail and each tells us in essence what happened and to whom – not with a name but a handy label.

Sometimes one element of a story will be particularly striking and the journalist's nose for news should make sure it appears in the intro, as in this example:

> ❝ Always grab the reader by the throat in the first paragraph, sink your thumbs into his wind pipe in the second, and hold him against the wall until the tag line. ❞
> – Paul O'Neill.

An anguished girl of 13 hanged herself while waiting for the result of a pregnancy test that proved negative. (BABY FEAR GIRL OF 13 IS FOUND HANGED, Geoff Marsh, *Daily Express*, October 24 2002)

environment, cannot fail to brush up against thousands of living dialogic threads. … After all, the utterance arises out of this dialogue as a continuation of it and as a rejoinder to it. … [Every] word is directed toward an answer and cannot escape the profound influence of the answering word that it anticipates… (Bakhtin, 1935: 76)

Where does the journalist figure in all this? Cultural analysis of texts sometimes gives the impression that the work of the journalist is irrelevant to the production of meaning by the audience. But just because a text is *capable* of being interpreted in many ways does not mean it necessarily *will* be, and "many media genres are understood by most of their receivers most of the time in predictable ways" (McQuail, 2000: 485). According to Colin Sparks:

To acknowledge that any text is polysemic is not the same thing as to say that it is capable of *any* interpretation whatsoever. Put more concretely, the sense which people can make of newspapers depends at least in part in *what the journalists have actually written in them in the first place.* (Sparks, 1992: 37, my emphasis)

As McQuail notes: "There is a power of the text that it is foolish to ignore" (McQuail, 2000: 485).

Media texts are sometimes subjected to what is described by academics as "critical discourse analysis", a method of textual, linguistic analysis that aims "to reveal what kinds of social relations of power are present in texts both explicitly and implicitly" (Machin and Niblock, 2008: 246). However, although such analysis may tell us what can be read into a text, it may be more limited in explaining how and why a particular piece of work came to be the way it is. As David Machin and Sarah Niblock point out, a discourse analyst may believe that a photograph has been selected to convey a particular ideological message, yet it may turn out that the picture was chosen primarily because it was cheap (or free) and handy. "Simply, we cannot understand a text in isolation from its production" (Machin and Niblock, 2008: 246–247).

Or this:

> A father of four died of a brain tumour after a hospital sent him home, insisting he was drunk. ('DRUNK' PATIENT DIES OF A BRAIN TUMOUR, Martyn Sharpe, *Sun*, July 20 2002)

Even the *absence* of information might provide a lead, as in:

> Mystery surrounded the death of a heavily pregnant teenager whose body was found today at the foot of a tower block in the Black Country. (FLATS DEATH RIDDLE, Simon Hardy, *Birmingham Evening Mail*, September 17 2002)

It might be something about the subject's *life* rather than the manner of their *death* that provides the angle, as in:

> A ten-pin bowling champion who dedicated her life to helping youngsters, has died suddenly. (BOWLING CHAMP DIES, *Yorkshire Evening Post*, October 24 2002)

Or the focus might be on the bereaved:

> A grief-stricken mother today told of her shock when her teenage son suddenly collapsed and died after complaining of a swollen throat. (MOTHER'S GRIEF OVER DEATH OF SCOTT, 19, Kim McRae, *Bradford Telegraph and Argus*, November 27 2001)

Some intros manage to combine the victim with grieving loved ones and the act of discovery, as in this example:

> A property tycoon and his wife found the body of their "sweet and gentle oddball" son lying in a pool of blood at his home. (PROPERTY TYCOON FINDS "GENTLE" SON KILLED AT HOME, Laura Peak, *Times*, October 25 2002)

The above intros, and countless other variations, tend to focus on one or two elements. They give us what the journalist has decided is the best news line, and they do it quickly and clearly. Occasionally you will find an intro that breaks with such conventions

of news writing. Here are two examples of delaying the most important information even in the most serious of news stories. Both seem to work, maybe because the stories were so big that most readers could be assumed to have heard the basic facts by the time they read the following day's front pages:

> Although he could not see right inside, the customs officer knew something was terribly wrong the moment he opened the heavy swing doors. The container on the white Mercedes lorry was a refrigeration unit, yet the air that belched out was warm and smelled putrid. In the half light, he saw two Chinese men sprawled in front of him, gasping for breath. Behind him in the gloom, the officer saw what a colleague described as a scene "out of a nightmare". Fifty-eight bodies lay haphazardly on the metal floor in between seven crates of tomatoes. (GRIM FIND OF 58 BODIES IN LORRY EXPOSES SMUGGLERS' EVIL TRADE, Nick Hopkins, Jeevan Vasagar, Paul Kelso, Andrew Osborn, *Guardian*, June 20 2000)

A similar technique is at work here, when a reporter describes the moment police realised they were dealing with a serial killer:

> The man walking along Old Felixstowe Road, near the village of Levington, could not be sure at first. In the failing light he stepped off the road and approached the darkened form. Only then was he sure. She was naked, lying in the wet scrubland where she had been dumped. It was 3.05pm.
>
> Forty minutes later a police helicopter hovered over the open ground south of Ipswich as detectives sealed off the area and covered the body with tarpaulin. The glare of the helicopter's searchlight lit up the wasteland below and there, 100 metres away from the bustle of police activity, the pilot saw the second body. (SNATCHED, KILLED AND DISCARDED, Sandra Laville, *Guardian*, December 13 2007)

Although the style is not conventionally newsy, even the above intros begin their narratives not at the beginning of a journey but at the moment just before the bodies were discovered, when the most

> ❝ Always, always, tell the news through people. ❞
> – Arthur Christiansen, legendary *Daily Express* editor.

important fact of each story is revealed. Both stories have been written to convey an atmosphere – to paint a scene – in addition to conveying information.

Sometimes, however, a journalist will delay an obvious news angle simply because they have thought of a more interesting approach, as in this example about a community campaign for a zebra crossing:

> ❝ Words are facts. Check them (spelling and meaning) as you would any other. ❞
> – Keith Waterhouse.

> Woe betide anyone who crosses Jade Hudspith when she grows up. For the Bramley schoolgirl has already shown her mettle at the tender age of nine by collecting no less than 100 names on her petition for a zebra crossing outside Sandford Primary in busy Broad Lane. (JADE ON WARPATH FOR ZEBRA CROSSING, Sophie Hazan, *Yorkshire Evening Post*, October 30 2002)

Apart from the misuse of the word "less" (it should be "fewer"), it shows that an imaginative intro can lift even a relatively straightforward story.

However, something such as the delayed drop, that might work in print, does not necessarily work so well online. For that reason, so-called "shovelware", the uploading of the text of newspaper or magazine articles straight to the web, tends to be frowned upon. At MEN Media in Manchester, Sarah Hartley says: "Each individual piece is worked on by one of the online team. They will be looking at changing the headline, partly so it fits but also because a lot of newspaper headlines just don't work on the web." While they are at it, do they also change the tense of news stories from past to present, to reflect the "nowness" of the web? Sometimes, but not as much as she would like: "We do have 'said' quite often. It's something that jars with me. It is essentially a broadcast medium, so in an ideal world, yes, we'd like to see it changed to the present tense. But there's only so many hours in the day."

Online journalists must also keep an eye on writing headlines and intros that will appeal to people using search engines, which is how a lot of users now come across stories rather than via the front door of the news organisation's homepage.

"We do it a little bit but we're not slavish to search engines," says Hartley. At the *Times*, online editor Anne Spackman says that monitoring the terms entered into search engines by users who end up on the *Times* website can help journalists better understand the interests of their audience. However, there are limits to how much they want to be dictated to by such data, as Spackman explains: "*Times* readers are obsessed with house prices and road tax. If we want to play the traffic tart game, there are certain things that we could write about all the time, like Britney Spears. But that's not really what the *Times* is for" (quoted in Stabe, 2008).

Online storytelling techniques are discussed further in Chapters 11 and 13.

The rest of the story

If the pyramid is a good starting point for thinking about intros and basic news stories, it can come to seem inadequate for more complex and/or lengthy stories, particularly those based on many different sources. David Randall talks of constructing such stories through "building blocks" which should be linked logically to each other (Randall, 2000: 175). Richard Keeble prefers the concept of stories having a *series* of inverted pyramids:

> News stories, whether of five or thirty-five pars, are formed through the linking of thematic sections. The reader progresses through them in order of importance, except on those few occasions when the punch line is delayed for dramatic reasons. The journalist's news sense comes into operation not only for the intro but throughout the story. Who is the most important person

to quote? Who is the next most important person? What details should be highlighted and which left to the end or eliminated? How much background information is required and where is it best included? All these questions are answered according to a set of news values held by the reporter. (Keeble, 2001a: 108)

Let's take two examples from the stories introduced earlier.

The *Daily Mirror* story about the dead yachtsman is tightly written, consisting of 71 words in five single sentence paragraphs, giving an average sentence length of just over 14 words. After the intro we have a par giving us the location of the accident and the age of the man, then a third par telling us that his body was found by a Navy helicopter. This is followed by two pars giving us details of the separate search for a missing fisherman. Any cutting from the bottom upwards would still leave a readable story. Fairly simple stuff.

The *Times* story about the property tycoon's oddball son is longer and more complex as it brings in a variety of sources, yet it is still written in a concise news style. It consists of 602 words in 34 sentences and 19 paragraphs, giving an average sentence length of just under 18 words – not *that* different from the tabloid story above. After the intro we are quickly given names, time, location and the information that somebody is being questioned by police. The basic story having been told, we are then given detail, colour, context, attribution and quotes. There are descriptions of the victim based on interviews with neighbours, background on the location, the results of the post-mortem examination, and quotes from the police about the death and appealing for information. The continuing police presence at the house is then linked to the fact that the bereaved parents are being comforted by police family liaison officers, which leads in turn to quotes from a statement issued by the family. The story ends with some extra biographical details about the father.

> ❝In news, order is everything but chronology is nothing.❞
> – Allan Bell.

This device of telling the basic story, and then telling it again in more detail, is common in news. In most cases chronology goes out the window when it comes to writing news. But it is important that, in a desire to include all the most important information, you do not end up writing a story that reads like a *list of points*. Ideas, sentences, paragraphs should be linked and follow on in some kind of logical sequence, or series of sequences. Facts, description, context, reported speech and direct quotes must all be *woven* into the text, to achieve a whole. Study the structure of news stories and you will see how neat are the links, how smooth are the transitions, and how additional information is slipped in without disrupting the flow.

Note, too, the use of quotes and **attribution**. Direct quotes can add authority, drama, immediacy or emotion to an account as well as giving the reader a sense of the quoted person's voice and personality. Direct quotes will normally be outnumbered by reported speech and/or the attribution of facts and opinions to sources. Together, they tell the reader "who says so". Keeble says that clear attribution is particularly important when covering allegations and counter-allegations (Keeble, 2001a: 103). Yet some journalists fail to give adequate attribution in stories for fear of what Randall terms "a certain loss of journalistic virility". He argues: "The reader should never have to ask, 'How does the paper know this?'" (Randall, 2000: 179). As a reporter with the Press Association, Merrick observed this differing attitude at first hand:

There is always attribution in our intros, to prove to our customers that it's properly sourced. We have to say "police said today…" or "an inquest heard today…" Newspapers then get rid of the attribution in their intros.

But good journalism retains the attribution somewhere in the story.

When writing a story for any news organisation you should always retain the idea that your *text* is to be read – and understood – by others. As Keith Waterhouse notes, we rarely hear people at bus-stops using words such as "bid" or "probe", or phrases such as "love-tug mum" or "blaze superstore". Nor do we hear them saying things like, "Did I tell you about young Fred being rapped after he slammed his boss? He thinks he's going to be axed." He warns:

Words that have never managed to get into the mainstream of the language are suspect as a means of popular communication. They are, and remain, labels. They do not convey precise meanings. The reader looks at the label, opens the tin – and finds a tin of labels. (Waterhouse, 1993: 230)

Labels have their uses, but precise meanings are what we should be aiming for.

■ ■ Summary ■

News is written in active and concise language with an emphasis on short sentences and short paragraphs. News is structured with the most newsworthy information first. News is told in the form of stories but these stories are not normally recounted in a chronological order. Journalists may have storylines already in mind when approaching events and this may affect how those stories are constructed. It has been suggested that many news stories are the re-telling of ancient myths in contemporary settings. Although readers may interpret news stories in different ways, their interpretations will be based, at least in part, on what the journalist has written.

■ Questions

Why is most news not told in chronological order?

Why are news articles called stories?

Can a story ever write itself?

Is news populated by unfamiliar names yet familiar characters?

What is the role of attribution?

■ ■ Further reading ■

The books by Randall (2007) and McKane (2006) both contain a wealth of good advice on writing news, and also well worth checking out are Phillips (2007), Pape and Featherstone (2005), Sissons (2006), Hicks, with Adams and Gilbert (1999), and Keeble (2006). Reah (1998) offers an introduction to the textual study of news stories, while Bell (1991), Conboy (2007) and Richardson (2006) all subject the language of news to detailed linguistic analysis. Conboy (2002) draws on the work of Bakhtin to explore the "carnivalesque" nature of the popular press. Lule's (2001) thought-provoking work on news as myth provides an alternative perspective to both practitioner and linguistic accounts of news construction. Finally, make sure that you read, watch and listen to a wide range of news stories from a wide range of media.

Sources for soundbites

Milne, quoted in Mansfield, 1936: 221; *The Front Page*, from Hecht and MacArthur, 1974; Berlyn, quoted in Hudson and Rowlands, 2007: 161; O'Neill, quoted in Randall, 2000: 162; Christiansen, quoted in Williams, 1959: 191; Waterhouse, 1993: 249; Bell, 1991: 172.

ten

writing features

It begins like this. A short sentence, followed by another. Nothing is explained, not even what "it" might be, let alone what "this" is. In this case it is an example of the way in which a feature article might start. Because, unlike hard news stories, a feature intro might make a diversion up what appears to be a dead end, it might beat about the bush, it might go round the houses, and it might take a leisurely, scenic route to its destination. As long as there *is* a destination and as long as the reader goes along for the ride too.

How features differ from news

The word **features** typically covers all editorial content apart from news, sports news, reports of sporting fixtures, letters, blogs and users' comments. So it covers reviews, horoscopes, TV listings, advice columns, gardening tips and so on, as well as news backgrounders, analytical articles, thinkpieces, picture spreads, profiles and celebrity interviews. Magazines may have news sections but most are dominated – and defined – by their features. In broadcasting, as Andrew Boyd notes, the term "feature" often means a human interest or "soft news" story:

> The hard news formula calls for the meat of the story in the first line. ... The feature style, which leads the audience into the story rather than presenting them with the facts in the first line, is used more freely wherever greater emphasis is placed on entertainment and a lighter touch than on straightforward and sometimes impersonal, hard news. (Boyd, 2001: 73)

Features should not be thought of as synonymous with entertainment, though. Features also deal

Features

The distinction between news and features is widely accepted. However, a different perspective is offered by David Randall, who argues that too many journalists "see the reporter as an earnest collector of 'facts' and the feature *writer* as someone who wanders around thinking of fine phrases which save them the trouble of doing much research" (Randall, 2000: 193, emphasis in original). He continues:

> The truth is that trying to make distinctions between news and features does not get us very far. In fact, it is positively dangerous. It produces narrow thinking which can restrict coverage of news to conventional subjects and puts writing it into the unimaginative straitjacket of a formula. With features, it encourages the insidious idea that normal standards of precision and thorough research don't apply and that they can be a kind of low-fact product. ... The opposite, of course, is the case. Most news pages could benefit from a greater sense of adventure and a more flexible approach to stories. Similarly, most features sections cry out for sharper research and less indulgent writing. There is no great divide between news and features. *Best to think of it all as reporting.* (Randall, 2000: 193–194, my emphasis)

Yet the market appears to value celebrity columnists more highly than it does the reporters who get their hands dirty actually finding things out, as Francis Wheen complains:

> [The] getting and giving of information now seem to be a minor function of the press, as newspapers become "lifestyle packages" stuffed with It girls and solipsists who witter on profitably about their love lives or their shopping habits. ... [The] status of the reporter – as against the lifestyle gusher, or the sad sap who rewrites PR handouts about minor pop stars for a showbiz column – has been dangerously downgraded. (Wheen, 2002: xii–xiii)

Not all columnists are lifestyle gushers, of course; many concentrate on more social and political issues.

with serious topical issues at greater length, and in greater depth, than is possible in simple news reports (Boyd, 2001: 127).

Irish journalist Nell McCafferty touched on some of the differences between what we think of as news and what we think of as features when she wrote:

> It is the modest ambition of every journalist to write a front-page story – the big one at the top left-hand side, with large headlines, that tells the world the main event of the day. The front-page story tells what happened, where, when, and gives the explanation usually of the person in charge. If you want to know how the rest of us feel about it, you turn to the inside pages. I discovered, early on, that I'd never be able to write a front-page story. I'd be inclined to argue with the person in charge, and feel obliged to give the other version in brackets. I discovered this particularly on Bloody Sunday in Derry, when I was lying on the street while people around me got shot dead. I saw everything while the other reporter was at the back. He, rightly, wrote the front-page story, because somebody had to establish the name of the officer in charge, interview him, and provide all the deadly details. Had it been up to me to phone the officer, the row would still be going on and the story would never have been written. My version appeared on the inside pages. I wrote about how the rest of us felt, lying on the ground. (McCafferty, 1984: 14)

Writing a news splash remains the ambition of many aspiring journalists, but having a personal column – complete with picture byline – seems to be an increasingly common goal.

Columnists have certainly proliferated as both newspapers and magazines have got fatter and as print has conceded some of its traditional breaking news role to online and broadcast platforms. Some columnists are engaged for their knowledge and insight and others because they can turn out an entertaining sentence or two. It is usually their task to be controversial, to get the publication talked about. But there are limits, if the case of John MacLeod is anything to go by. He was sacked by the *Herald* in Glasgow because his piece on the death of two schoolgirls in Soham was deemed a bit *too* controversial (Morgan, 2002a).

The most high-profile of such columnists and commentators, ranging from Polly Toynbee of the *Guardian* to Trevor Kavanagh of the *Sun*, have been described as constituting a "commentariat" that is "taken seriously by most of those who constitute the political class" (Hobsbawm and Lloyd, 2008).

Subject

Why is it that features can be about virtually any subject, when news tends to be more restricted? Features need not necessarily conform to the notions of "newsworthiness" discussed in Chapter 3, but how much *agency* do journalists have in choosing subjects and style? Certain subjects will be either *in* or *out* at certain titles or at certain times, and journalists quickly absorb expectations of what is required of them, sharing a set of "formulas, practices, normative values and journalistic mythology passed down to successive generations" (Harrison, 2000: 108).

Some subjects are selected for feature treatment "solely to attract certain advertisers" (Randall, 2000: 21). This is particularly the case in magazines and the growing number of magazine-influenced newspaper supplements – covering subjects as diverse as fashion, media, education, computers, gardening, cars, travel, and food – where editorial features act as bait to attract readers to the advertisements that provide the sections with their economic *raison d'être*. For Bob Franklin, formerly serious publications are increasingly producing advertiser-friendly feature copy and relying on opinion over fact, often about subjects he dismisses as "cripplingly banal" (Franklin, 1997: 7–10). Writing in a US context, Hanno Hardt argues that such a business-friendly system of "patronage" is anti-democratic in its effects:

> Emerging from the practices of contemporary advertising and public relations efforts is a journalism of a new type which promotes the construction of corporate realities at the expense of a common-sense desire for a fair and truthful representation of everyday life. … It is one of the dangers of the anticipated or realised business mentality of the media that content – which represents an expression of freedom – will be defined by those who seek to serve the public as *consumers* rather than by society as *participant* and source of democratic power. (Hardt, 2000: 218–219, my emphasis)

Whether they represent strong opinion, expert analysis, an individual profile or a piece of descriptive writing, good features require both content *and* style. They have a beginning, a middle and an end – usually in that order – not to be confused with Philip Larkin's phrase about a beginning, a *muddle* and an end (cited in Adams, 1999: 50). Features should also have a theme, an idea, something to say; though readers of some of our newspapers and magazines might be forgiven for thinking that content has gone out of fashion. Style is everything for some, as parodied on the radio programme *Sunday Format*:

> ‘ Our feature pages should be sprinkled with star dust or whatever it is that women wear that catches the light at first nights. ’
> – Arthur Christiansen.

CONTENTS PAGE. In this week's Sunday Format. RELATIVE VALUES: a famous celebrity and a relative discuss how much they think the other is worth, page 5. BOOKS BY MY NAMESAKE: former All Saint Shaznay Lewis discusses The Lion, the Witch and the Wardobe, page 3. ME AND MY DUVET: Salman Rushdie, page 49. … MY NAME SOUNDS LIKE YOUR NAME: pop singer Geri Halliwell talks to former drugs tsar Keith Helliwell about fame, the Spice Girls, and comparative arrest rates between different police authorities, pages 42 to 59. … Do teeth matter in a modern romance? … How we haven't yet met yet… Celebrity legover… Ten fruits that are now… Ten occupations that are in… Ten Downing Street… Ten things that are bigger than a cat… Ten new buzzwords… Ten occupations that are out… Ten ways to improve yourself… Ten things that could kill you… (BBC Radio Four, *Sunday Format*, September 18 and 25 2001)

Harsh but fair. Many features are indeed rather formulaic affairs, as Brian Whittle points out:

> If you look at women's mags, the stories have got to be TOT – triumph over tragedy. There's got to be a happy ending, otherwise they won't run them. It's unbelievable, they're so formulaic, they're homogenised. They are the Mills and Boons of today.

But that is only part of the story. There are also features that illuminate, features that have the power to make us laugh out loud or cry into our

The presence of the journalist

The personal pronoun "I" is absent from "normal printed texts", according to Roger Fowler (1991: 64). But it appears in many features. Jon Dovey notes that "confessional modes of expression" have proliferated in journalism and beyond since the 1990s (Dovey, 2000: 1). Letting the journalist appear as an *actor* in the drama may be driven by a desire to tell stories in more interesting ways, but for Dovey it also reflects a changing cultural climate:

> [We] are witnessing the evolution of a new "regime of truth" based upon the foregrounding of individual subjective experience at the expense of more general truth claims. … Subjectivity, the personal, the intimate, becomes the only remaining response to a chaotic, senseless, out of control world in which the kind of objectivity demanded by grand narratives is no longer possible. (Dovey, 2000: 25–26)

This account raises (at least) two questions. First, how new *is* this foregrounding of the journalist? Not very, according to Lynn Barber:

> [This] supposedly new postmodern development of the picaresque interview actually has very long antecedents. Rudyard Kipling's 1889 interview with Mark Twain starts with a good ten paragraphs about the difficulty of finding Mark Twain's house, complete with the statutory cabdriver who doesn't know the way. (Barber, 1999: 199)

Second, if features *have* shifted towards reflexivity in recent years, will this eventually challenge the "regime of truth" represented by the traditional, impersonal method of telling the news? Such issues are touched on in Chapter 5.

Anecdote

Behr's argument that an anecdote can illustrate a "general truth" raises the question of what exactly *is* a general truth? In any event, couldn't an anecdote just as easily illustrate a generally held falsehood?

cornflakes, features that impart information or question our assumptions, that make us look at things in different ways, that shine a torch into some darkened corner. And features that are simply good writing. The best way to learn about features is to *read* lots of features, to *write* lots of features, and to get other people to *read* your features. Like all journalism, features should be produced for the *reader*, not the *writer*.

Where do features come from?

Virtually anything can be the **subject** of a feature, and sources for feature ideas are similar to the news sources discussed in Chapter 4. With features, however, there is a tendency for more ideas to come from personal experience. For example, Leah Wild wrote a double-page feature about her battle with bureaucracy to get a toilet seat suitable for her disabled daughter, to which a sub added the rather unimaginative headline: THE STORY OF MY DISABLED DAUGHTER'S TOILET SEAT (*Guardian*, March 7 2002). If a lot of your 20-something mates are still hanging around the parental home, you might think of writing a feature on the choices and problems confronting this generation. You might abandon the car and start cycling to work, prompting a feature on how lorry drivers seem to be out to kill you. You might be on a postgraduate journalism training course, so you could think of submitting an account of your experiences to the media pages of one of the national papers or to the trade rag *Press Gazette*. That last one's already been done several times, by the way, but you get the idea.

Just as news feeds on itself, features are often prompted by other features and by news. For example, a redtop splash (WORLD'S TALLEST BLOKE LIVES IN NEASDEN, *Sun*, February 18 2002) became food for a "quality" feature (TOUGH AT THE TOP,

> **❛ Most British news- papers now have more columns than the Acropolis. ❜**
> – Ian Jack.

Guardian, February 21 2002). Although the latter was ostensibly a serious discussion of health issues prompted by the claim that "the tallest die young", it was illustrated with one of the pictures used by the *Sun*, showing 7ft 7in Hussain Bisad towering over a pillar box. Six weeks later Hussain's story became a 30-minute radio feature, *It's My Story* (BBC Radio Four, April 8 2002).

A common cycle is that a news story is followed up with more news stories, then background features, and by the third or fourth day it becomes a peg for columnists to hang their personal opinions on; then, when lots of high-profile colum- nists (the so-called "commentariat") get their teeth into a subject, it can in turn influence the news agenda. Sometimes the topic will be rounded off with a "why oh why?" piece in one of the Sunday papers. It can reach farcical proportions, as when film star Kate Winslet mentioned in an interview with *Radio Times* that she wanted to lose some weight after giving birth. This prompted a feeding frenzy by tabloids and broadsheets alike, who ran feature after feature on obesity, dieting, Hollywood waifs, eating disorders, and working out, topped off with a columnist's complaint that Kate Winslet should stop going on about her weight. As *Private Eye* commented at the time, it was "a perfect example of the reverse-alchemy whereby one nugget of news can be transformed into several tons of base metal" (*Private Eye*, 2001).

Let's suppose you've got a better idea than the above. And that you've done your research along the lines suggested in Chapters 4, 5 and 6. Before you lay a finger on your keyboard, Sally Adams suggests that you consider the results of your research and ask yourself:
What's

- the most startling fact you've discovered?
- the best anecdote unearthed?
- the most astonishing quote?
- the most surprising event?
- the item with the greatest "Hey, did you know that...?" factor? (Adams, 1999: 74)

When you've done that, you should have a fair idea of the angle you want to take, so it's time to start writing.

Beginning

The feature intro, sometimes known as the lead, is hard to pin down because there are so many different styles. The main purpose of the intro is to make the reader want to read on, so the key question is: what works?

Sometimes it might be a *general statement*, as in this exploration of the case of a Texan woman who killed her five children:

> Mental illness has never been much of a mitigating factor in the great retributive machine that is the US criminal justice system. (Andrew Gumbel, *Independent*, March 14 2002)

Gumbel goes on to detail two other cases before getting around to asking, "why would anyone imagine that the heartbreaking case of Andrea Pia Yates would be any different?" It seems like he is taking a long time to give us the "meat" of the story, but we do not read these opening sentences in isolation. They are put in context by the "page furniture" so important to features; in this case the stark headline IN GOD'S NAME superimposed on a picture of the mother, accompanied by the explanatory standfirst:

> Andrea Yates was a respectable wife and mother, raising a God-fearing family. Then, one fine morning last summer, she drowned her five children. Why? Only now can the full, dreadful story be told. (Andrew Gumbel, *Independent*, March 14 2002)

Presentation is important to the ways in which journalism is consumed, and features depend more than hard news on being sold to the reader "by means of a complex of headlines, pictures, blurb, standfirst … caption and significant quotation"

drawing out "the mood and underlying substance" of the feature (Hodgson, 1993: 247–248).

Some features begin by getting to the point directly with a *bold statement*, as in this discussion of smacking:

> The parents I really despise can be spotted all over the place. You will have seen them – they are the ones in supermarkets or shopping centres who suddenly address their child in the sort of vicious tones you wouldn't even use on a disobedient dog. (Jayne Dawson, *Yorkshire Evening Post*, April 3 2002)

It demands attention because of the strength of feeling, notably "despise" rather than any of the softer alternatives. The wording involves us – "you" – as assumed witnesses to such behaviour, able to tut-tut along with the writer.

News writing tends to concentrate on giving answers rather than asking questions, but features are more open to the unresolved question. Occasionally you might even begin a feature with a *question*:

> What on earth is going on at the National Theatre? We certainly know what is not going on. Previously announced productions of *Alice and Wonderland* and *The Playboy of the Western World* have been postponed indefinitely … (Michael Billington, *Guardian*, October 10 2000)

Note the double meaning of the phrase "going on". Billington's intro gives us a pretty clear steer that the feature is going to discuss recent events at the National Theatre, and if we want to find out what's been going on then we will read on.

At other times, though, writers take a more oblique route, hoping to draw in the reader with a piece of *descriptive* writing:

> Nik Entwistle unwraps the first of his newly delivered white leather sofas. He strokes a cushion tentatively, slides his hand into the crevice between arm and back as if searching for a missing coin and finally allows himself a shy smile. "S'great," he says. "S'really diff'rent.

Modern. Minimal. Goes with the flat." Less than two years ago, Nik was still a student at Leeds Metropolitan University, living in digs on the edge of town. Now, aged 23, he is something whizzy in information technology and the proud owner of a light-filled, one-bedroom apartment, newly converted from a former textile factory in Leeds city centre. (Susannah Herbert, *Daily Telegraph*, February 19 2000)

Or the more stark:

Drissa takes off his T-shirt. His numerous wounds are deep and open – down to the bone. If it weren't for the maggots that have nested in his skin, he would surely have succumbed to gangrene.

Drissa was a slave on an Ivory Coast cocoa plantation. Forced to work for 18 hours a day on little or no food, and locked in a small room with his fellow captives at night, he was regularly, systematically, brutally beaten. It is scarcely credible that such cruelty and disregard for human life should be employed in the production of a chocolate bar. (Fiona Morrow, *Independent*, September 27 2000)

> ❛ Read over your compositions, and where ever you meet with a passage which you think is particularly fine, strike it out. ❜
> – Dr Samuel Johnson.

The intro about Nik Entwistle contains many details, descriptions, quotes and the wonderfully vague phrase "something whizzy in information technology", none of which would make it anywhere near a news story. In contrast, it is possible to imagine the material in the Drissa intro being rewritten as a news story along the lines of: "Slaves on a cocoa plantation are systematically beaten and denied food, according to…" But the feature intro is effective because of its focus on the individual, because of the rhythm of the writing ("…regularly, systematically, brutally beaten…"), and because of the delayed contrast between the horrors described and the realisation that the purpose of this brutality is the production of a mere chocolate bar.

A frequently used device is to include **the presence of the writer** in the story, as in this example:

It was a simple assignment: go and interview the editor of *Who's Who*. I duly bunged in a request to Messrs A & C Black, the publishers. "I'm afraid not," the firm's spokeswoman, Charlotte Burrows, informed me sternly. "All the editors have to remain anonymous, to protect them." Protect them from what? "From people wanting to be in *Who's Who*." (Francis Wheen, *Sunday Telegraph*, March 17 1996)

This interface between journalist and subject is a popular one with feature writers, not just to attract the reader but also to set the tone for what follows. From the above paragraph, for example, we are left in little doubt that Wheen feels the publishers need to be brought down a peg or two. A rather different mood to the following intro, from a sympathetic profile of New York Mayor Rudolph Guiliani:

Rudy is late. He has gone to see his tailor about a suit to wear for tea with the Queen. But I don't care how long I have to wait. Rudy the Rude is now Rudy the Rock. (Alice Thomsen, *Daily Telegraph*, February 12 2002)

One brief paragraph at the head of a lengthy interview, but we are already introduced to the idea of the former Mayor's informality ("Rudy"), the fact that he went from zero to hero ("the Rock") in the wake of September 11, and the cultural relevance of his visit to the UK ("for tea with the Queen"). These themes are then developed throughout the feature.

Sometimes a bit of *dramatic licence* is employed, as in this example from a profile of a crime writer:

Harry Patterson, aka thriller writer Jack Higgins, is a man of cast iron habits. I find him sitting at his usual table in his favourite Italian restaurant, his perennial glass of champagne in hand. On the table in front of him lie the tinted glasses of unvarying design that make him look like a hit man. (Cassandra Jardine, *Daily Telegraph*, February 25 2000)

Or this intriguing opening with the echo of a thousand westerns:

> A silence descended on the little grassy racing track behind the car park of the Jolly Friar pub in the former pit village of Blidworth, on the border between Nottingham and South Yorkshire, when Mark Pettitt appeared. It was an uncomfortable silence, the kind you get in cowboy films when the gunman walks into the small town. For Mark Pettitt is currently the most unpopular man in whippet racing. (Paul Vallely, *Independent*, August 11 2000)

Unlike the who, what, where, when and why of the hard news story, the feature intro sometimes leaves the reader with little clue as to the subject about to be addressed. Consider this *anecdotal* and colloquial example:

> Standing in a night club in Banja Luka in the Republic of Serbska, I'm starting to feel a wee bit nervous. We've bunked out of Nato's vast metal factory base with five pissed squaddies for a Friday night on the town, and the locals have got wise to the fact that we're Brits, mainly because the squaddies are wearing Sheffield United shirts. Three terrifying Serb boneheads are gathering nearby, getting just that bit too close for comfort. No one is talking to us. We stand out like sore thumbs. (Stephen Armstrong, *Guardian*, September 25 2000)

It turns out to be a feature about a music radio station in former Yugoslavia, run by the British Army to win the "hearts and minds" of young locals.

Some idea of a target audience can inform the way a feature begins. See, for example, the use of detail, description and cultural references in the following intro that was perfect for *Word* magazine but which may not have been deemed appropriate by other less self-consciously "in the know" publications:

> The office where Will Self writes gives you the astonishing feeling that you're sitting inside the writer's brain. Situated right at the top of his house, there are dictionaries and cigars and pipes and ashtrays. There are spindly

steel chairs and a bike. There's a window with a view of Stockwell. And then there are the Post-It notes. Hundreds of them. They cover each wall in perfect yellow ranks like erudite rising damp, each one bearing a mnemonic phrase in Self's intense, italic handwriting: "GUIDE TO NON-EXISTENT COUNTRIES" or "CRACK WHORES" or "THE PASSION OF BENNY HILL". Frankly, Will Self's office feels very much like the obsessive loony's inner sanctum in the climactic scenes of a *Seven* or a *Silence Of the Lambs*. (Andrew Harrison, *Word*, May 2008)

Freed from the constraints of hard news, feature writers sometimes make use of a more poetic style. Take this extended *metaphor* that, combined with description, anecdote and the presence of the journalist, introduces an analysis of problems at Coca-Cola:

> There is a slight problem with the front door at Coca-Cola's European headquarters. It is gleaming and wide, like a movable wall of glass, with the outline of a row of giant Coke bottles gleaming across, but it will not open properly. The lock seems to be broken; visitors must knock to gain the attention of reception. The glass, though, is very thick, and the headquarters is in the middle of a noisy shopping centre, in the middle of perhaps the busiest roundabout in west London. The receptionists take quite a while to look up, clack across the lobby, and unfasten the door. There is time to take in the lobby's blaze of logos and bright red walls, as if the building were a vast Coca-Cola vending machine, with a malfunction. (Andy Beckett, *Guardian*, October 2 2000)

The key phrase comes in the last three words, and the feature goes on to explore whether Coca-Cola is indeed malfunctioning as a global corporation.

A slightly less elaborate example of *imagery* at work comes from a local newspaper feature about inner-city areas in a so-called boom city:

> On a clear day people in parts of Beeston and Holbeck can see the cranes towering over Leeds city centre at yet another multi-million pound development.
>
> For many in the communities north of the Aire, the cranes helping to build the latest upmarket apartments or plush offices are symbols of hope and opportunity.

But for some in poverty-stricken Beeston and Holbeck, they are a depressing reminder of a successful local economy that is largely passing them by. (David Marsh, *Yorkshire Evening Post*, March 20 2002)

Rhythmic writing and use of contrast to paint a picture can be as effective on a page as when spoken, as this transcript of the intro from a radio dispatch by Alan Johnston demonstrates:

Gaza is battered, poverty-stricken and over-crowded. It's short of money, short of space, short of hope and many other things. But it's not short of guns. There are about a dozen different, official security forces. Alongside the police and the army, there's the Presidential Guard, there's the Preventive Security Unit and so on. There are more security men here per head of population than almost anywhere on earth, but sadly they deliver very little in the way of security. (Alan Johnston, *From Our Own Correspondent*, BBC Radio Four, 7 October 2006)

The above passage works partly because of the quality of the writing and partly because we know that it has not been written in a London newsroom far from the action but from "here", in Gaza. It is based on good reporting as much as a good prose style.

Feature intros, as we have seen, often focus on something quite *specific*, something human, some tiny detail – painting the little rather than the big picture. Of course, it can all go horribly wrong, as in this profile of satirist Chris Morris:

A few days ago, as Phil Collins, the man who once memorably made boatloads of money with an action-ably mawkish song about the homeless called Another Day In Paradise, then threatened to leave the country if we didn't vote Tory, was beginning to seethe at Chris Morris's latest trick, his nemesis was walking out of Oxford Circus tube station into a blattering rain. (Euan Ferguson, *Observer*, July 22 2001)

There are some nice turns of phrase in that swollen 63-word sentence – "actionably mawkish" and "blattering rain" – but the focus is confused and there are too many sub-sub-sub-clauses. Back in the day when journalists

dictated their words of wisdom down the phone, they would often be asked by a deeply unimpressed copytaker: "Is there much more of this?" It was a useful reminder that we do not write for ourselves.

Middle

If the beginning is the single most important element in feature *writing* – because it doesn't matter how good the rest is if readers never venture beyond a dull intro – then the middle is the *point* of it all. Even the best intro in the world can't salvage a feature with nothing to say, with no substance.

The content and structure of a feature will vary depending on the subject matter, the style of the publication, the perceived interests of the readers, the intentions of the writer, and on the time and energy available for research. Unlike hard news stories, features rarely write themselves; they must be worked at so they do not come across as a series of unrelated points or as a meandering but aimless stroll around a topic. So there must be some logic to the order in which subjects are introduced, shifts of emphasis are made, and the tone of writing is altered. It is an internal logic rather than a formula and will differ from feature to feature, from journalist to journalist.

A feature will utilise some or all of the following, often overlapping with each other:

- facts
- quotes
- description
- anecdotes
- opinions
- analysis.

Facts

All features need facts. Apart from straightforward opinion pieces and the most personalised "lifestyle" columns, that means research. The process of gathering facts for features is essentially the same as for news – interviewing people, searching databases, reading reports, witnessing events, and so on – with the main difference being that features tend to be written over a longer period of time and tend to contain more words. So there is often the time to consult a wider range of sources and the space to include more of the information gathered during your research. Andy Beckett's feature on Coca-Cola, for example, is full of facts gleaned from a variety of sources, including cuttings, websites, and books, as well as a range of interviews with actors and "experts" alike; dates, prices, percentages and ingredients are all introduced to support the analysis, description and anecdote that structure the feature. When you have a lot of facts to include, you may wish to make your feature more digestible by including the facts at appropriate points in the text rather than in off-putting chunks; alternatively, you can separate some facts into a "factbox".

> ❝ Most features sections cry out for sharper research and less indulgent writing. ❞
> – David Randall.

Quotes

As with news stories, direct quotes can add authority, drama and powerful expression to an account. In the Texas mother feature discussed above, the first quote is a long time coming, after the writer has already given us a lot of the story in his own words. When it arrives it is worth the wait, being a controversial opinion simply expressed by a credible source:

> "It seems we are still back in the days of the Salem witch trials," one of Yates's lawyers, George Parnham, commented after the verdict was returned on Tuesday afternoon. (Andrew Gumbel, *Independent*, March 14 2002)

More direct speech will normally be included in profiles of individuals, because the subject's voice, their use of language, can be as important to the

story as what they are saying. Hence we are treated to Rudolph Guiliani's own words about himself:

> "It's weird getting used to being loved. … My scowl has turned into a smile. I'm becoming soft. … Sometimes, I would have to slip into the bathroom and cry." (Alice Thomsen, *Daily Telegraph*, February 12 2002)

Description

There's an old journalistic maxim: "Show, don't tell." In other words, use description to express what you see, and let readers make up their own minds what to think about it. We have already seen many examples of description in the intros quoted above. David Randall offers the following guidance:

> Description brings the story alive, takes readers to where you have been and evokes atmosphere. … So long as you remember that description goes into a story to aid readers' understanding and not provide you with an opportunity to display your latest vocabulary, it will be an aid to clarity and not an obstacle to it. … Avoid vague, judgmental adjectives and descriptions. To say that an office is "imposing" tells you something, but not very much. Far better to say that it is so big that you could park two cars in there, that it has plush red carpet, a new black desk with brass fittings and that the windows command a view of the capital. That gives a far better idea. Apply this thinking to people, too. … Descriptive writing is about finding ways of *bringing something to life*, not the random sprinkling of adjectives through a piece. (Randall, 2000: 182–183, my emphasis)

Anecdotes

Anecdotes play a far greater role in features than in news stories, where they are often squeezed out by tight word limits and an emphasis on the facts. As well as sometimes being funny or moving, anecdotes can help to explain how the actors in a story felt or reacted, tell us something about the human condition, and create a big picture by painting small pictures in sufficient detail. Foreign correspondent Edward Behr says that even the most "trivial, nonsensical **anecdote** can be made to illustrate a general truth" and may reveal more than the "careful marshalling of facts" (Behr, 1992: x). While interviewing schools careers' advisers for a background feature on a strike, I took a note of the sort of incident that wouldn't have made it into a hard news story but which helped to bring a worthy but potentially dull feature to life:

> Staff first realised something was brewing in the summer, when their leased yucca plants were unceremoniously removed and office supplies of pens and paper suddenly dried up. "One of our managers was telling us there was no financial crisis just as a yucca was wheeled out behind her," recalls Lisa Cooper. (Tony Harcup, *Guardian*, October 10 1995)

In a stroke of genius, a sub came up with the headline FIRST THEY CAME FOR THE YUCCAS, a reference to Pastor Niemoller's famous lament: "First they came for the Jews…".

Opinions

Some features make the opinions of the writer clear, others do not – it depends on the style, the subject, the publication, and on whether the writer *has* an opinion. But there is usually more opinion in features than in news, from a greater variety of sources. Rather than the traditional "both sides of a story" adopted in much news, features often allow room for more subtle or nuanced differences of opinion to emerge. And it is not unknown for the stated opinion of the writer to have changed by the time the feature ends.

> ❝ Nothing wrong with opinions. … But they need some sort of anchorage in fact. ❞
>
> – Francis Wheen.

Analysis

Again, not all features are analytical, but they have more scope for analysis than do tightly written news stories with a more immediate focus. Beckett's Coca-Cola feature includes a range of analyses of the company's performance, based on its historical position, on its product diversification, and on its brand image. Apart from the writer's own analysis of what is going on, he invites Coke's UK chief and a range of independent experts to put forward their own explanations. In the Texas mother feature, the case is analysed by reference to how a similar case would have been handled in the UK, with a British lawyer explaining that Yates would probably have been cleared on the grounds of temporary insanity, if she had been tried at all. More likely, she would have been sent to a psychiatric hospital until she was declared fit enough to be discharged. The purpose of such analysis in features is to take journalism beyond reportage and description with a view to helping us not just know *what* is going on, but to *understand* it a little more.

The end

As with the intro, the feature ending – known as the "payoff" because it rewards the reader for sticking with you – can come in all shapes and sizes. Whereas news stories often end on the least important information, allowing them to be cut from the bottom upwards, features tend to have a more rounded ending. This might mean a summary of what has gone before, a return to the scene of the intro, or a new twist to leave the reader pondering.

Gumbel's story of the mother who drowned her children ends by referring to the unrepentant state prosecutor, leading to the payoff:

Her conviction is clearly another feather in his cap. Whether it advances the cause of civilisation, however, is another matter. (Andrew Gumbel, *Independent*, March 14 2002)

The writer tells us an individual tale in sometimes gory detail, but the subject of the feature is not actually Andrea Yates at all. Rather, it is the US justice system.

The Rudolph Guiliani profile discussed above ends with the former Mayor's own words:

> "You know what I'm looking forward to most in London, apart from meeting the Queen? Prime Minister's questions. I'd do anything to be on it. I don't even understand half the issues, but it's so dramatic. You have to focus, focus, focus." He laughs. "Maybe I should go into politics in England." (Alice Thomsen, *Daily Telegraph*, February 12 2002)

A return, then, to the topic of his visit to England that was signalled in the intro – with the twist that a hero-worshipped US politician actually admires the much-derided British institution of PMQs. The suggestion in the final sentence is not to be taken seriously ("he laughs"), but it helps make the subject of the feature comfortably familiar for UK readers.

A bigger twist, as well as a return to the opening scene, is offered in the payoff to Armstrong's feature about the British Army running a radio station as part of Nato's SFOR force in Bosnia:

> Back in the club, you could believe there is some hope. The squaddies have split and they're all in the middle of the dance floor, hands in the air as the DJ builds a storming set. There are Croats and Serbs and Bosnians here and people may be slagging off SFOR but they're buying the squaddies rounds of Amstel. The guy on the podium with the lurid green glo-sticks steps down and chats to me about music, always music, and doesn't want to know when I get on to politics, so that just for one, naïve, 1988 Summer Of Love moment you actually do think that music could make a difference. Or maybe that's just the beer talking. (Stephen Armstrong, *Guardian*, September 25 2000)

So we are back in the opening scene but everyone is more relaxed, and we have heard an upbeat story about music promoting peace, love and understanding. Then the final sentence arrives to raise a question mark about the meaning of everything we have just read. Similarly, Beckett's lengthy piece on Coke's problems in Europe is put into perspective by the payoff quote from an analyst:

> "If Coca-Cola get people in China and India to drink one more a year, they needn't give a toss about people like us." (Andy Beckett, *Guardian*, October 2 2000)

We may well be better informed than at the start of the feature, but let's not kid ourselves that we know everything.

Putting it all together

Whereas news stories for print are normally written in the past tense, features are often written in the present tense. The only hard-and-fast rule on the tense of a feature is to be consistent throughout. However, variety is important when it comes to the length of sentences, as too many long sentences can become a stodgy read, and too many short ones can have a jerky effect.

In a good feature the transition between different sections and different ideas should be smooth. Like a duck in the water, you will have to work hard to produce a smooth effect on the surface. The reader should not have to break sweat to find out what you are getting at. Linking words and phrases are essential in good writing. Do not simply give the reader a succession of points apparently unrelated to each other, and do not leave your quotes flapping in the breeze. Strive to link one idea with the next, one paragraph with the previous one.

Linking words and phrases can be as simple as *and* or *but*. Again, variety is important. This chapter, for example, has so far included the following linking words and phrases, among others: in this case...because...so...though... also...but...as...for example...just as...although ...then...the above...note...at other times, though...or the more stark...this...consider this...it turns out that...see...take this...the above passage...as we have seen...again...as with...a return, then...a bigger twist.

It is a useful exercise to take a feature from a newspaper or a magazine and go through it highlighting the linking words or phrases.

■ ■ Summary ■

A feature may give background information and analysis on a topical issue; may profile a person, place or organisation; may convey controversial opinion; and may be entertaining in style and/or content. Virtually anything can be the subject for a feature, although subject matter will be selected according to the perceived interests of readers and advertisers. Features tend to be longer than news stories and tend to use more sources. There are many styles of feature writing and features do not conform to the "inverted pyramid" formula of most news reporting. Journalists working on features often have greater freedom to experiment with style, and the journalist is frequently included in the story. The "confessional" mode of feature writing has been increasingly prevalent in recent years, and it is argued that this reflects wider social changes that challenge "general truth claims" in society.

■ Questions

What are features *for*?

How do features differ from news?

Are some subjects more suited to features than news?

Why do star columnists tend to be paid more than reporters?

Why do we see "I" in features but not in news?

■ ■ Further reading ■

Angela Phillips' (2007) excellent *Good Writing for Journalists* reproduces and deconstructs a range of feature articles; in the process it provides numerous pointers to better writing. Also worth checking out are Pape and Featherstone (2006), Keeble (2006), and Adams (1999), while McKay (2006) includes a useful chapter specifically on magazine features. Although critical of the strict division between news and features, Randall's (2007) emphasis on reporting is welcome and his writing tips are invaluable. For an introduction to the process of writing reviews, see Gilbert (1999). Dovey (2000) is a useful starting point for discussion of reflexivity within journalism and beyond. And make sure that you read a wide range of features from a wide range of media.

Sources for soundbites

Christiansen, quoted in Williams, 1959: 190; Jack, 2006; Johnson, quoted in Hicks et al., 1999: 124; Randall, 2000: 194; Wheen, 2002: xiii.

eleven

telling it in pictures

key terms

Audio; Broadcast journalism; Convergence; Crowd sourcing; Interactivity; Internet; Radio; Television; 24-hour news; User-generated content; Video

It lasts just 11 seconds yet it has proved to be far and away the most popular video story on the website of the *Manchester Evening News*. Taken from CCTV footage, it shows a car following a bus through a restricted traffic "gateway" only to crash into two steel bollards that rise from the ground automatically to prevent unauthorised vehicles driving through. Ouch! Not only was it watched by thousands of **internet** users, many of whom emailed the link to friends or colleagues, but it also prompted dozens of posts to the site's Your Comments facility, as people debated everything from the placing of traffic warning signs to the comedic timing of the video clip. It was a LOL moment.

The bollards story is made by the video. It is also an example of the possibilities opened up by developments in online technology and by the ways in which users – the web term for readers and viewers – can become part of the story by contributing their own comments and anecdotes. It was even more popular than the site's previous big hitter, which featured a prank captured on mobile phone footage of a firefighter going round and round in a tumble dryer. But the *Manchester Evening News* site – also known as *Manchester Online* – is not all about amusing yet inconsequential video clips, as Sarah Hartley, head of online editorial at MEN Media, explains:

It's a variety and there are different levels of what video does. There are the funny ones. The best viewing figures we've ever had is the bollards, with thousands of people watching it. The fireman did quite well but not as well as the bollards. It's silly things. You can go from that level to a big investigation type thing into Styal prison where our video journalist got access to interview the women and the

Internet

Whether or not it includes video, animation, still pictures, maps, audio or other ways of telling a story, journalism on the internet is still journalism. According to Mike Ward: "The application of *core journalistic principles and processes* should inform all stages of online content creation and presentation, from the original idea to the finished page or site" (Ward, 2002: 6, my emphasis). He identifies these processes as:

- *Identify* and find news and/or information which will attract and interest the key audience/readers;
- *Collect* all the materials needed to tell the story/provide the information;
- *Select* from the collection the best material; and
- *Present* that material as effectively as possible. (Ward, 2002: 30, my emphasis)

However, online journalists differ from other journalists in the ways they relate to their respective audiences, according to a study in the Netherlands:

[The] bottom-up concept of "the public" suggests that this group of journalists is much more aware of an active role for the people they serve than their offline colleagues. This is an interesting result, as it ties in with the discourse of new-media technologies in which they are perceived to empower people and further democratise the relationships between consumers and producers of content (be it news or information). It also connects to online media logic as a concept which includes the notions of *the audience as an active agent* in redefining the workings of journalism. (Deuze and Dimoudi, 2002: 97, my emphasis)

Thus website users have the power to go where they please "from information chunk to audio file, to database, to graphic, to text summary, to video, to archive", and then either back again or off to an external

prison officers. It's a much more formal mini-series, three separate pieces, and there's also a whole text feature to go with it. Or you can have an interview with somebody or a voxpop, it's a variety.

The converged newsroom

As part of a media company that now combines the production of newspapers with television and radio, Hartley's online team can draw on a pool of video and audio material as well as text. But all journalists are now encouraged to submit visual material, as indeed are the users:

> We're trying to do something here that's an integrated newsroom. We're lucky that we have a television company so we do have reporters going out and doing videos for that every day which we've got access to. Equally, though, we wanted to bring the print journalists more into online news gathering so they are issued with mobile phones so they can take video clips to just illustrate something where they happen to be. On top of that we have a reasonable quality Sony A1 camera based in the office, which somebody from the print team or the online team or whatever can use to put together a more formal package than you would with a phone. So we've got a mix there. Our sources for video, apart from what we do ourselves, are the services [such as police] and users. People are quite comfortable with cameras and mobile phone footage these days.

> **❝ The non-linear online package is the closest thing to a new form of journalism since the advent of broadcasting. ❞**
> – *Gary Hudson and Sarah Rowlands.*

Not just moving pictures, but still photographs too. In 2008 an MEN Your Pictures site was set up on www.Flickr.com and within two months more than 2,500 pictures of Manchester had been posted on it. As with user comments on the site, all pictures are pre-moderated by staff to remove offensive content and/or hoax pics before they can appear online. Admittedly, there are some fairly dull looking pictures of buildings, but there are also lots of pics of people taking part in events ranging from community fêtes to political protests in

site to consult primary sources and original documentation (Ward, 2002: 121). Compared to the traditional linear form of broadcast journalism, featuring a beginning, a middle and an end, "graphics-based online story telling can be different," explain Gary Hudson and Sarah Rowlands:

> Online, using a programme like Flash, different story telling elements can be linked. Video, still photographs, sound, text and graphics can all be used to tell the story. And because of the way they are linked, users can decide how much or how little they want to see or hear. There's a linear thread, but the user controls the length of the experience. ... When you are planning an online package you will probably be unclear what features might be added as the story develops. Some might be suggested by feedback from users. Then your content will be truly interactive. (Hudson and Rowlands, 2007: 300–301)

Increasingly, as far as we can tell, journalists will deliver material *across* different media platforms; this is already blurring many of the boundaries between the formerly distinctive worlds of print, radio, TV and online journalists. Yet journalists have always fed on each other's work across media. Just as broadcast journalists scan the newspapers for stories, so print journalists monitor TV and radio; print and broadcasting both feed off the internet, and vice versa. David Walker writes that, in his experience, stories often "do not exist" for BBC newsdesks unless they have already appeared in print (Walker, 2000: 239). Local radio stations have long had a cannibalistic relationship with local papers and all elements of the media now consume each other in an increasingly orgiastic frenzy. The development of the internet means that the process is far quicker, more international in scope, and that the audience gets more of a look-in.

User-generated content

The phrase "user-generated content", known to some as "UGC", may be recent, but the phenomenon itself is not new. A reader's letter published in a newspaper or a magazine is an example of it at work in traditional media, and other examples would be the historical photographs often sent in by readers, the reports of flower shows and sporting events contributed by non-journalists, radio phone-ins, and the seemingly

the city; many of these events would not have been covered by MEN staff and, even if they were, the website could display numerous pictures whereas the newspaper might select just one or two. Hartley explains the thinking behind this initiative:

> It's about going to where people already are, as much as anything. In the past we might have said, "This is our newspaper website, if you'd like to send us something, thank you very much." Whereas now we say, "All these people are out there taking pictures of Manchester, we'll go and join them rather than the other way round." And it's worked well. I also do a page every week in the paper called *e view* and I use some of the pictures in there. This is an online community of people keen on pictures, so every time we want to use one in the paper we go back and ask permission and involve them in that process. What we didn't want to do was be plundering these people's work for nowt. It requires a lighter touch than some newspapers have used.

In addition to video clips, video packages, and galleries of still photographs, online news sites are now using a range of ways of telling stories via pictures, including slideshows, combined slideshows with text and audio, graphics and maps. And the beauty of an online map is that it can become inter-active. The first one on the MEN site showed the locations of gun killings in the Greater Manchester area; when you clicked on a specific location, up popped a photograph and biography of the victim combined with a link to online articles about the case. Things have since moved on, as Hartley explains:

> The one on gun crime wasn't truly interactive, because it just pinpointed places. But we have since done an interactive map of traffic blackspots across the region, and people can come and add their own traffic infor-mation to it. You just click on it and add your problem and we've had hundreds of people taking part. People plot their own experiences – it's the principle of crowd sourcing.

Such "crowd sourcing", along with people uploading pictures and video and/or commenting

endless scribblings of amateur community or village correspondents that are still carried in some local and regional newspapers. However, digital communication has transformed the phenomenon in terms of both speed and volume so that it is now a major part of the thinking of most journalistic operations. "What is criti-cal about this public behavioural shift towards an explosion of UGC is that mainstream media are making space for this production within newsrooms … and within news items," observes Rena Kim Bivens (2008: 116–117). "On some occasions, the flood of UGC linked to a breaking news item has actually reversed the traditional flow of news."

Broadcast journalism

Journalism on radio and television shares with print journalism the basic techniques of news gathering and storytelling, although the importance of sound and pictures for broadcast journalism can affect both *which* stories are selected and *how* stories are covered. Paul Chantler and Sim Harris argue that radio is "the best medium to stimulate the imagination" because "pictures on radio are not limited by the size of the screen; they are any size you wish" (Chantler and Harris, 1997: 5). Just as pictures (in the head) are important for radio, so sound is vital for television, especially the sound of people's own voices (Holland, 2000: 79). Therefore, stories with the potential for good pictures and/or audio stand a far higher chance of being covered by broadcast journalists than those without either; and reporters covering impor-tant but dull stories without good sound or vision may try out imaginative ways of *creating* them through stunts, extended metaphors, or imaginative pieces to camera.

Broadcast journalism tends to have a more immediate *feel* than does print journalism, reporting things that are happening *now* rather than things that happened earlier (even when this is an illusion). According to a classic study of the television industry, broadcast journalism is far from the "random reaction to random events" that it sometimes appears:

> On the contrary, it is a highly regulated and routine process of manufacturing a cultural product on an electronic production line. In stages of planning, gather-ing, selection and production broadcast news is moulded by the demands of composing order and organisation within a daily cycle. The news is made, and

on stories and blogs, is part of the phenomenon known within the trade as "user-generated content".

User-generated content is now also becoming more common within mainstream **broadcast journalism**, and it can prove very useful to the professional journalists, argues Lindsay Eastwood of ITV Yorkshire:

Especially on a weekend when we are limited with cameras and people, you do get lots of footage emailed in. People generally don't want anything for their footage, I think they get quite a thrill. Some of it's ropey but some of it's really good, so that's a real help now. Sometimes there's stuff that's a real Brucey Bonus. And it struck me that we are restricted for filming at places like airports, you have to ring hours in advance to get permission. We did a follow-up story to the attack on Glasgow airport, saying that security had been stepped up at our airport, and it took me quite a long time of phone bashing trying to set up for a reporter and camera to go and just film the armed police at the airport. But if Joe Public with his video camera can just film whatever he wants, it might throw up some issues for the airports themselves, because they're very controlling of us.

It's not just Joe and Jo Public out with their digital video cameras these days. Traditional TV crews going out on assignment are also likely to bump into print or online journalists videoing events for the websites of their increasingly "converged" newsrooms, as Eastwood explains:

If you go out on a story now you see your usual suspects from other TV channels and you also see these other people with little video cameras, and you think, where are they from, are they students? And they're from the *Yorkshire Post* or the *Hull Daily Mail* or wherever. The thing is, not to be disparaging, but they kind of sometimes get in the way. There's a limit to what people will do for the cameras; if you're asked too many times, eventually the last person to ask is going to get a "No". But, although we're "proper TV", they've got as much right to do it as we have.

> ❛ The internet is only the street corner meeting on a big scale. ❜
> – Tony Benn.

> ❛ I see a future where there are millions and millions of reporters. ❜
> – Matt Drudge.

like any other product it carries the marks of the technical and organisational structure from which it emerges. (Golding and Elliott, quoted in Manning, 2001: 51)

Notwithstanding the powerful image of an "electronic production line", individual journalists can still affect content to some extent through their own contacts, skills and attitudes (Manning, 2001: 53). Reading the words of TV journalist Lindsay Eastwood in this book, for example, it is clear that although she operates within constraints laid down by her employer and by broadcast regulators, she still has room to develop her own contacts, her own stories and her own creativity as a journalist.

Recent years have seen the emergence of 24-hour rolling news programmes on both radio and TV. According to Andrew Boyd:

The 24-hour news format has since developed a number of distinct styles: the magazine approach, which presents a variety of programmes and personalities throughout the day; and the news cycle, which repeats and updates an extended news bulletin, and lasts usually between twenty minutes and an hour. (Boyd, 2001: 130)

Concern has been expressed about the tendency for such news to "over-emphasise the live and dramatic" and to deliver over-simplified "nuggets" (Harrison, 2000: 209). In reality, 24-hour news quickly becomes repetitive and, despite its continuous nature, it still relies on selection and mediation by journalists. Yet there is now so much news being pumped into newsrooms electronically that there are fears that some broadcast journalists may forget where news actually comes from in the first place:

We must guard against one of the biggest dangers of all, especially with the increasing use of new technology. There could be a tendency to think of news as that which simply appears on the screen or the printer. Never forget that real news is what you go out and find through your own efforts. (Chantler and Harris, 1997: 64)

A distinction should therefore be made between properly resourced journalism and the "churnalism" discussed in Chapter 1.

For Jackie Harrison, a shift towards a "faster, racier style of news presentation" raises further questions about the quality of information and interpretation

Getting the pictures

Eastwood started out in newspapers before anyone dreamed that print reporters might one day need to think in terms of moving pictures, let alone go and film the pictures themselves before editing them into a package for a website. When she left print for broadcast journalism she was struck by the central importance of pictures for television reporting. "It's pictures that you're looking for all the time," she says. Other differences include the difficulty of persuading people to appear on screen compared to chatting with someone holding a notebook, the fact that her own clothes and hair suddenly assumed new importance on screen, and the "frustrating" amount of time it takes to do everything. As somebody who had covered parish council meetings for her local newspaper as a 16-year-old on work experience, she also noticed that an awful lot of regional TV news involved following up stories that had already appeared elsewhere, mostly in newspapers.

Frustrating is a word Eastwood uses frequently when discussing the differences between print and television. But that is only one side of the story. She recognises that there are other stories on which broadcasting comes into its own:

Where we obviously excel is breaking news, because you're there when it happens. You get it on first whereas a newspaper is the day after. That's where you get your kicks. That's the main thing to be proud of if you're working for TV, and radio is even more immediate. Television is good at showing things as they are, like fires, devastation, or when John Prescott punched that guy [during the 2001 general election campaign]. Fires and destruction make good TV. Also, you can show how people talk. In a newspaper you have a quote but you don't get the personality of the person. I love doing voxpops because you get a range of people and you can see and hear what they're like.

The Bradford riots in the summer of 2001 count as one of her most satisfying stories because all the above criteria were met. The riots were breaking news, and few things are more visually

provided to citizens: "[What] appears to be a tinkering with production techniques and format style by news organisations eventually has an effect on news content and the amount of information available, and ultimately on the relationship of terrestrial television news to the public sphere" (Harrison, 2000: 29 and 42). Not that there is anything wrong with "fancy video effects" in themselves:

[A]s long as the viewer can tell they are fancy video effects (layered shots, graphics or electronic wipes, for example) rather than a use of the technology to cheat the viewer, that's acceptable. Re-enactments of events by actors should be clearly labelled as such, and you should only show details of which you are certain. There is no place in journalism for making pictures up, any more than you can make up the facts of a story. (Hudson and Rowlands, 2007: 318)

That last point should not really need making but, in the light of some of the TV "fakery" scandals of recent years, perhaps it should be painted on the walls of television centres and production companies.

dramatic than petrol bombs being hurled through the air by masked youths. Being on the spot meant that broadcast journalists could report events as they happened and use the authentic voices of people on the streets.

> The riots stick in my mind because I was out there filming in the thick of it. That was an unbelievable experience really. Very scary. We ended up in a car behind the rioters. We thought they were people going to watch but they were people going to join the riot. So we were driving in the same direction as them and we gradually realised we were getting into a situation where it would be impossible to turn around and get away. We spotted these guys with scarves over their faces, carrying hammers and a crowbar and we thought, "We'd better get out of here". We were trying to cover up our equipment and we managed to drive off and got behind police lines. There were bricks coming over. We were trying to find a spot to film because obviously behind police lines you can't see the rioters in front, so we were trying to get on high places on either side of the road. But we were also trying to watch our backs. Then there were rowdy people coming round the side of us. I interviewed some. You want to be interviewing the young folk that are involved, saying, "Why are you doing it?" I did feel a bit of hostility a couple of times, but nothing too in-your-face. There were a lot of university students involved so they were quite articulate about why they were doing it.

Reporters can get embroiled in the excitement, as she notes:

> We should have been dodging bricks, but the adrenalin gets you and you're just caught up in the moment. But as a reporter you're responsible for the health and safety of the crew, and you can't ask them to do what they don't want to do.

In fact, some TV crews *did* film from in front rather than behind police lines, resulting in even more dramatic footage from a different perspective, but at much greater physical risk. However, financial cutbacks combined with developments in technology have since reduced the size and number of crews as well as the number of technical and editing staff in regional TV newsrooms. This has impacted on the reporters' jobs in a number of ways, as Eastwood explains:

> They had this massive swathe of redundancies here and taught us all how to edit, so now you're drawn back here [to the studio] quite a lot because the technology is here. The deadline's a bit tighter because you think, "I've got to come back and edit this".

> I'm completely non-technically minded, but I find basic editing quite all right. When you've got time, if you've shot a story the day before and then you've got the next day to edit it, it's fantastic. Being a control freak, I do quite like being in control and I can choose the shots. Before, when you were sitting with an editor, after a certain number of times trying a certain thing, you'd feel a bit like you were doing their heads in and you'd stop; whereas now, if you're doing it yourself, you can try and try and try and try and try to see if there's a better clip a bit further along. *If* you've got the time. When it becomes stressful is if you've had quite a hard day out on the road, you're up against it when you come back here and the pressure's on, and something goes wrong with the machine. It all gets a bit fraught.

> The other thing that's happened is we've lost all the sound men and the two man crews. In certain situations it was really good to have another person there, say if it was a rowdy situation, to watch your back. But it can hinder. On a breaking story it's sometimes a lot quicker for you to be holding the microphone while running around with a cameraman, you're much more portable, really.

As well as being portable, a television reporter needs to be prepared for anything for the sake of telling a story with pictures, including putting on a pair of waders to stand waist deep in water while reporting from inside a house hit by the floods of 2007:

> That's another difference from reporting it for a newspaper. The photographers were going out in the boats with their wellies on, but the [print] reporters were nowhere to be seen, they were in the community centres where everybody had been evacuated to, getting the human

story. But we have to be in there in the houses that are waist deep, which is fun. You do get the smell and the sense of absolute devastation, the shoes and the photos floating around in the house and everything is ruined, which you wouldn't experience as a newspaper reporter. But you've still got to try to get the human side as well, of course. It's not quite as glamorous as it's made out to be, but it gets the old adrenalin going.

Also, on the first day of the floods all the technology kept packing in because it was raining so hard, the cameras were getting wet and stopping working – we were drying a camera with a hairdryer. Give me a notepad! My top tip is: pencils rather than pens, when it's raining.

Eastwood was on the case again when Prime Minister Gordon Brown subsequently visited the flood-hit areas:

We worked our socks off all day tearing around the region trying to keep up with his schedule of visits. He obviously had a police escort, and me and the cameraman were constantly playing catch-up. We had a really tight turnaround time to make the programme but managed to get a really good item on air by the skin of our teeth. A couple of residents affected by floods were quite angry and vocal and we managed to barge through the media scrum and get close enough to get some good "actuality" sound of them having a go at him. One woman in Hull told him to, "Get your finger out".

We also managed to get quite close to him as he was heading for his car to leave Toll Bar near Doncaster. I shouted a question at him and was amazed when he turned back and came over and gave us a really good reply; the press liaison people had said he wouldn't be doing any interviews. That was satisfying. It just proves it's always worth pushing the boundaries in these situations to see what you can get. Nothing ventured, nothing gained.

Pictures, then, are central to TV. As Andrew Marr explains, that means TV news is biased towards news that has exciting or unusual pictures and against anything that looks visually dull:

Television news has been good at covering the controversy over whether fox-hunting should be banned. This has something to do with the visual appeal of foxes, hounds, horses, red coats and picturesque lanes, not to mention colourful urban demonstrations. Television news has been less good at covering the struggle over the European constitution, or the fight for better long-term care for the elderly. Television news likes plane crashes and train crashes because of how they look. It is mostly bored rigid by car crashes, which kill many more people, but not all at once. Similarly, television news looks overseas and it likes boy soldiers and tanks rather than peacemaking and reconciliation. (Marr, 2005: 291)

Increasingly, it seems, the reporter is expected to be in the picture too, whether standing pointlessly outside what may well be an empty building or interacting with those whom the story is supposed to be about. This is not a trend of which Lindsay Eastwood wholly approves:

We get policies dictated from the central office [of ITV News] and they very much like reporter involvement at the moment, that's flavour of the month. They like more interesting pieces to camera, not just standing outside court but walking and talking and going into rooms. Being a bit more interactive in the story. I'm in two minds about that. It's nice for the viewers to feel like you're their friend and to build some relationship with the reporter and presenters. But to me the story is always about the person and not about me, and I'd rather keep myself out of the story unless absolutely necessary. To me, a piece to camera is a tool that you use when you don't have any pictures to tell that bit of the story.

> ❛ It is a standing joke in the BBC that any award-winning news package should have helicopters in it, no matter the story. ❜
> – Andrew Marr.

Sometimes she gets the chance to make documentaries, such as the one about post-natal depression discussed in Chapter 4. Getting the right pictures to tell such a story at length can be both a challenge and an opportunity to be more creative than there is usually time for in the more hectic world of news reporting. Filming for the post-natal one took place off and on over several months:

We followed three women and I managed to keep the same cameraman, which helps. He was a fantastic cameraman, and the editor was superb as well, and I felt that I'd got to a stage where I could be a bit more artistic. We tried to be quite creative. The women were in mental torment and thinking horrible thoughts about their babies, but how do you illustrate that in pictures? We did blurry kind of shots and treated the shots. One of the women said she used to walk around her village in a daze and she would just find herself somewhere, so rather than having her walking we did the cameraman walking through the village, filming it from her point of view. So there are techniques you can use without it looking too reconstructed.

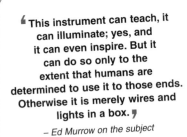

❝ This instrument can teach, it can illuminate; yes, and it can even inspire. But it can do so only to the extent that humans are determined to use it to those ends. Otherwise it is merely wires and lights in a box. ❞
– Ed Murrow on the subject of televison.

Pictures were particularly tricky for a documentary about the work of an air ambulance, because the helicopter had room only for the pilot, paramedic and patient. So, to get some dramatic footage from the scene of real incidents, the pilot and paramedic were equipped with a minicam and filmed it themselves. It was not so much user-generated content as participant-generated content, but it worked.

❝ Each new mass medium has been hailed for its educational and cultural benefits, as well as feared for its disturbing influence. ❞
– Denis McQuail.

Pictures and videos being submitted by non-journalists have now transformed the ways in which some events are reported, with digital communication meaning that material can be transmitted around the world within minutes, even seconds. "The opportunities are fantastic," says *Channel 4 News* presenter Jon Snow, "I just can't see the secret society surviving" (quoted in Kiss, 2006). The Asian tsunami of Boxing Day 2004, the London tube and bus bombings of July 2005, the Burma pro-democracy protests of 2007, and the Chinese earthquake of 2008 are just four examples of the ways in which images captured by "amateurs" have been used by journalists to help tell dramatic stories. From the most serious of life and death stories such as these, to the most frivolous such as a fireman in a tumble dryer, the use of footage from non-journalists has quickly become a fact of life for virtually all sections of the media.

We are probably still nearer the beginning of this "digital revolution" than we are to the end, assuming it has an end, so only a fool would be certain as to what is going to happen next. People have a tendency to use technology in unpredictable ways. I can remember writing magazine features in which technological whizkids talked about the possibility of using new-fangled mobile phones to send text messages. Back then they thought this new technology would be of most use to businesspeople who wanted to check the price of shares during meetings; nobody seemed to predict that texting would become a social phenomenon.

A rich mix of storytelling techniques

Different branches of journalism do not exist in isolation. Digital communication is transforming many of the ways in which we do journalism and is allowing for increasing convergence between delivery platforms. Each form of journalism informs others, and journalists are increasingly having to think across traditional divides and delivery mechanisms. When I interviewed Martin Wainwright for the first edition of this book, he told me:

There's a feeling that people get their immediate news from radio, television and internet, so the *Guardian* [newspaper], rather to my sadness, has become a bit stodgy with very long analytical articles. One good way out of that is we have the website. We have audio which is just like radio, so at the Great Heck rail crash I did a couple of audio reports, saying, "I'm standing here in front of the train". I love doing stuff for them.

When we met up again in 2008 I reminded him of those words and asked if he still felt the same way. He did, only more so:

Oh, I was very far sighted. That was in the early days of using mobile phones for the audio. I no longer consider the paper product as a newspaper in the old-fashioned sense of the word, it's more of a magazine. That's a matter of taste and, to be honest, it's not particularly to my taste. But the whole product *is* to my taste, because the paper has now become part of something much bigger. I really enjoy working online, there's the sheer quantity of stuff you can get out of one story now. I had to go up Skiddaw [a mountain in the Lake District] the other day to report on a three-course meal that was cooked up there. It wasn't a very big story in the paper – as usual my wonderful words were cut by about two-thirds and there was one picture – but we had a longer story online, we had a picture gallery online, I had to do two blogs about it, and we also had audio in the newsdesk podcast. Another positive thing about it for journalists is that, in order to do audio and video, you've actually got to be there – so there is hope.

Just as traditional print organisations now have websites featuring audio and video along with RSS feeds, podcasts, downloads and all the rest, so broadcasting journalists may be expected to contribute written text for use online. Many of the core skills of reporting may be similar but there are some significantly different relationships involving sound, vision, time and space; online allows for stories to be told in non-linear formats and, arguably, in greater depth and breadth.

For web journalist Jemima Kiss, although the core skills are the same, there are some significant differences between journalism online and offline.

She identifies these core skills as: "Accuracy, research, respecting sources, clarity, understanding an audience, knowing which questions to ask, using your initiative and being extremely persistent." And the differences? She points to four examples:

One, writing and structure: like one sentence paragraphs, keeping stuff short, writing headlines for search engines, including links for background. *Two*, stories are very often the start of something online rather than the end of the process. I think we've only just started to explore this properly but at the very least, you'd expect an online journalist to go back and manage the comments stream on a story or blog post to answer points, pick up extra questions and curate the debate. *Three*, aggregation: human editing on top of automatic aggregation is extremely important. Editors and bloggers become "trusted guides" for readers through so much information. *Four*, speed: there is no deadline anymore because it is always now. The skill of writing accurately with speed is more important than ever, but the web has inspired new formats, such as minute-by-minute coverage of sports and live events. Much more could be done with messaging services like Twitter.

Apart from her own *Guardian* site, is there any website that she thinks gets anywhere near to fulfilling the potential of online journalism? Yes, it turns out, there is: www.newsvine.com. According to Kiss:

This is pretty much the best news site on the web, in my humble opinion. Newsvine combines mainstream news with feedback and customisation tools, and is just incredibly sexy. It's the best attempt yet at combining all the elements of the "new" journalism.

Check it out. But be aware that, by the time you read this, there will almost certainly be some new kids on the block. There might even be a new block.

Editorial conferences within major media organisations now typically look at how stories can be run across platforms as well as the circularity of one form of media pointing the audience in the direction of another, for added extras rather than simple duplication. And, given the information now available to the producers of websites, such discussions can be informed by precise knowledge of what most interests the audience; or, at least, that section of the audience that is online. Sarah Hartley explains how this works at MEN Media:

> We've three conferences a day and in those conferences you've got print, online, radio and TV people. We all sit down together and decide what we're going to be, and not going to be, doing. We embed an online journalist within a department, so we've got an online journalist in news, one in business, one in sport, one in entertainments, and one in lifestyle areas. Those people look after the channels of output from those departments: managing the content; bringing different content together to make a package, which could be text, pictures, audio-video, a mix of those things; and managing that area of the site so that it appears when it should and, equally importantly, disappears when it should. We add extra pictures and obviously lots of links, because that's the main point of online, the depth of information that you can let people access.

> So the online journalist is doing all that, they're repurposing, they're putting links in, they're getting the extras to bring to it. Some things lend themselves to video because they are just so visual. We do some separate audio too. We encourage the print reporters to record interviews with people, so we do get some quite nice little podcasts with celebrities we're interviewing. Sometimes we can use an audio package from the radio with a series of pictures and make a slideshow package.

The result of all this can be a rich mix of storytelling techniques, with more ingredients – wikis, live interactive chat, animated graphics, things we haven't yet thought of – being added to the mix all the time.

It is a pity, then, that some publishers have seen such technology and user-generated content simply as a means to gather cheap material and therefore as an excuse for cutting the jobs of journalists. But

that's not the way it's got to be, as is perhaps best demonstrated by the *BAE Files*. This area of the *Guardian* website (www.guardian.co.uk/world/bae) is the polar opposite of cheap and/or lazy journalism. An investigation into allegations of corruption involving giant arms company BAE Systems – and drawing in the governments of the UK and Saudi Arabia as well as the Serious Fraud Office – the site includes numerous news stories, background features and comment pieces. And that's not the half of it. It also tells the story via video, audio, picture galleries, slideshows, interactive maps, cartoons, an extensive cast of characters, a timeline, original documents, and even an article in which journalists David Leigh and Rob Evans (2008) detail how each document was sourced, complete with links to the full documents themselves. The story simply could not have been told in such a way in print alone; but nor could it have been told without the investment of time and money in meticulous reporting by experienced and skilful journalists. One of the journalists involved, David Leigh, has expressed concern that such "proper" reporting could become endangered in the age of the internet:

> My fear is that today everybody is rather too obsessed with new platforms. But not enough people are talking about values. The internet is an incredibly rich information resource. And a great tool for worldwide sharing. But it soaks up a lot of people's time, just messing about. As well as overloading us with instantaneous terrors, it also degrades valuable things – the idea of discrimination, that some voices are more credible than others, that a named source is better than an anonymous pamphleteer. ... The notion of authoritativeness is derided as a sort of top-down fascism. I fear that these developments will endanger the role of the reporter. Of course, there'll always be room for news bunnies – to dash in front of a camera and breathlessly describe a lorry crash, or to bash out a press release in 10 minutes. There'll probably be a lot more news bunnies in the future: high-speed, short-legged creatures of the internet age. There will probably also be hyper-local sites: postcode journalism fuelled cheaply by neighbourhood bloggers. But not proper reporters. (Leigh, 2007)

That's a gloomy prospect for those of us who take the reporting side of journalism seriously. But the work of Leigh and others – including the work of the journalists interviewed for this book – suggests that the reporter is not dead yet.

Journalism remains journalism, whether it be printed, broadcast, online, or multimedia. Trevor Gibbons, a magazine journalist who became a radio journalist and then went on to become a journalist for *BBC Online* (before returning to radio), believes that the same fundamentals should apply:

> Internet journalism is journalism. It's about ideas, it's about what you're actually going to put on the page. Our sources are the same, we check them the same, we put in the same calls, we ring up the same people. Just like TV, radio or print, you need to know who you're writing for. There is the unique ability to construct this web behind a story, and that's what people who use the internet like about it, but the same attributes should apply really.

These attributes, the basics of journalism as discussed throughout this book, include the ability to ask questions, to think laterally, to maintain curiosity, to check sources, to look for evidence, and to tell stories. But it is not simply a one-way process of core journalism skills being used to inform online reporting. The innovations associated with the internet also influence how traditional media report events. So, for example, TV news and sports channels now routinely split their screens to include captions and tickers delivering many different strands of information at once, and sometimes two or more bits of footage being shown side by side. We have the speedy feedback and polling made possible by email and text messages, with the audience able to interact with TV and radio programmes being broadcast live. We have the increasing trend in newspaper and magazine reporting of emulating the non-linear and "layered" approach of online journalism

> 〝 Of course the world wide web is full of lunatics and lies; but it's not technology that is responsible for this, but simply human failings like sloppy journalism and ignorance. 〞
>
> – *Andrew Brown.*

by breaking up information into different sections with boxes, summaries, background material and graphics. Print and broadcast reporters can use the web to place background material, original documents, full interviews, photo galleries, links and discussions that would not fit into their reports for non-online media; and they can blog about their journalism, enabling them to engage in more of a conversation with more of their audience than was ever possible previously. Interactive input from users is vital for BBC Online, adds Gibbons: "Increasingly the online audience doesn't just want to be *told* the story, it wants to be *part* of the story."

Journalists can also be part of the story at times. It is now common, for example, for radio programmes to have their own websites featuring webcams showing the presenters at work; and jolly dull most of them are too. But radio websites are also being used more imaginatively to present visual and textual information that can complement audio. BBC Radio Four's *PM* programme has a particularly interactive relationship with its listeners via its website (www.bbc.co.uk/radio4/news/pm), which features blogs, photo galleries, webcam, video, maps produced by "crowd sourcing", podcasts, listen again, biographies of the journalists, and much more besides. The Saturday edition of the show, *iPM*, goes even further and allows listeners to suggest news items and to comment in advance on the proposed running order. Not surprisingly, the "i" stands for "interactive"; check it out at: www.bbc.co.uk/blogs/ipm.

However, no amount of technological bells and whistles should deflect journalists from an understanding that it is the quality of reporting that remains the most important thing. And sometimes, as many a radio journalist will tell you, the best pictures are the ones that exist only inside your head when you listen to a good piece of audio.

▪ ▪ Summary ▪

Journalists are increasingly working across different media sectors in a process referred to as integration or convergence. Broadcast and online journalism may differ in style and detail but they also share certain core processes with each other and with print journalism: the identification of news, the collection of information, the verification of evidence, the selection of material, and the presentation of stories. Although pictures have long been important for newspaper and magazine journalism, they are central for television and much online journalism. Much video footage and many still photographs are now supplied by the audience (user-generated content) and online journalists are developing non-linear ways of storytelling. Online journalists make greater use of interactive elements, although interactivity is also a growing element within broadcast and even print journalism.

▪ Questions

What core skills are needed by *all* journalists?

What makes good pictures?

How do pictures affect what stories are covered?

Have non-linear packages really transformed journalism?

Is everyone now a journalist?

▪ ▪ Further reading ▪

For detailed instruction and discussion of the ways in which pictures are used on television and online, plus an awful lot more, including radio, the best place to start is the excellent *Broadcast Journalism Handbook* by Gary Hudson and Sarah Rowlands (2007). Less up-to-date but no less authoritative, Boyd (2001) offers a practical introduction to TV and radio reporting, plus a brief look at online journalism. Also worth reading is the edited collection by Jane Chapman and Marie Kinsey (2009), *Broadcast Journalism: A Critical Introduction*.

A useful introduction to academic analysis of broadcast journalism and the public sphere can be found in both Harrison (2000) and Bromley (2001). Jim Hall's (2001) *Online Journalism* offers a polemical account of the technology's impact; more recent research into and theorising about online journalism can be found in journal articles by Robinson (2007), Singer (2004 and 2005), and Bivens (2008). For interviews with online practitioners, not just journalists, as well as a more theoretical context, Dewdney and Ride's (2006) *New Media Handbook* is worth checking out; for a practical guide to journalism on the internet, see Ward (2002); and for detailed guidance on how and why to use multimedia and interactive online packages and graphics, see Mindy McAdams' (2005) *Flash Journalism*.

The sixth edition of Kobre's (2008) book on photo journalism includes a guide to shooting moving pictures for use online. And finally, as a reminder of the power of the still photograph in newspapers and magazines, and as a discussion of the role of the image within journalism, you still can't beat Harold Evans' ([1978] 1997) *Pictures on a Page*; you might have to hunt around in libraries or secondhand bookshops, but it will be worth it.

Sources for soundbites

Hudson and Rowlands, 2007: 300; Benn, quoted in Cottle, 2001; Drudge, quoted in Boyd, 2001: 400; Marr, 2005: 291; Murrow, 1958; McQuail, 2000: 38; Brown, 2000: 185.

twelve

style for journalists

The name may not mean much to younger readers, but Elizabeth Taylor was once one of the most famous – and glamorous – women in the world. According to journalistic folklore, when she was asked how she was feeling during a visit to London towards the end of the 1950s, she duly replied with a quotable quote: "I'm feeling like a million dollars." Her remark was faithfully reported in most of the following day's newspapers, but only in the *Daily Telegraph* did it become: "I'm feeling like a million dollars (£357,000)." Its style guide stipulated that any amount given in a foreign currency must be followed with a conversion into sterling; as *Telegraph* historian Duff Hart-Davis (1990: 9) put it, the absurd Liz Taylor quote was an example of the paper's "slavish devotion to its house rules".

All news organisations have a concept of house *style*; that is, the **language** in which stories should be written. Why? Because consistency in matters of detail "encourages readers to concentrate on *what* its writers are saying" (Hicks and Holmes, 2002: 19, emphasis in original). A publication's strictures on style can say as much about what the publication is *not* as what it *is*, as this entry from the current *Telegraph* (2008) style book indicates: "*Brave* is an acceptable adjective to apply to somebody who has perpetrated a courageous act. Its usage to describe the demeanour of somebody suffering from a serious illness is tabloid."

Many newsrooms have their own style books, some have searchable electronic guides, and some rely on new recruits picking up unwritten rules

> ❝ Never use a long word where a short one will do. ❞
> – George Orwell.

> ❝ We misspelled the word misspelled twice, as mispelled, in the Corrections and clarifications column. ❞
> – Guardian.

Style

Like all such style guides, the one presented in this chapter contains a mixture of common practice, pointers towards correct use of English, points of clarification, and attempts at attaining consistency. The aim is to "eliminate undesired idiosyncrasies" in copy (Bell, 1991: 83). However, it no doubt contains its fair share of "personal idio-syncrasy and whimsy" (Cameron, 1996: 323).

The underlying ethos of most such guides, as of Chapter 9 on writing news, is the plain, terse style of writing advocated by the journalist, novelist and essayist, George Orwell:

> A scrupulous writer, in every sentence that he writes, will ask himself at least four questions, thus: What am I trying to say? What words will express it? What image or idiom will make it clearer? Is this image fresh enough to have an effect? And he will probably ask himself two more: Could I put it more shortly? Have I said anything that is unavoidably ugly? (Orwell, 1946b: 151–152)

Orwell went on to list six rules to be relied upon "when instinct fails":

- Never use a metaphor, simile or other figure of speech which you are used to seeing in print.
- Never use a long word where a short one will do.
- If it is possible to cut out a word, always cut it out.
- Never use the passive where you can use the active.
- Never use a foreign phrase, a scientific word or a jargon word if you can think of an everyday English equivalent.
- Break any of these rules sooner than say anything outright barbarous. (Orwell, 1946b: 156)

from more experienced colleagues. Such guides contain rules, reminders and points of clarification, and the details will change over time:

> There are unmistakable trends in house style: in grammar, loose, colloquial usage is more accepted than it was; there is less punctuation, ie there are fewer capital letters, full stops for abbreviations, apostrophes, accents etc; in spelling, shorter forms are increasingly common and the ... –ize ending has lost ground to – ise... (Hicks and Holmes, 2002: 21)

Arguments over style can get pretty heated, as when the use of a dash prompted an *Independent* journalist to write to his union journal and rail against such slapdash standards of punctuation drifting from the tabloids to more serious titles; readers were informed that the author of an offending piece on style was unfit even to be sent for the teas (Johnston, 2002).

> ❝ Every word must be understood by the ordinary reader, every sentence must be clear at one glance, and every story must say something about people. ❞
> – Harold Evans.

When it comes to style, it seems, the number of opinions is matched only by the vehemence with which each one is expressed. But, amid the rules and regulations, style guides can also be repositories of humour, as in the following entries:

> *Goths* (uc) Germanic tribe that invaded the Roman empire
>
> *goths* (lc) Sisters of Mercy fans who invaded the Shepherd's Bush Empire
>
> (*Guardian* style guide; Marsh, 2007)
>
> Lazy journalists are always at home in *oil-rich* country A, ruled by *ailing* President B, the *long-serving strong-man*, who is, according to the *chattering classes*, a *wily political operator* – hence the present *uneasy peace* – but, after his recent *watershed* (or *landmark* or *sea-change*) decision to arrest his prime minister (the *honeymoon is over*), will soon face a *bloody uprising* in the *breakaway* south. ... Towards the end, after an admission that the author has no idea what is going on, there is always room for *One thing is certain*, before rounding off the article with *As one wag put it...* (*Economist* style guide, 2008)

While aiming to eliminate inconsistency within a title, a style guide also identifies those "minor style choices by which one news outlet's finished product is different from another's" (Bell, 1991: 82). As Deborah Cameron points out, style guides produce distinctive voices for different titles by submitting the voices of individual journalists (big name columnists usually excepted) to "corporate norms". Such rules help differentiate one news organisation from another and, by reflecting the usage or aspirations of a target audience, contribute towards what might be termed a "brand image" (Cameron, 1996: 320–324). This may go some way towards explaining why the *Daily Telegraph*, for example, issues its journalists with a list of banned words that include "toilet" and offers advice such as: "Christmas lunch is what most of our readers would eat, not Christmas dinner" (*Telegraph*, 2008). Jenny McKay (2006: 62) points out that magazines such as *Rolling Stone* and the *Spectator* avoid the "corporate monotone" of a restrictive house style by allowing "more scope for the individual voice of the writer to be heard". However, this very absence of house style can itself be seen as part of a brand image.

It has been argued that the issue of house style goes beyond simple choices over presentation to have an ideological effect. The BBC, for example, has felt it necessary to issue its journalists with a style guide specifically concerned with coverage of the Israeli–Palestinian conflict, covering contentious terms such as "assassinations", "occupied territories", "terrorists" and even "wall", although the BBC prefers "barrier" (http://news.bbc.co.uk/newswatch/ukfs/hi/newsid_6040000/newsid_6044000/6044090.stm). Ideological implications are not limited to stylistic rules concerning the coverage of conflicts. For Paul Manning: "Formats are never neutral in their ideological implications." He argues that the journalist's concern to meet restrictive stylistic requirements can result in "less discursive news treatments and fewer opportunities for a wider range of news sources to inject critical or oppositional voices" (Manning, 2001: 60). Thus the mode of address of the *Sun* newspaper, for example, has been categorised as "heterosexual,

amok: no Daily Telegraph style book would be complete without the observation that only Malays can run amok. See also berserk...

berserk: no Daily Telegraph style book would be complete without the observation that only Icelanders can go berserk. See also amok. (*Telegraph* style book, 2008)

What follows in this chapter is an example of a style guide. That means it is likely to contain a fair number of prejudices, pet hates and arbitrary preferences as well as what some would no doubt dismiss as *political correctness* gone mad. Many of the house rules below will be almost universal among journalists within the UK but many will not. Student journalists should study the styles of different organisations and be aware that, even if it is not codified in a written guide, some form of house style will certainly exist. Anyone entering a newsroom on work experience or as a new recruit will quickly need to get to grips with that particular organisation's preferences on a range of stylistic issues – whether to abbreviate Councillor to Coun or Cllr, whether to cap up Prime Minister, whether to end words with –ise or –ize – and to apply such rules consistently. When you change jobs you will have to do it all over again. Eventually, of course, you might be in a position to break or even change the rules – but first you need to know what they are. The following guide will give you an indication of what issues might arise and, in the process, it might help you to write better copy.

> ❛ A piece of writing can drone or it can splutter or it can mumble or it can sing. Aim for the singing kind – writing that has life, rhythm, harmony, style – and you will never lose your reader. ❜
>
> – Keith Waterhouse.

male, white, conservative, capitalist, nationalist" (Pursehouse, cited in Stevenson, 2002: 101).

So style guides themselves can be seen as ideological, irrespective of whether their authors see them as such:

> Though they are framed as purely functional or aesthetic judgements, and the commonest criteria offered are "apolitical" ones such as clarity, brevity, consistency, liveliness and vigour, as well as linguistic "correctness" and (occasionally) "purity", on examination it turns out that these stylistic values are not timeless and neutral, but have a history and a politics. They play a role in constructing a relationship with a specific imagined audience, and also in sustaining a particular ideology of news reporting. (Cameron, 1996: 316)

Yet journalists can on occasion break with consensus, both in terms of style and in terms of ideology. When Nell McCafferty covered the Dublin criminal courts for the *Irish Times* she abandoned the conventional rules of court reporting and journalistic style, as she explained in the introduction to a collection of her descriptive and often plaintive articles:

> Because these people have suffered more than enough by appearing in court in the first place, I never used their real names and addresses. I have named the Justices who decided their fate. Hopefully, this collection of articles will put them in the dock for a change. (McCafferty, 1981: 2)

Language

Journalists are often dismissive of academics' close, textual analysis of the language used in journalism. However, choices over language are inseparable from issues of truth and "what really happened", argue linguists Robert Hodge and Gunther Kress:

> It is common for linguistically-oriented critics to attend too much to language, and to overvalue the importance of what is contained in words, especially words in written texts; but the opposite can also be the case. All the

major ideological struggles will necessarily be waged in words, through texts that circulate in various ways by virtue of various technologies, in forms of language that bear the traces of these struggles in innumerable ways. (Hodge and Kress, 1993: 161)

For Cameron, even the plain language celebrated by Orwell – and embraced by most UK news media to this day – also has ideological implications:

The plain and transparent style recommended by Orwell is particularly well suited to the prevailing ideology of modern news reporting as simply "holding up a mirror to the world", and it is not coincidental that this style is most strictly adhered to in news rather than feature items. The use of a plain, terse, concrete language in news items – a language that deliberately aims not to draw attention to itself as language – is a code, not unlike the code of realism in fiction, and what it conventionally signifies is unmediated access to the objective facts of a story. It implicitly conveys to us, in a way a less self-effacing kind of language could not hope to do, that what we are reading is not really a representation at all: it is the simple truth. ... [It] is the linguistic analogue of the camera never lies, and should be treated with similar suspicion. (Cameron, 1996: 327)

> ❛ Words are the tools of a journalist's trade and, in common with any craftsman, he should keep them keen and well-polished, using them appropriately; he will cherish them. ❜
>
> – The Inky Path.

Political correctness

What is often referred to as political correctness is largely a matter of simple courtesy, argues Jenny McKay, but that does not mean it has no political significance:

In the early days of the struggle by ethnic minority groups and women for social equality many journalists dismissed the idea that choice of words made any difference. (This was perhaps surprising since they had staked their lives and livelihoods on the fact that words did matter.) Now, however, many of the bigger publishing houses have recognised that there is something excluding about, for example, writing which uses the male pronoun, he, all the time when the people who are being described are in fact a mixture of he and she. ... [T]he phrase "politically correct" is often used to denigrate worthwhile attempts to think about the full significance of a writer's choice of words. Of course, the prescriptive aspect of this can be taken too far but the underlying motive is, in many cases, less sinister than polite. (McKay, 2006: 72)

A dismissive attitude towards what is often seen as a politically correct approach to issues such as racism, sexism and disability can limit the extent of ethical debate among journalists who work within mainstream media (Keeble, 2001b: 1–2). Yet journalist Gary Younge (2006) argues that the widespread abandonment of once common words, such as "darkie" and "spastic", should not be seen as political correctness at all; rather, such changes occurred as a result of social progress, "not imposed by liberal diktat, but established by civic consensus".

Style Guide

A

a or an before h?   If the h is silent, as in hour, use an; otherwise use a, as in *a* hero.

abbreviations   Abbreviations such as *can't* or *that's* are increasingly common in today's media but some still frown on them unless they are in direct quotes. Shortened versions of words such as doctor (Dr) or Labour (Lab) do not need full stops, nor do initials such as GP, BBC or MP (which should be upper case with no spaces). Explain all but the most famous abbreviations either by spelling out: National Union of Students (NUS); or by description: the transport union RMT. If the initials can be spoken as a word (such as Nato) they form an *acronym*.

accommodation   Double cc and double mm.

acronyms   A word formed by using the initial letters of other words, as in Nato. Explain all but the most famous like this: train drivers' union Aslef; or Acas, the arbitration service.

Act   Upper case in the full name of an act, as in the Official Secrets Act.

addresses   Most addresses in news articles give the street, not the number. But if giving the full address for contact details, write it as follows: 999 Letsby Avenue, Sheffield S1 3NJ.

adrenalin   Prefer to adrenaline.

advice, advise   Advice (noun) is what you ask for or give. Advise (verb) is what you might do.

adviser   Prefer to advisor.

affect   Not to be confused with *effect*. To affect is to change. Such a change may have effects.

ageing   Not aging.

ages   Freddie Sears, 19; or 19-year-old Freddie Sears; or Freddie is 19 years old.

Aids   Prefer to AIDS.

A-levels   Hyphen and lower case l.

all right   Two words unless you are quoting a title such as *The Kids Are Alright*.

Alzheimer's disease   Upper case A, lower case d, and note the apostrophe.

amongst   Prefer *among*.

ampersand   (&) Use in company names when the company does: Marks & Spencer. Otherwise avoid.

and   You may begin sentences with the word *and*. But not every sentence, please.

> ❝ It sometimes seemed that the main effort of the sub-editors, armed with that formidable weapon, the Style Book, was directed towards suppressing innovation. ❞
> – Duff Hart-Davis on the Telegraph.

apostrophes   Use an apostrophe to show that something has been left out of a word (eg *don't*, short for *do not*) and to mark the possessive (eg *John's foot*). Plural nouns such as children and people take a singular apostrophe (eg *children's games, people's princess*).

armed forces   Lower case.

Army   Upper case A if referring to *the* (ie British) Army. Army ranks should be abbreviated as follows: Lieutenant General (Lt Gen); Major General (Maj Gen); Brigadier (Brig); Colonel (Col); Lieutenant Colonel (Lt Col); Major (Maj); Captain (Capt); Lieutenant (Lt); 2nd Lieutenant (2nd Lt); Regimental Sergeant Major (RSM); Warrant Officer (WO); Company Sergeant Major (CSM); Sergeant (Sgt); Corporal (Cpl); Lance Corporal (L Cpl); Private (Pte). Do not abbreviate Field Marshall or General.

asylum seeker   Two words, no hyphen.

B

B&Q   No spaces.

backbenches   One word, as in backbencher.

bail, bale   Somebody might be on police *bail*, and a cricket player will be familiar with *bails*. But a boat could be *baled* out, and a pilot could *bale* out of an aeroplane.

Bank of England Upper case B and E. Subsequently the Bank.

bank holiday Lower case.

banknote One word.

barbecue Not Bar-B-Q, BBQ or barbie.

Barclays Bank Upper case Bs, no apostrophe.

bare, bear Often confused. *Bare* means unclothed, unadorned, just sufficient, and to reveal; *bear* means to carry, to produce or give birth, and a furry animal.

begs the question Best avoided because even the experts seem to disagree about what it means.

biannual Means twice a year. Not to be confused with *biennial*, every two years. Probably best avoided.

Bible Upper case. But biblical is lower case.

billion One thousand millions. Write the word in full (£1.4 billion) except in headlines (£1.4bn).

birthplace One word.

boffins This word lives on as journalese for scientists and other researchers, but it really shouldn't.

Boxing day Upper case B, lower case d.

breach Means to break through or to break a promise or rule. Not to be confused with *breech*, which is either part of a gun or something to do with short trousers.

breastfeeding One word.

brownfield One word.

brussels sprouts Lower case, no apostrophe.

BSE Bovine spongiform encephalopathy, but not normally any need to spell out. You may refer to it as "mad cow disease".

Budget Upper case B if this is *the* Budget set by the Chancellor of the Exchequer, otherwise lower case.

but You may begin sentences with the word *but*. But not too many.

byelection Prefer one word.

bylaw Prefer one word.

bypass Prefer one word.

C

cabinet, shadow cabinet Lower case.

caesarean section Lower case.

canvas, canvass Tents are made of *canvas*, whereas politicians may *canvass* for support.

capitals UK media now use upper case letters far more sparingly than they did even just a few years ago. Clarity and consistency can sometimes be at odds with each other, in which case clarity should be allowed to win.

cappuccino Lower case.

Caribbean One r and two bbs.

cashmere A fabric, not to be confused with *Kashmir* in the Indian subcontinent.

cemetery Not cemetry or cemetary.

censor Means to suppress and should not be confused with *censure*, meaning to criticise harshly.

centre Not center.

century Lower case, with numbers, as in 9th century or 21st century.

chairman, chairwoman Prefer chairman if it's a man, chairwoman if it's a woman, and chair if it is simply a position (eg The committee's first job will be to elect a chair). Lower case.

Chancellor of the Exchequer Upper case C and E. Subsequent mentions: the Chancellor.

Channel tunnel Upper case C, lower case t.

cheddar, cheshire cheese Lower case.

Chief Constable Upper case Cs for a particular Chief Constable, lower case for a meeting of chief constables.

Christian Upper case C, though unchristian is lower case.

Christmas day Upper case C, lower case d.

churches Full name, upper case, eg Sacred Heart Roman Catholic Church; then Sacred Heart, or just the church if it is the only one mentioned in the story.

citizens advice bureau Lower case, no hyphen.

city centre Two words, no hyphen.

CJD Creutzfeldt-Jakob disease, but not normally any need to spell out. You may refer to it as "the human form of BSE".

Clichés Some say, "avoid clichés like the plague", but opinions vary. Keeble (2001a: 117), for example, advises reporters to avoid saying that so-and-so is "fighting for her life" when a hospital reports her condition as "critical", on the grounds that it is a cliché. Maybe it is, but so is critical, and at least fighting for her life gets closer to the drama of the situation. Clichés are hard to avoid completely, they change over time, and just occasionally they might be used ironically. If you are tempted to use a cliché in your copy, stop and ask yourself if it really is the best way of expressing what you want to say. Particularly tired words and phrases are listed below:

a big ask
a bridge too far

acid test
after the Lord Mayor's show
as so-and-so looks on (in picture captions)
at the end of the day
back to square one
baptism of fire
between a rock and a hard place
bitter end
bombshell
brutal murder
bubbly character
budding (in stories about young people)
burning issue
chickens coming home to roost
closure (as prerequisite for moving on)
cold comfort
crack troops
cyberspace
drop-dead gorgeous
early doors
fairytale ending
fairytale romance
fears are growing
first the good news…
flash in the pan
flushed with success (in stories about toilets)
genuine six-pointer
gobsmacked
goes without saying
handbags (among footballers)
high-level summit
high-speed chase
hit the ground running
hopes were dashed
horns of a dilemma
I have to say
interesting to note
…is the new black
…is the new rock'n'roll
it has to be said
it remains to be seen

> ❛ Plain English is always the democrat's best defence. ❜
> – Andrew Marr.

jaw-dropping
kept himself to himself
kick-start
last but not least
leave no stone unturned
level playing field
mass exodus
mega
meteoric rise
morning after the night before
move on (following closure)
only time will tell
personal demons
pillar of the community
political correctness gone mad
purrfect (in stories about cats)
quiet confidence
revellers
rich tapestry
rich vein of form
ripe old age of…
sea change
speculation was rife
step change
storm in a D-cup (in stories about bras or
    breasts)
sweet smell of success
SW19 (in stories about Wimbledon)
take the bull by the horns
taken its toll
the devil is in the detail
to die for
torrid time
tragic mum (or tot, or whoever)
tsunami (except when it actually
is one)
tucking into festive fare (in picture captions)
untimely death
up in arms
veritable feast
wake up and smell the coffee
wake-up call
war of words

> ' All the major ideological
> struggles will necessarily
> be waged in words. '
> – Robert Hodge and
> Gunther Kress.

company names   Use spellings, upper or lower case letters, and apostrophes as the companies do themselves.

conman, conwoman   Both one word.

connection   Not connexion.

Conservative party   Upper case C, lower case p. *Conservatives* and *Tories* are also acceptable. The Conservative party is singular; Conservatives are plural.

Continent   Upper case C only if you are referring to *the* Continent, ie mainland Europe.

convince   You convince someone of the fact; you do not convince someone to do something, you *persuade* them.

co-operate, co-operative, co-op   With a hyphen because that's how it's pronounced.

Coroner's Court   Bradford Coroner's Court, with upper case and apostrophe. But lower case if general, eg "The cause of death will be decided in the coroner's court".

council leader   Lower case.

councillors   Lower case for councillors in general, but upper case and for individual councillors. Some newsrooms prefer Coun, others prefer Cllr.

councils   Upper case on first use – Sheffield City Council – then the council if it is the only one referred to in the story. The council *is* rather than the council *are*. Cabinets, panels and boards can all be in lower case.

couple   Plural, so the couple *are* planning a holiday, not *is*.

Crown Prosecution Service   Upper case first letters. May subsequently be abbreviated to CPS.

curate's egg   Does not mean a bit good and a bit bad, because an egg that is good in parts is still rotten.

D

dashes   Two dashes may be used – as in this example – to mark a parenthesis. One dash may also be used to introduce an explanation, to add emphasis, or to mark a surprise. But avoid littering your copy with too many dashes.

dates   Most UK publications go for March 21, or March 21 2009. Not March 21st; nor 21 March; nor March 21, 2009.

day-to-day   Hyphenated.

D-day   Just the one upper case D, plus a hyphen.

decades   1980s, 1990s, 2000s, with no apostrophe. Swinging 60s is acceptable only if used ironically (and sparingly). Some prefer noughties for the 2000s; others ban it.

decimate   Means to kill or remove a tenth of the population – not to defeat utterly.

defuse   Means to render harmless or to reduce tension. Often confused with *diffuse*, meaning spread about.

disabled people   Not the disabled or the handicapped.

discreet   Means circumspect and should not be confused with *discrete*, meaning separate.

disinterested   Means impartial, but is often confused with *uninterested*, meaning bored or not interested.

Doctor   Abbreviate to Dr without a full stop.

dotcom   Dotcom companies, not .com or dot.com.

dots   Use three dots (ellipsis) to indicate that something has been omitted when quoting a document; also if you want to indicate that more could be said on the subject, eg "But that's another story…".

double-decker bus   Not double-deck.

drink driving   Not drunk driving. Court reports should include the measurements and the relevant legal limit: 80 milligrams of alcohol in 100 millilitres of blood; 35 micrograms of alcohol in 100 millilitres of breath; or 107 milligrams of alcohol in 100 millilitres of urine.

E

earring   No hyphen.

Earth   This planet's name takes an upper case E.

east   Lower case e if it is a description (east Leeds) or a direction (head east), but upper case E if it is the name of a region or a county (the North-East).

E.coli   Upper case E, lower case c, with a full stop and no space.

e-commerce   Hyphenated, lower case.

ecstasy   Lower case. Write Es only if you are quoting somebody.

Edinburgh   Not borough. *See also Middlesbrough and Scarborough.*

eg   Means for example. Lower case, no full stops.

email   No hyphen.

enclose   Not inclose.

enormity   Monstrous wickedness. Do not use to mean very big.

euro   Lower case for the currency.

exclamation marks   Known in the trade as "screamers", these are found by the dozen in the work of amateur journalists and editors of parish newsletters. They should generally be avoided except in titles, when quoting somebody shouting at the top of their voice, or when someone genuinely exclaims ("Ouch!"). They should certainly not be used to signal that something is supposed to be funny! Ha ha ha!!!!

exhaustive   Means comprehensive, but is often confused with *exhausted*, meaning tired.

expense   Not expence.

eyewitness   One word, but what's wrong with witness?

F

fairytale   One word.

fast food   Two words, no hyphen.

fewer   Means smaller in number, eg fewer hours of sunshine, fewer people. Should not be confused with *less*, which means to a smaller degree, eg less sunshine, less money.

fireman   Prefer firefighter.

first, second   Not firstly, secondly.

first aid   Lower case.

flaunt   Means to show off or display something, but is often confused with *flout*, meaning to disobey contemptuously.

focused   Prefer to focussed.

foot and mouth disease   Lower case, no hyphens.

fulsome   Means excessive or insincere, so *fulsome praise* means excessive praise rather than generous praise. Often misused.

G

GCSE, GCSEs   Upper case, no full stops, and the plural takes a lower case s.

general election   Lower case.

gentlemen's agreement   Not gentleman's agreement. But *verbal agreement* might be less sexist, unless you are referring specifically to gentlemen.

getaway   One word (as in getaway car).

God   Upper case if you are using it as a name, lower case for gods in general.

government   Lower case.

government departments   Prefer upper case for formal names, like this: Department for Environment, Food and Rural Affairs; Ministry of Justice. Use lower case for descriptions, as in environment department or justice ministry.

graffiti   Two ffs, one t.

green belt   Two words, lower case, no hyphen.

green paper   Lower case.

greenfield   Prefer one word.

Greens   Upper case for the Green party, lower case for the wider green movement and for the food that you should eat up.

gunman   One word.

Gypsy   Upper case. Prefer to Gipsy.

H

half   Prefer half-a-dozen, half-past, half-price, halfway, two-and-a-half.

hardcore   One word.

headteacher   Prefer one word.

heaven/hell   Both lower case.

height   Most UK newsrooms still give people's heights in feet and inches (6ft 1in) but usually put other heights (eg buildings) in metres (12.25m) or centimetres (25cm).

hello   Not hallo or hullo.

heyday   Not hayday or heydey.

hiccup   Not hiccough.

high street   Lower case if referring to general shopping but upper case if it is the name of an actual street.

hijack   One word.

his, hers   No apostrophe

hi-tech   Hyphenated. Probably also a bit of a cliché now.

hitman   One word.

housewife   Unless you are reporting on somebody who has married a house, find a better description.

humour   Not humor.

hyphens   Many words begin life as two words, become hyphenated, and eventually become one word – but rushing in too soon can create confusion. Check individual entries and in other cases be guided by current media practice, by pronunciation, and by the need for clarity.

I

ie   Means that is to say. Lower case, no full stops.

in order to   An over-used phrase usually best avoided.

income support, income tax   Lower case.

infinitives   Avoid split infinitives when they may confuse or sound inelegant. But, as Raymond Chandler told one of his editors: "When I split an infinitive, God damn it, I split it so it will stay split" (Chandler, 1984: 77).

inner-city   Normally hyphenated.

inquests   A coroner *records* a verdict. A coroner's jury *returns* a verdict.

inquiry, inquiries   Prefer to enquiry, enquiries.

internet   Lower case.

ise   Prefer to ize, eg organise.

its, it's   There is no apostrophe in the phrase *its death*, meaning the dog's death, just as there is no apostrophe in the phrase *her death*. The apostrophe is introduced when *it's* is short for *it is*. It's that simple.

J

jack russell   Lower case for the dog (but upper case for the wicketkeeper).

jail   Prefer to gaol.

jibe   Not gibe.

jobcentre, jobseeker's allowance   Lower case.

judges   Full name and title for the first mention, eg *Judge Roger Scott*; then *Judge Scott* or *the judge*. High Court judges are known as Justice, as in *Mr Justice Henriques*; then *the judge* or the full version – not Judge Henriques. Recorders (part-time judges) are known as *the recorder Mrs Mary Smith*. Full-time magistrates who used to be known as stipendiary magistrates are now district judges (magistrates courts).

junior   Abbreviate to Jr without a full stop.

K

kick-off   Normally hyphenated.

kilogram, kilometre, kilowatt   Abbreviate as kg, km, kw.

knockout   Prefer one word.

Koran   Upper case.

L

Labour party   Upper case L, lower case p. Subsequent mentions: Labour. Both are singular.

labour   Not labor.

lamp-post   Hyphenated.

landmine   One word.

lay, lie   He was *laying* the table while she was *lying* on the bed.

layby   One word.

lead, led   Celtic *lead* the table now, but Rangers *led* at the start of the season.

less Means to a smaller degree, eg less sunshine, less money. Should not be confused with *fewer*, which means smaller in number, eg fewer hours of sunshine, fewer people.

liaison Not liason.

Liberal Democrats Upper case L and D. She is a Liberal Democrat (singular). She is a member of the Liberal Democrats (plural). May also be abbreviated to Lib Dems.

licence You need to buy a TV licence (noun). You will then be *licensed* (verb) to own a TV.

linchpin Prefer to lynchpin.

lists Introduce a list with a colon: separate elements with semicolons; end with a full stop.

literally I'll literally explode if I see another example of this word being used inappropriately.

Lloyds Bank No apostrophe.

loathe A verb meaning to hate, not to be confused with loth, meaning reluctant.

Lord's Note the apostrophe in the name of the cricket ground.

lottery Lower case.

lovable Prefer to loveable.

M

McDonald's Upper case M and D, plus an apostrophe.

mankind Use only if you intend to exclude females, otherwise use humankind, humanity, or people.

Marks & Spencer Subsequently M&S.

Mayor Upper case when referring to a particular person (eg "London Mayor Boris Johnson"), but lower case when referring to the job of mayor in general.

measurements For long distances, use miles; for people's heights, use feet and inches; for people's weights, use stones and pounds; for drinks, use pints; otherwise, use metric measurements. In time we will no doubt switch fully to metric measurements as advocated in an informative guide produced by the UK Metric Association (2002), but that time does not seem to have arrived yet.

media Plural (the media *are*), not singular (the media *is*).

medieval Prefer to mediaeval

memento Not momento.

mentally handicapped Do not use. Prefer person "with learning disabilities".

mentally ill Refer to "mentally ill people" or someone "with mental illness" rather than to "the mentally ill".

mic Abbreviation for microphone. Prefer to mike.

midday One word, no hyphen.

Middlesbrough Not borough. *See also Edinburgh and Scarborough.*

midweek One word.

mileage Not milage.

million One thousand thousands. Write in full (£1.4 million) except in headlines (£1.4m).

miniskirt One word.

minuscule Not miniscule.

misuse One word, no hyphen.

Morrisons Not Morrison's.

Mosques Full name, upper case, eg Drummond Road Mosque. Then: the mosque.

mph Lower case, no full stops, as in 20mph.

MPs No apostrophe.

Miss, Mr, Mrs, Ms   Courtesy titles are now usually used only for subsequent mentions in news reports, so John Smith becomes Mr Smith after the first time. The exception is court reporting, for which many organisations refer to defendants by their surname alone (Smith) while others use that discourtesy only for those who have been found guilty.

Muslim   Prefer to Moslem.

N

names   Always check the spelling and use both first and family name on first mention. Do not use initials except in those rare circumstances where somebody famous is known by their initials (eg OJ Simpson), in which case there are no full stops.

national lottery   Lower case.

nationwide   One word.

Nazism   Not Naziism.

nearby   One word.

nightclub   One word.

no one   Two words.

north   Lower case n if it is a description (north Leeds) or a direction (head north), but upper case N if it is the name of a county or a region (North Yorkshire, the North-East).

north–south divide   Lower case, one hyphen (en-rule).

numbers   One to nine inclusive should be spelled out; 10 to 999,999 should be given in numbers, with commas to mark thousands; then 2 million, 4.5 billion. Exceptions: speeds will be expressed in numbers, eg 5mph; temperatures take numbers, eg 30C (85F); sports scores will have numbers, eg 2–1; but numbers at the beginning of a sentence will normally be spelled out, eg "Seventeen England fans were arrested last night…"

O

off-licence   Hyphenated.

Ofsted, Ofcom   Just an upper case O.

oh!   Not O!

OK   OK is OK; okay is not.

O-levels   Note the lower case l and the hyphen.

online   One word.

P

parliament   Lower case.

passerby   One word. Plural: passersby.

pensioner   Not OAP.

per   Prefer *£10,000 a year* to *per year* or *per annum*.

per cent   Some prefer %, percent or pc.

persuade   *See convince.*

phone   No apostrophe.

place names   Use an official website, an atlas, a gazetteer or an A–Z to check spellings. Never guess or assume.

play-off   Prefer two words, hyphenated.

plc   Lower case.

police   South Yorkshire Police, then the police. Also lower case for the police in general. Note that police are plural, while police force (or service) is singular, so "police *are* investigating…" but "the South Yorkshire force *is* short of money". Police ranks should be abbreviated as follows: Chief Superintendent (Chief Supt); Superintendent (Supt); Chief Inspector (Chief Insp); Inspector (Insp); Detective Inspector (Det Insp); Detective Sergeant (Det Sgt); Sergeant (Sgt); Detective Constable (DC); Constable (PC). Do not use WPC. Do not abbreviate Chief Constable, Deputy Chief

Constable or Assistant Chief Constable – write it in full at first, then Mr or Ms.

postgraduate   One word.

postmodern   One word, lower case.

post mortem   Lower case, two words, no hyphen; and you should always refer to a *post mortem examination*.

Prime Minister   Upper case P and M.

principal   The first in rank or importance, who may or may not have *principles*.

prodigal   Means recklessly wasteful, not simply someone who returns.

programme   Not program, unless it is a computer program.

prostitutes   Not vice-girls, please.

protester   Prefer to protestor.

Q

queuing   Not queueing.

quotes   As a guideline, use double quote marks unless there is a quote within a quote, which should have single quote marks; but note that many magazines in particular do the opposite. If a quote runs over more than one paragraph, open each paragraph with quote marks but close them only once, at the end of the full quote. Punctuation marks such as commas and full stops normally come inside quote marks when a full sentence is quoted but outside if just a phrase or partial sentence is quoted.

R

refute   Means to disprove, not to deny.

reported speech   Should be reported in the past tense.

restaurateur   Not restauranteur.

reviews   Always give full details of title, venue, when the run ends and so on, including certificates for films.

ring-road   Prefer lower case, hyphenated. Also: inner ring-road and outer ring-road.

robbery   Means theft using force or the threat of force, and should not be confused with theft in other circumstances or with burglary.

rock'n'roll   One word with two apostrophes.

Rolls-Royce   Upper case, hyphenated.

Royal Air Force   Prefer upper case, then the RAF. RAF ranks are abbreviated as follows: Group Captain (Group Capt); Wing Commander (Wing Cmdr); Squadron Leader (Sqn Ldr); Flight Lieutenant (Flight Lt); Warrant Officer (WO); Flight Sergeant (Flight Sgt); Sergeant (Sgt); Corporal (Cpl); Leading Aircraftman (LAC). Do not abbreviate Marshal of the Royal Air Force, Air Chief Marshal, Air Vice Marshal, Flying Officer, or Pilot Officer.

Royal Navy   Prefer upper case, then the Navy. Naval ranks are abbreviated as follows: Lieutenant Commander (Lt Cmdr); Lieutenant (Lt); Sub Lieutenant (Sub Lt); Commissioned Warrant Officer (CWO); Warrant Officer (WO); Chief Petty Officer (CPO); Petty Officer (PO); Leading Seaman (LS); Able Seaman (AS); Ordinary Seaman (OS). Do not abbreviate Admiral, Vice Admiral, Rear Admiral, Commodore, Captain, Commander or Midshipman.

rugby   Where relevant, distinguish between rugby league and rugby union. Use of the term *rugger* should probably be a sacking offence.

S

Safeway   Not Safeway's.

Sainsbury's   Not Sainsbury.

Scarborough   *See also Edinburgh and Middlesbrough.*

schizophrenia   This is a complicated illness – do not use it lazily to mean "in two minds".

school names   As in Bracken Edge primary school.

scrapheap   One word.

seasons   As in autumn, winter and so on, lower case.

Secretaries of State   Prefer upper case titles, as in *Foreign Secretary David Miliband*, but the trend is for the caps to go.

senior   Abbreviate to Sr without a full stop.

September 11   Preferred to 11th or 9/11.

shear, sheer   It will be *sheer* luck if you manage to *shear* the wool off that sheep.

Siamese twins   Prefer conjoined twins.

sit, sat   He was *sitting* on the left until the teacher *sat* him in the middle. You may write that he sat on the left; do not write that he *was* sat on the left, unless by a third party.

soccer   This term should be banned because, in the UK at least, it is hated by most people with an interest in it. Say *football* instead.

south   Lower case s if it is a description (south Leeds) or a direction (head south), but upper case S if it is the name of a region or a county (the South-West or South Yorkshire).

spokesman, spokeswoman   The former if it is a man, the latter if it is a woman, and spokesperson if it is neither (eg an emailed statement).

standing, stood   She was *standing* at the back until the photographer *stood* her at the front. You may write that she stood at the back; do not write that she *was* stood at the back, unless by a third party.

stationary, stationery   With an *a* it means not moving, with an *e* it means writing materials (think "e for envelope").

streetwise   One word.

swearwords   Swearwords can offend many people for little purpose, especially outside direct quotes. Stop and think before using, and be aware that different publications can have *very* different attitudes.

T

targeted   Not targetted.

taskforce   One word.

temperatures   Prefer celsius with fahrenheit in brackets: 7C (45F).

Tesco   Not Tesco's.

that or which?   That defines, which informs. This is the style guide *that* is published in my book. This book, *which* is published by Sage, includes a style guide.

theirs   No apostrophe.

times   Use am and pm, not hundred hours. Do not write 12 noon or 12 midnight because what other noon or midnight are there? Just noon and midnight will suffice.

tonne   Prefer to ton unless instructed otherwise, but be aware that they are different. A tonne (1t) is 1,000kg or 2,204.62lb; a ton is 2,240lb.

trademarks™   Take great care with these, and use an alternative unless you mean the specific product in question. So, if you mean ballpoint pen, don't write Biro.

trillion   A thousand billion; that is, a million million.

tsar   Not czar.

T-shirt   Prefer to tee-shirt.

U

under way   That *under way* should be written as two words was drummed into journalists of a certain vintage, which means that many of us get irrationally annoyed when we see it reduced to one word. I have no idea why, to be honest, but there you go: you have been warned.

unique   Something is either unique or it is not. It cannot be very unique.

universities   Like this: Leeds Metropolitan University or the University of Sheffield.

V

Valentine's day   Prefer upper case V, lower case d, and note the apostrophe.

VAT   Upper case, no need to spell out.

versus   Prefer a lower case v for Warrington Wolves v Leeds Rhinos. Not vs.

W

Wall's   Note the apostrophe.

Wal-Mart   Note the hyphen.

wander, wonder   You may *wander* from place to place while others *wonder* why you don't settle down.

war   Prefer lower case, eg Iraq war, apart from the First World War and Second World War.

web, website, world wide web   All lower case.

weights   A common rule is to still give people's weights in stones and pounds (12st 3lb) even if other weights in tonnes (17t), kilograms (36kg), grams (75g) or milligrams (12mg).

welfare state   Lower case.

west   Lower case w if it is a description (west Leeds) or a direction (head west), but upper case

W if it is the name of a region or a county (the North-West, West Yorkshire).

whatsoever   One word.

wheelchair-bound   Few people are strapped into a wheelchair for 24 hours a day, so this should be banned in favour of saying someone has to *use a wheelchair*, is a *wheelchair user*, or was *in a wheelchair*.

whereabouts   Are plural.

whilst   Prefer *while*.

whiskey, whisky   *Whiskey* is for Irish and *whisky* for Scotch.

withhold   Not withold.

workmen   Prefer workers unless you are describing a specific group of workers who were indeed all men.

World Trade Centre   Not Center.

wrongdoing   One word.

X

x-ray   Lower case, hyphenated.

Y

yo-yo   Lower case, hyphenated.

yorkshire pudding, yorkshire terrier   Lower case.

yours   No apostrophe.

Z

zero   Plural zeros, not zeroes.

zigzag   One word, no hyphen.

▪ ▪ Summary ▪

All news organisations have rules governing style, whether or not such rules are codified in written guides. Their purpose goes beyond minimising mistakes in spelling, grammar and vocabulary to ensuring consistency *within* outlets and differentiation *between* outlets. The most common style in UK journalism is based on the plain style advocated by George Orwell. It has been claimed that style is not neutral and that stylistic choices and presentational formats can have ideological implications by reducing openings for critical voices. The rejection of such rules can be seen as stylistically and ideologically challenging or transgressive. The plain style of news reporting draws attention away from itself as language, leading to suggestions that it purports to be unmediated truth rather than a representation.

▪ Questions ▪

What is the point of house style?

Where does house style come from?

Have you noticed changes in style over time?

Are words never neutral?

Do style guides privilege some social groups over others?

▪ ▪ Further reading ▪

The classic practitioner text on newspaper style probably remains Harold Evans' (2000) *Essential English for Journalists, Editors and Writers*. Although slightly whiskery even in its revised edition – but not as dated as its original title of *Newsman's English* – it remains full of good advice on essentials such as active writing and wasteful words. For a useful chapter on broadcasting style, see Boyd (2001), while Hicks (2007), Hicks et al. (1999) and McKane (2006) offer good general advice and Waterhouse (1993 and 1994) is always worth reading on the subject of writing. House style is discussed further in Hicks and Holmes (2002), which also includes a brief style guide containing some interesting differences from and similarities to the one used in this chapter. Fowler (1983) is a handy companion for any journalist, along with a decent dictionary and possibly an occasional visit to the website of the Plain English Campaign at: www.plainenglish.co.uk.

Style guides themselves can increasingly be found online. See the *Telegraph* version at: http://www.telegraph.co.uk/news/main.jhtml?xml=/news/exclusions/ stylebook/nosplit/SBintrostyle.xml; the *Economist* one is located at: http:// www.economist.com/research/StyleGuide/index.cfm; the *Guardian* style guide, which is also published in book form, can be viewed online at: http://www.guardian.co.uk/styleguide; and the guide for BBC radio news is at: http://news.bbc.co.uk/1/hi/programmes/radio_newsroom/1099302.stm. As with the *Guardian* (Marsh, 2007), the *Times* (Austin, 2003) and *Economist* (2008) are among those publications which have published their style guides in book form.

For critical reflection on – and academic study of – the language of journalism, the best places to start are probably Fowler (1991), Bell (1991), Richardson (2006) and Conboy (2007). See also a special issue of *Journalism Studies* (Vol 9, No 2, April 2008) on language and journalism. Deborah Cameron's research paper, "Style policy and style politics", remains a rare example of journalists' style guides being subjected to the kind of academic scrutiny usually reserved for journalists' outputs (Cameron, 1996).

Finally, Graeme Whitfield of the *Newcastle Journal* has initiated an online Journalese–English Dictionary, to which readers are invited to contribute suggestions. You should be able to find it at: http://blogcentral.journallive. co.uk/2008/02/journaleseenglish_dictionary_f.html.

Sources for soundbites

Orwell, 1946b: 156; *Guardian*, September 28 2007; Evans, 2000: 15; Waterhouse, 1994: 143; Hart-Davis, 1990: 245; *The Inky Path*, Bedford, 1997: 148; Marr, www.plainenglish.co.uk; Hodge and Kress, 1993: 161.

thirteen

conclusion: the challenge for journalism

In his book *The Invention of Journalism*, the sociologist Jean Chalaby argues that journalists have little interest in informing or educating people about the society in which we live. Instead, journalists "bypass the social dimension of individuals, address their fantasies and reconstruct a world of illusions around their readers' dreams" (Chalaby, 1998: 193). Few critical observers would deny that there is an element of the above going on in journalism, not only at the more fanciful end of the market exemplified by splashes such as WORLD WAR 2 BOMBER FOUND ON MOON, once brought to you by the *Sunday Sport*, FREDDIE STARR ATE MY HAMSTER by the *Sun*, or 45 MINUTES FROM ATTACK, courtesy of the *Evening Standard*. But is that the whole picture? We have heard from many journalists in the preceding twelve chapters of this book and we have seen something of the good and bad of journalism – some of its principles and practices – at work in the real world. One thing that should have become apparent by now is that, rather like academics, perhaps, journalists are not all the same.

In the process of looking at journalists at work, we have considered a range of influences that impact on their practice. Influences do not necessarily have to be thought of negatively, as **constraints**. Some influences may be interpreted as positive, even liberating. For example, although the codes of conduct produced by the National Union of Journalists, the Press Complaints Commission and the BBC can certainly be seen as constraining the behaviour of journalists in some ways, such codes may also help journalists to *resist* what they see as unethical behaviour and to *defend* journalistic integrity (Harcup, 2002a, 2002b and 2007). As the novelist and journalist

Constraints

In Chapter 2 we came across David Randall's suggested journalistic disclaimer. Having heard a bit more about the principles and practice of journalism, perhaps we might now rewrite it along the following lines:

> This product has been produced by underpaid and overworked journalists who were recruited from a small section of the population before being socialised into the routines and news values of journalism. Much of the material originated from press officers and public relations professionals working on behalf of well-resourced organisations. Many news items were selected to meet the perceived interests of audiences thought to be most desirable to our advertisers. Stories were produced against the clock and things may have changed since then. Stories have been made to fit largely arbitrary word or time limits determined by decisions on format, design and production. In the processes of research, writing and editing, stories may have been simplified and made more dramatic. The sources consulted may not have known the full story and/or may have had their own interests to promote, and some of the journalists may have been concerned not to jeopardise relations with some sources. The journalists involved may have their own opinions, and these opinions may or may not have influenced the finished product. The journalists may also have been influenced in story selection and construction by the attitudes of their proprietors, editors and colleagues. They will have been mindful of legal constraints and regulatory rules, knowing how far things can be pushed and who is most likely to complain or take legal action. They will also have been aware of what will most impress current and prospective employers. By the time you read this, the journalists may have lost interest in many of these stories and will probably have moved on to a fresh selection.

It's become a bit long now, so we could sub it down to:

> *Don't believe everything you read.*

It could go next to the corrections column.

HG Wells put it in a message to his fellow NUJ members back in 1922:

> We affect opinion and public and private life profoundly, and we need to cherish any scrap of independence we possess and can secure. We are not mere hirelings; our work is creative and responsible work. The activities of rich adventurers in buying, and directing the policy of, groups of newspapers is a grave public danger. A free-spirited, well-paid, and well-organised profession of journalism is our only protection against the danger. (Quoted in Mansfield, 1943: 518)

Ethical responsibility

If journalists are not to be the "mere hirelings" of the wealthy, as Wells put it, and if we are to avoid being the purveyors of fantasy described by Chalaby, then we must take seriously our commitment to independent-minded observation, investigation, verification, scrutiny, accuracy and fairness in addition to honing an ability to communicate clearly and entertainingly. Jake Lynch argues that the challenge facing journalists is to take seriously the "ethic of responsibility" that goes with the job, particularly in this era of instantaneous mass communication. He believes that an emphasis on entertainment-driven "news-lite" can have damaging consequences both for our work and for the world on which we report:

> In this information age, journalists are not disconnected observers but *actual participants* in the way communities and societies understand each other and the way parties wage conflict. ... We live in a media-savvy world. There's no way of knowing that what journalists are seeing or hearing would have happened the same way – if at all – if no press was present. This means that policies are born with a media strategy built in. There's nothing pejorative in that, it's a condition of modern life; but it closes the circle of cause and effect between journalist and source. The only way anyone can possibly calculate journalists' likely response to what they do is from their experience of previous reporting. Every time facts get reported, it adds to the collective understanding of how similar facts will likely be reported in future.

Informing citizens

As introduced in Chapter 1, the concept of a space in which informed citizens can engage in critical discussion and reflection – a public sphere – is an ideal against which journalism has come to be measured and is often found to be wanting: "Analysts and critics may dispute the extent to which Britain *has* a properly functioning 'public sphere'... but all agree that such a space *should* exist, and that the media are at its core" (McNair, 2000: 1, first emphasis in original, second is mine). The concept of the public sphere is associated with the writings of Jürgen Habermas, who – from a 20th century vantage point – looked back on late 17th and early 18th-century Britain and identified "the advent of a public sphere of reasoned discourses circulating in the political realm independently of both the Crown and Parliament" (Allan, 1997: 298). Although this public sphere was a conceptual space, it also had physical manifestations, for example in the coffee houses of London where this "reasoned discourse" would take place, albeit among a limited section of the (male) population. Habermas also points to the existence of multiple or competing public spheres, including a "plebian public sphere" with its own radical forms of alternative media (Habermas, 1989: xviii, 425, 430; and, 1992: 425–427; see also Downing et al., 2001: 27–33; and Harcup, 2003).

Yet the idea of journalism serving an informed citizenry is undermined by a tendency to treat audiences as little more than consumers, argues Granville Williams. He locates this as one of a series of key oppositions, signifying very different ways of viewing the world (see *Box 13.1*).

For Williams, who is a journalist and an academic as well as one of the brains behind the Campaign for Press and Broadcasting Freedom, the competing world views represented in *Box 13.1* impact on journalism in the following ways:

> There are basically two views about the function of the mass media in society. One puts a commercial value on everything, turning citizens into consumers; children into vulnerable merchandising targets via video games, magazines, film and television; and information into "infotainment". ... Such a view assigns the media merely the role of a commodity, to be manufactured and assessed by market criteria. ... Counterposed to this is a view of the media as a liberating force for human enlightenment and progress, informing, entertaining, nurturing

Box 13.1

Citizens or consumers? Contrasting ways of conceptualising the media audience and society, according to Granville Williams (1996: 2–3)

- Society v Market
- Citizen v Consumer
- Need v Want
- Value v Price
- Community v Globalism
- Regulation v Efficiency

That understanding then informs people's behaviour. This is the feedback loop. *It means every journalist bears some unknowable share of the responsibility for what happens next.* (Lynch, 2002, my emphasis)

And so we return to the point made in Chapter 1: journalism is not simply an interesting job; journalism *matters* because it informs discussion in the public sphere. This social role in *informing citizens* means that a good journalist will be a *reflective practitioner* and will be aware that he or she is not simply an entertainer or a teller of stories. Reflection is required because skills alone "are not enough" (de Burgh, 2003: 110).

Despite all the constraints discussed in this book, and despite the fact that most journalists work for monolithic and/or commercial organisations, journalists retain some agency. The actions of journalists, individually and collectively, can make a difference to journalistic outputs and thereby, as Wells argued, can make a difference to people's lives. Journalists make choices every day: what stories to cover, which sources to consult, whose door to knock on, what questions to ask, who to believe, what angles to take, what quotes to use, how much context to include, what words to use, what pictures to use, what to leave out, and so on. They may not be entirely free choices, they are not taken in a vacuum, and sometimes they will be orders from on high, but for the most part

creative talent and being financially and editorially independent from powerful vested commercial or political interests. At the heart of this view is a respect for diversity and pluralism, and a recognition that unchecked media power can undermine democracy. (Williams, 1996: 2–3)

His words echo those of US broadcast journalist Ed Murrow, who famously told the 1958 convention of the Radio-Television News Directors Association in Chicago:

Our history will be what we make it. And if there are any historians about 50 or 100 years from now, and there should be preserved the kinescopes for one week of all three networks, they will find there recorded in black and white, or colour, evidence of decadence, escapism and insulation from the realities of the world in which we live. … In this kind of complex and confusing world, you can't tell very much about the why of the news in broadcasts where only three minutes is available for news. … I am frightened by the imbalance, the constant striving to reach the largest possible audience for everything, by the absence of a sustained study of the state of the nation. Heywood Broun once said, "No body politic is healthy until it begins to itch". I would like television to produce some itching pills rather than this endless outpouring of tranquillisers. It can be done. Maybe it won't be, but it could. … This instrument can teach, it can illuminate; yes, and it can even inspire. But it can do so only to the extent that humans are determined to use it to those ends. Otherwise it is merely wires and lights in a box. There is a great and perhaps decisive battle to be fought against ignorance, intolerance and indifference. (Murrow, 1958)

Half a century on, that battle continues.

they still involve *choices*; and the journalist whose choices are not anchored in some sense of ethical responsibility may simply be blown this way and that by prevailing economic and political winds. As Lynette Sheridan Burns writes:

> Professional integrity is not something you have when you are feeling a bit down at the end of a long week. It is a state of mindfulness that you bring to everything you write, no matter how humble the topic. ... Put simply, given the power that you have to do good or harm by virtue of the decisions you make, under pressure each day, the least you can do is think about it. (Sheridan Burns, 2002: 11)

> ❛ It's handy to have as many skills as you can. ❜
> – *Lindsay Eastwood.*

Not just to *think* about it but also to *talk* about it and even occasionally to *do something* about it (Harcup, 2002a, 2002b and 2007).

Journalism as conversation?

One of the things that some journalists – and others – are doing about it is to more openly discuss stories as they develop and to engage in multidimensional conversations with the audience – blurring or even, according to some, abolishing the distinction between the sender and receiver of messages. In its relatively short life, the phenomenon of blogging – a sort of online discussion with links – has already suggested some interesting answers to the communication question posed in Chapter 1 of this book: Who says what to whom, through what channel and with what effect? Although it must be remembered that not everyone is online – and not everyone who is online wishes to post comments – blogging is said to have "reshaped globalised communications and in doing so has demanded that journalists re-evaluate and reform their practices" (Knight, 2008: 118). Together with user-generated content, blogging is sometimes referred to as *citizen journalism*.

The reflective practitioner

If journalists are not to absolve themselves of all social responsibilities then they must become reflective practitioners, argues Sheridan Burns (2002: 11). Journalists should reflect critically on what they do, because "a journalist who is conscious of and understands the active decisions that make up daily practice is best prepared to negotiate the challenges involved" (Sheridan Burns, 2002: 11). That does not mean taking time off and sitting back in leisurely contemplation; rather, it means "an active commitment in journalists to scrutinise their own actions, exposing the processes and underlying values in their work *while* they are doing it" (Sheridan Burns, 2002: 41–44, emphasis in original). Of course, a concept such as the reflective practitioner presupposes that journalists have both the individual capacity to reflect upon their own practice and sufficient room to manoeuvre to effect some change in their practice. For Sarah Niblock, a reflective journalist is "one who can make confident editorial judgements that are informed by a strong awareness of their role in society. Consequently, they can anticipate and effectively negotiate a dynamic and evolving context for journalism production and reception" (Niblock, 2007: 26).

Similarly, Pat Aufderheide (2002: 14) argues that there is a need to cultivate "a more self-aware journalistic culture". Writing in the context of US television after the attacks on the World Trade Centre in 2001, Aufderheide argues that journalists need "time, money and imagination to experiment with the kind of reporting that gives viewers an understanding of large conflicts and issues in the world, before they become the stuff of catastrophe", adding:

> They need ways to bring other voices into their coverage, and to explain the implications and differing readings of US government behaviour. They need a relationship with viewers that permits them to introduce disturbing and conflicting perspectives, to go beyond the two masks of sentimental patriotism and coolly objective fact-vending. (Aufderheide, 2002: 12–13)

It could be argued that *all* journalism would benefit from such a willingness to report conflicting perspectives, to offer differing readings, to challenge the common sense of audiences and journalists alike, and

As a journalist whose entire career has been online, Jemima Kiss says: "I get very tired of the discussion about the definitions of what a blogger is, what a journalist is and what a blogging journalist is." For Kiss, the purpose of journalism remains "to inform and educate, to hold people in authority to account, to document and interpret development and change"; blogging is merely one way of making such material available, but a more interactive way. She explains:

> Blogging is primarily just a publishing system – it was born of the web and suits it perfectly – easy to browse, in reverse chronological order and easily indexed and linkable. Blogs work just as well for news as they do for opinion. In terms of how blog culture has developed, blogging demands a strong individual voice, but using a personality works well to counter the impersonal nature of the internet. Profile pictures and names also help to improve the relationship between a blogger and readers to some extent. I think that communication is now also more central to news and opinion than it has ever been, because platforms are now more easily two-way.

> I have faith in most people to be able to discern wheat from chaff, so I think the role of writers and editors will remain important, but I do think that once the industry eventually gets over its historical snobbery of involving the public, there is enormous potential in collaborative journalism between news sites and readers.

At MEN Media Sarah Hartley writes two blogs, one about food and one about online and tech issues; a blog about blogs, in other words. Both attract a healthy traffic in users' comments, to which Hartley will often post a response. It can sometimes get heated – and some posters can be quite abusive – but she feels: "If you're going to put yourself out there and say, 'I know about this topic', you've got to be prepared to be taken to task about it." As someone who began her career in newspapers and who now works in a converged media environment incorporating text, video and audio delivered via print, broadcasting and online, she has fully embraced blogging:

> ❛ I see myself as a reporter rather than a writer. ❜
> – Jane Merrick.

to think twice before making assumptions about who "we" and "us" might be. In short, by working both sides of the street.

Citizen journalism

The twin phenomena of user-generated content and blogging are often referred to as "citizen journalism", seen as part of the more general blurring of boundaries between journalist and audience – sender and receiver – facilitated by the internet. Although it can be difficult to discern what exactly practices such as sending in pictures taken on mobile phones or creating some of the more self-obsessed blogs have to do with either citizenship or journalism, many bloggers do concern themselves with journalistic attributes such as reporting and verification. Andrew Sullivan describes blogging as "peer-to-peer journalism", more like a 24-hour broadcast than "a fixed piece of written journalism". When readers of his blog began responding not merely with opinions but also with fresh information, he saw that the blog's advantage over traditional one-way journalism was that it could "marshal the knowledge and resources of thousands, rather than the few" (Sullivan, 2002). For Hall, this potential passing of control from journalists to users holds out the promise – or threat – that journalists will lose their role as gatekeeper (Hall, 2001: 53). Much theorising on the subject of the internet goes along with Hall in arguing that everything has changed, while others counter that nothing fundamental has changed. For Jackie Harrison: "[T]he availability of greater sources of news does not guarantee an engaged or enlightened citizenry (any more than anything else does), and earlier claims to this effect about the internet and the digital citizen now seem exaggerated" (Harrison, 2006: 206).

As Nick Stevenson points out, on the one hand we have the "communicative possibilities that are suggested by horizontally rather than vertically organised information structures"; on the other hand, it is argued that new technologies are part of "the accumulation of capital, commodification and the disappearance of public space" (Stevenson, 2002: 184). In other words, the most important issue is not technology itself but the uses to which it is put, and such uses are unlikely to be uniform. While the internet can be used

What you're trying to do with a blog is to conduct a conversation. We've tried to encourage staff to get into them and experiment with them as much as anything, and if they're into something like local politics or Bollywood or even the Eurovision Song Contest, they tend to write more passionately about it. Sometimes a blog will be the start of a conversation about finding something out, asking people to join in, asking people to give you information. The best blogs should be like that, really. What you're first putting out there isn't the definitive and isn't the history, it's the start of a process. It's all the revisions and the feedback, and the things that come along after, that are probably more important than what you first started with.

A good online journalist now will be able to bring that right round, because it is a never-ending story. You've got no deadline, you've got no bedtime, you just keep on forever. And things can stay online forever. On my food blog, two years ago I wrote about Marmite and I'm still getting feedback and responses to that two years later because some people are only reading it today, so it's a new story to them and they've got something to add to it. It really doesn't end.

Does Hartley's enthusiasm for this new form of communication lead her to believe that all journalism could, or should, end up being more like online journalism, even when not delivered online? She thinks it is already happening:

Probably even those involved aren't noticing it to that extent, it's a slow incremental change, but if I think back even a couple of years ago it was very rare that you'd see at the bottom of a print story, "What do you think about this? Has this ever happened to you?" Now it's very rare not to see that in print. In just a couple of years it's shifted entirely, so I'm sure that will keep on moving.

So all journalism could become more of a conversation? "We haven't got much choice because people don't like just to be shouted at," she says. "They want to take part, so that shift has happened."

> ❝ You have to be really tenacious and thorough, and just not give up. ❞
> – Deborah Wain.

to facilitate a more active citizenship, most people seem content to use it for shopping, entertainment or social networking. Within this context, Manuel Castells argues that, although the "information society" may be a product of post-industrial capitalism, the internet is also capable of enabling the building of networks among oppositional social movements (Stevenson, 2002: 192–195). For Castells, the economy has become organised "around global networks of capital, management, and information, whose access to technological know-how is at the roots of productivity and competitiveness" (Castells, 1996: 471). Yet, within the belly of this beast, "the historical law that where there is domination there is resistance continues to apply", online as much as anywhere else (Castells, 1998: 351). Thus, "communes of resistance" – from anarchists to Zapatistas – are using the internet to further "people's horizontal communication" and to challenge society's dominant voices (Castells, 1997: 358). Arguably at least, then, the production of journalism for such alternative forms of media – from the radical working-class press of the 19th century to the anti-capitalist websites of today – could be seen as having a stronger claim to the title "citizen journalism" than do some of the practices that have been so labelled in recent years.

It cannot be denied, however, that producers of journalism now seem to be more cognisant of the interests and opinions of the audience for journalism. For Sarah Hartley of MEN Media, although the internet age means that a journalist should think of journalism as more of a dialogue than a monologue, it also means retaining a sense of "brand credibility" to make their voice worth listening to among the babble of other voices competing for attention. For Hall, however, it means that journalists should be offering "commentary, fact-checking and inflection" on material that may already be in the public domain, acting as map-makers to help people make sense of everything that's out there online: "The maps contextualise and mediate the sources that they point to but *the interpretation of sources becomes the responsibility of the readers themselves*" (Hall, 2001: 54, my emphasis). Finding a continuing role in such circumstances is one of the many challenges facing journalism.

If journalism *is* becoming more of a conversation, then perhaps the participants need to remember their manners a bit more often. Martin Wainwright of the *Guardian* is a web enthusiast but he is not a fan of abusive and anonymous blog posters:

> Interaction is very good, and it's much easier now to be picked up for making mistakes. Mistakes are built in to daily journalism, and all that matters is that you correct them. But the tone of the comments – some of them you think, "I really would not want to meet these people". They dominate, and I can't understand why they are allowed to be anonymous. You get some blogs that have 300 comments, but when you look it's mainly two people going on and on at each other.

There are other downsides too, according to Abul Taher of the *Sunday Times*:

> The internet is a blessing, as it is a ready tool to find information very quickly to tight deadlines. But it is also having a direct result in newsrooms across Fleet Street, in that jobs are being lost because significant advertising revenue has moved from newspapers to their websites, and newspaper budgets are being squeezed so that extra money can be found to invest in the websites. I feel the internet has not yet had its full impact on newspapers, and it will still be a few more years before we know how newspaper websites and news websites in general have changed people's ways of reading the news. So, at the moment, the newspaper–internet relationship is in a flux, and it's hard to predict how it will pan out.

A sense of curiosity

As always, then, the future is uncertain; and that is part of **the challenge for journalism**. But there is no sign yet of journalism losing its popularity as a career choice for the intelligent, the questioning, the sociable and the articulate. So what words of wisdom do some of our more experienced journalists have for new recruits to journalism?

The challenge for journalism

In journalism, as in so many things, everything has changed and yet nothing has changed. Alan Knight, an Australian journalist-turned-academic, spells out some of the new challenges facing journalism today:

> Journalists were once defined by where they worked; in newspapers, or radio and television stations. The internet promises everyone can be a publisher. But not everyone has the skills or training to be a journalist; defined by their professional practices and codes of ethics. Such journalists will continue to authorise information, providing signposts for discerning audiences. ... Anyone applying professional practices within recognised codes of ethics will be differentiated from most bloggers as well as our friends at Fox News. ... Journalists should be trained to produce fair and accurate stories about their communities, and if journalism educators make ethics and professional practices the core of their courses, journalists should still be the best equipped to deliver such information. If they do so, journalists will adapt to the internet, in the same ways they embraced the telephone, the telegraph and the printing press. (Knight, 2008: 123)

As with the impact of the internet and technological convergence, the extent to which individual journalists retain sufficient agency to *make a difference* is an area of disagreement within journalism studies. Some academic theorists and commentators have been criticised for a tendency to downplay the room for agency in the production of journalism. So, for example, the *political economy* model emphasises the determining role played by economic power and material factors in creating media products. In the view of Peter Golding and Philip Elliott: "News changes very little when the individuals that produce it are changed" (quoted in Curran and Seaton, 1997: 277).

For Jean Chalaby, not only does the news not change much when individual journalists change, but much journalism within commercial media is actually doing the opposite of producing an informed and enlightened citizenry:

> [J]ournalists do not venture beyond what they think are the limits of their readers' cognitive abilities and seek to produce a newspaper without a cognitive gap with the average reader's mind. Newspapers, those reaching a popular audience in particular, may try to influence or even manipulate their readers, but they will never

"All jobs entail compromises of some sort," observes Taher, "and journalism has its share of them too." One of the compromises is that rates of pay can be extremely low, particularly at the beginning. Yet he feels that journalism still looks attractive to many young people today, just as it did to him:

> 'A lot of people go into journalism to make sure the baddies are exposed.'
> – Kevin Peachey.

I was attracted to journalism because I had always wanted to be a writer. Journalism is easily the most widely read type of literature in modern societies, beating novels, books and poetry. There is a huge pleasure from writing a good, well-researched article, and you really do get a unique window into society through journalism. Journalism informs and educates people about the world beyond their own personal experience. It is a good profession, but it is also one where there is very little financial reward unless you are at the top. Money is the biggest problem … and it is especially hard if you have moved to London and are having to pay rent as well as student loans. … I have a lot of friends who have become sick of finding that elusive break and want to do other things in life.

What advice would Taher give to anybody reading this book because they want to become a journalist?

> 'It's a daily ritual of moral and intellectual compromise – it is a good job, but it is hard.'
> – Abul Taher.

Be prepared for hard work and for travel at the drop of a hat. If you have a sense of excitement for the job, then you'll do well. If you are coming into print journalism, then you'll have a feeling that you are entering an industry that is in terminal decline. Don't be discouraged by that – the newspaper industry has been in that state for sometime now.

Brian Whittle feels that "naturally nosy" people make the best reporters: "You want somebody who's nosy, somebody with enthusiasm, somebody who wants to do it more than anything else." Jane Merrick stresses the importance of learning "the basics" such as shorthand and law. She points out that a humble attitude is also an attribute:

attempt to educate them. … As a result, journalists rarely challenge readers' preconceived ideas and prejudices or transcend readers' present state of consciousness. Journalists open no new levels of perception for their readers and do not expand their intellectual horizon. …

[T]he popular media not only put limits to their readers' intellectual horizon but, by making readers unaware of their lack of information, undermine the conditions for the appropriation of further knowledge. With such a relation to knowledge, the commercial popular press could only annihilate the promises of the project of enlightenment … (Chalaby, 1998: 190–191)

That's quite a claim; that far from enlightening citizens with information about society, journalists in fact "deny them knowledge about the world and knowledge about their position in the world" (Chalaby, 1998: 5). But it represents a strand of academic thought that seems to dismiss the possibility that many journalists *do* indeed seek to inform, to educate and even to stretch intellectual horizons, not just of their audiences but sometimes even of themselves. How much leeway do they have to achieve this? Cultural studies theorist Stuart Hall argues that journalists have "relative autonomy from ruling class power in the narrow sense", within certain ideological limits (Hall, 1977: 345–346). But his emphasis is on the "relative" because he argues that – whatever their personal thoughts and wishes – journalists *tend* to reproduce society's prevailing ideology. This is not because of the "conscious intentions and biases" of individual journalists, but as "a function of the discourse and of the logic of social processes", including sourcing strategies that privilege the powerful (Hall, 1982: 88).

Yet individual journalists *do* retain the power to resist the demands of the market and to insist on acting in an ethical manner, even if only by using the ultimate sanction of resigning from their jobs, argues John O'Neill. He adds that the relationship between the "virtues and vices" of journalism can be more fluid than is portrayed in the simplistic depiction of the journalist as either hero or villain:

Many, I suspect, find themselves forced to compromise the constitutive values of journalism, while at the same time insisting that some of the standards be enforced. … Journalists, like other workers, are not totally passive in their attitude to their own faculties. (O'Neill, 1992: 28)

Never think that you know more than the lowest journalist on the newspaper or agency, or wherever you start. Take *everything* on board. There's a balance between giving your newsdesk the confidence that you can do the job, and being level-headed. It's a matter of getting that balance right. Journalists will respect somebody prepared to take it all on board.

For Wainwright, "the best journalists go into situations with open and absorbing minds. The great virtue of a journalist is curiosity – a constant interest in what makes people tick." So what would be the main attributes he would look for in somebody who wants to become a journalist today?

> ‘ The best reporter is somebody who's naturally nosy. ’
> – Brian Whittle.

> ‘ The best journalists go into situations with open and absorbing minds. ’
> – Martin Wainwright.

Well, they haven't changed. Curiosity is the number one, wanting to know what's going on, what's it all about, what is the truth? And with that I would say enthusiasm, which is a general virtue that you look for in all young people. And then I think writing, which also applies to audio and video because you need a script: the ability to tell stories interestingly and coherently. Those are the three things and they haven't changed, but what has changed is that the internet has massively expanded the platforms on which all these things can be presented, which is wonderful. People do still need to be trained, though.

From the perspective of a journalist who has only ever worked online, what advice would Jemima Kiss give to someone wishing to become a journalist?

Blog. Why would anyone who wants to write for a living not platform their work, ideas and commitment by using a free, professional and potentially global publishing network? Also, get out and meet as many people as possible – join the union, go to meetings, go to conferences and talks, meet as many people as possible, always. And the old work experience thing.

Put another way, the agency of individuals may be limited by economic and social structures, but it exists; just as ethical journalists exist (Harcup, 2007). Journalists work in a field that is – or claims to be – constituted by a professional commitment to ethics and truth telling, yet at the same time journalists may be expendable employees expected to produce stories to sell in the marketplace (O'Neill, 1992: 27–28; Harcup, 2002b: 103). Discussion of the agency of journalists – of their ability to make a difference and/or to act in an ethical manner even when working within a commercial and/or bureaucratic operation – needs to take account of the tension between journalists' different identities. Those different identities include being skilled individuals, socially responsible citizens, factors of production at the whim of management, and workers with at least the potential to share a sense of collective identity and even occasionally to speak or act collectively (Harcup, 2002b: 101–114; and 2007). If journalism matters to society, then surely the actions of journalists matter too.

What skills does another journalistic blogger, Sarah Hartley, think the coming generation of journalists will need to develop?

> ❛ Meet as many people as possible, always. ❜
> – *Jemima Kiss.*

You've still got to be able to write. Increasingly, sifting what's important is going to become a key skill. It always was, but is now more so as publishers look to bring in material from lots of different sources, including users, so the ability to be able to spot what's important and bring the best of things to people is going to be where we're going.

As journalists I think our role is going to be, "We're bringing you the best on this subject, wherever that might come from, we've researched it for you, we've brought some kind of judgement to it that you understand because you know what kind of organisation we work for." We're providing that context for people, that brand credibility. You can go on YouTube and have fun, but would you sincerely believe a news story you saw on YouTube? It's going to come down to that in the end. Everything's got a role to play in the mix of things, but your new journalist intake has got to learn that skill of differentiating what's editorially important and what isn't – more so than before, I think.

> ❛ Whatever you see, there's a story behind it. ❜
> – *Paul Foot*

> ❛ It's exciting times to be a trainee journalist, I think. ❜
> – *Sarah Hartley.*

And also, being prepared to experiment with new formats and new audiences, and involve people in what they're doing. When you start on a weekly paper and you've got good contacts, it's only an extension of those core skills of maintaining contacts and everything – just the same, but you might be doing it on Facebook. Maintaining contacts and being able to find good people to contribute, they are essentially the same skills but there are new tools to help you. It's exciting times to be a trainee journalist, I think.

For a last word, I turned to Paul Foot – veteran reporter, investigator and columnist – and asked what advice he had for aspiring young journalists in the 21st century. This is what he said:

I think people should join the NUJ and if there isn't a union where they work they should do their best to try and form one. That's the first thing. The other thing is, don't lose your sense of curiosity or your sense of scepticism.

Understand the way the industry works and do your best to apply yourself against that. The last thing I mean is young people rushing in and telling their editors how to run the world, that's absolutely fatal. There's nothing worse than the arrogant young person – who knows *everything* – going and telling people what to do. Even if they're right, which often they are, that's not the way to behave. That's the way to get sacked. You've got to keep your head, you've got to bite your lip, and you've got to do what you're told a lot of the time. Nine times out of ten it's better to go ahead and do what you are told, but there's a tenth time when it is worth resisting.

The main thing is to keep your sense of independent observation as to what's happening around you, and to try to use what ability you have to get those things into print. Whatever you see, there's a story behind it. There is a truth and there's no doubt there are facts. Facts are facts, you can't bend them.

And that seems to be as good a note as any on which to conclude a book on the principles and practice of journalism. Over to you.

▪▪ Summary ▪

The social role of journalism in informing citizens, and the impact of journalism on people's lives, means that journalists have an ethical responsibility to engage in a process of critical reflection on their practice. Despite the structural forces and constraints that bear down on journalists, individuals and groups of journalists retain elements of choice in their work. In the era of the internet, journalism is said to be moving more in the direction of a conversation than a lecture, yet journalistic skills, such as selection and verification, are still seen as important. Recruits to journalism are advised to learn everything they can from more experienced journalists without ever losing their own sense of curiosity and independent observation.

▪ Questions ▪

Who is journalism for?

What is journalism for?

Where is journalism practised?

When is journalism at its best?

Why are journalists not trusted?

How might journalism develop?

▪▪ Further reading ▪

You could usefully start by reading this book once again and looking up the references and suggestions for further reading contained in each chapter. To delve deeper into the ethical issues raised throughout, see *The Ethical Journalist* (Harcup, 2007), for which a useful companion volume would be Frost (2007). For historical context behind the practice of journalism, Curran and Seaton (2003) and McChesney (2000) offer informative and critical perspectives from the UK and USA respectively, while Andrew Marr's (2005) memoir-cum-history, *My Trade*, is a delight. Roy Greenslade's (2004) *Press Gang* is a useful history of the UK national press from 1945 to 2003, while *Flat Earth News* by Nick Davies (2008) is a bleak and unforgiving attack on many of the practices of today's media.

Sheridan Burns (2002) and Randall (2007) are good places to start for critical reflection on journalism; for discussion of more theoretical perspectives, try Harrison (2006), Zelizer (2004), Allan (2004) or McQuail (2000). An overview of different academic approaches and methods for researching journalism around the world can be found in Loffelholz and Weaver's (2008) *Global Journalism Research*, which includes contributions from active researchers in a range of different countries; and original work by a range of international scholars has been brought together in the *Handbook of Journalism Studies* (Wahl-Jorgensen and Hanitzsch, 2009).

New academic research is published regularly in the peer-reviewed journals *Journalism Studies* (Taylor and Francis), *Journalism Practice* (Taylor and Francis) and *Journalism: Theory, Practice and Criticism* (Sage), while many discussion articles by practitioners can be found in *British Journalism Review* (Sage) and *Press Gazette* (Wilmington). *Free Press*, the journal of the Campaign for Press and Broadcasting Freedom, publishes thought-provoking and critical material on the media in general and journalism in particular, while the views of members of the National Union of Journalists can be found in the union magazine *Journalist*. Tim Gopsill and Greg Neal's (2007) fascinating book *Journalists* traces the first century of the National Union of Journalists; information and advice on journalism training and careers is also available from the NUJ's training website: www.nujtraining.org.uk.

David Randall's (2005) *The Great Reporters* is an enjoyable and admirable introduction to the work of some great reporters, while collections of articles by Paul Foot (2000), Francis Wheen (2002), and Greg Palast (2002) all demonstrate what can be achieved with a combination of journalistic flair, a questioning attitude, and a cantankerous insistence on getting at "the facts". Finally, if you are serious about journalism, don't forget to check relevant websites, to watch/listen to news and current affairs, and to read the papers – every day.

Sources for soundbites

Interviews with the author.

appendix: national union of journalists code of conduct (last updated in 2007)

A journalist:

1. At all times upholds and defends the principle of media freedom, the right of freedom of expression and the right of the public to be informed

2. Strives to ensure that information disseminated is honestly conveyed, accurate and fair

3. Does her/his utmost to correct harmful inaccuracies

4. Differentiates between fact and opinion

5. Obtains material by honest, straightforward and open means, with the exception of investigations that are both overwhelmingly in the public interest and which involve evidence that cannot be obtained by straightforward means

6. Does nothing to intrude into anybody's private life, grief or distress unless justified by overriding consideration of the public interest

7. Protects the identity of sources who supply information in confidence and material gathered in the course of her/his work

8. Resists threats or any other inducements to influence, distort or suppress information

9. Takes no unfair personal advantage of information gained in the course of her/his duties before the information is public knowledge

10. Produces no material likely to lead to hatred or discrimination on the grounds of a person's age, gender, race, colour, creed, legal status, disability, marital status, or sexual orientation

11. Does not by way of statement, voice or appearance endorse by advertisement any commercial product or service save for the promotion of her/his own work or of the medium by which she/he is employed

12. Avoids plagiarism.

Conscience clause

The NUJ believes a journalist has the right to refuse an assignment or be identified as the author of editorial that would break the letter or spirit of the code. The NUJ will fully support any journalist disciplined for asserting her/his right to act according to the code.

The public interest

Problems over media coverage often hinge on the "public interest". The NUJ code of conduct uses the concept as a yardstick to justify publication of sensitive material. This is the NUJ's definition, drawn up by the NUJ Ethics Council:

1. The public interest includes:
   - Detecting or exposing crime or a serious misdemeanour
   - Protecting public health and safety
   - Preventing the public from being misled by some statement or action of an individual or organisation
   - Exposing misuse of public funds or other forms of corruption by public bodies
   - Revealing potential conflicts of interest by those in positions of power and influence
   - Exposing corporate greed
   - Exposing hypocritical behaviour by those holding high office
   - There is a public interest in the freedom of expression itself.

2. In cases involving children, journalists must demonstrate an exceptional public interest to overide the normally paramount interests of the child.

(www.nuj.org.uk)

references and bibliography

Interviews

Unless otherwise indicated in the text, comments by the following are taken from interviews conducted by the author between 2001 and 2008:

Lindsay Eastwood
Paul Foot
Trevor Gibbons
Sarah Hartley
David Helliwell
Jemima Kiss
Jane Merrick
Kevin Peachey
Abul Taher
Deborah Wain
Martin Wainwright
Brian Whittle
Waseem Zakir

Bibliography

ABC (2002) 'National newspaper circulation', Audit Bureau of Circulations monthly report, August 2002, http://www.abc.org.uk/cgi-bin/gen5?runprog=nav/abc&noc=y.

ACPO (2001) *Guide to Meeting the Policing Needs of Asylum Seekers and Refugees*. London: Association of Chief Police Officers.

Adams, Catherine (2001) 'Inside story', *Guardian*, 13 March.

Adams, Sally (1999) 'Writing features', in Wynford Hicks with Sally Adams and Harriett Gilbert, *Writing for Journalists*. London: Routledge, pp. 47–98.

Adams, Sally with Hicks, Wynford (2001) *Interviewing for Journalists*. London: Routledge.

Addicott, Ruth (2002) 'Magazines warned not to ignore financial watchdog', *Press Gazette*, 17 May.

Aitchison, James (1988) *Writing for the Press*. London: Hutchinson.

Allan, Stuart (1997) 'News and the public sphere: towards a history of objectivity and impartiality', in Michael Bromley and Tom O'Malley (eds), *A Journalism Reader*. London: Routledge, pp. 296–329.

Allan, Stuart (1998) '(En)gendering the truth politics of news discourse', in Cynthia Carter, Gill Branston and Stuart Allan (eds), *News, Gender and Power*. London: Routledge, pp. 121–137.

Allan, Stuart (2004) *News Culture*. Maidenhead: Open University Press.

Allan, Stuart (ed) (2005) *Journalism: Critical Issues*. Maidenhead: Open University Press.

Arlidge, John and Cole, Sandra (2001) 'Jon Snow slams ITV's "crazy" cut in news budget', *Observer*, 2 December.

Armitstead, Claire (2002) 'Write the same thing over and over', *Guardian*, 31 January.

Atton, Chris (2002) *Alternative Media*. London: Sage.

Aufderheide, Pat (2002) 'All-too-reality TV: challenges for television journalists after September 11', *Journalism: Theory, Practice and Criticism,* Vol 3, No 1, pp. 7–14.

Austin, Tim (2003) *The Times Style and Usage Guide*. London: Harper Collins.

Bailey, Sally and Williams, Granville (1997) 'Memoirs are made of this: journalists' memoirs in the United Kingdom, 1945–95', in Michael Bromley and Tom O'Malley (eds), *A Journalism Reader*. London: Routledge, pp. 351–377.

Bakhtin, Mikhail (1935) 'The Dialogic Imagination', extract printed in Pam Morris (ed) (1994) *The Bakhtin Reader: Selected Writings of Bakhtin, Medvedev and Voloshinov*. London: Edward Arnold, pp. 74–80.

Banks, David and Hanna, Mark (2009) *McNae's Essential Law for Journalists* (twentieth edition). Oxford: Oxford University Press (forthcoming).

Barber, Lynn (1999) 'The art of the interview', in Stephen Glover (ed), *The Penguin Book of Journalism*. London: Penguin, pp. 196–205.

Barnett, Steven (2008) 'On the road to self-destruction', *British Journalism Review,* Vol 19, No 2, pp. 5–13.

Barnett, Steven and Seymour, Emily (2000) *From Callaghan to Kosovo: Changing Trends in British Television News 1975–1999*. London: University of Westminster.

Barnicoat, Becky (2007) 'The fine art of interrogation', *Guardian*, 8 September.

BBC (1999) 'UK politics: Old Bailey hearing for Aitken', http://news.bbc.co.uk/hi/ english/uk_politics/newsid_257000/257826.stm, 19 January.

BBC (2002) *The Message*, BBC Radio Four, 15 February.

BBC (2003) 'WTC attacks death toll falls', *BBC Online*, 29 October, http://news.bbc. co.uk/1/hi/world/americas/3225313.stm.

BBC Trust (2007a) *From Seesaw to Wagon Wheel: Safeguarding Impartiality in the 21st Century*. www.bbc.co.uk/bbctrust/research/impartiality.html.

BBC Trust (2007b) *Report of the Independent Panel for the BBC Trust on Impartiality of BBC Business Coverage*. www.bbc.co.uk/bbctrust/research/business_news_impartiality. html.

Beaman, Jim (2000) *Interviewing for Radio*. London: Routledge.

Beckett, Andy (2001) 'Mail order', *Guardian*, 22 February.

Bedford, Martyn (1997) *Exit Orange & Red*. London: Bantam.

Behr, Edward (1992) *Anyone Here Been Raped and Speaks English?* London: Penguin.

Bell, Allan (1991) *The Language of News Media*. Oxford: Blackwell.

Bell, Martin (1998) 'The journalism of attachment', in Matthew Kieran (ed), *Media Ethics*. London: Routledge, pp. 15–22.

Bell, Martin (2002) 'Glamour is not good news', *Independent*, 19 February.

Bennett, Catherine (2001) 'The waste of space that is Lord Wakeham', *Guardian*, 5 July.

Berenger, Ralph D (2007) 'Book reviews', *Journalism: Theory, Practice and Criticism,* Vol 8, No 4, pp. 474–481.

Bernstein, Carl and Woodward, Bob ([1974] 2005) *All the President's Men.* New York: Pocket.

Bivens, Rena Kim (2008) 'The internet, mobile phones and blogging: how new media are transforming traditional journalism', *Journalism Practice,* Vol 2, No 1, pp. 113–129.

Blastland, Michael and Dilnot, Andrew (2007) *The Tiger That Isn't: Seeing through a World of Numbers.* London: Profile.

Bloy, Duncan (2007) *Media Law.* London: Sage.

Blumler, Jay (1999) 'Political communication systems all change: a response to Kees Brants', *European Journal of Communication,* Vol 14, No 2, pp. 241–249.

Bonnington, Alistair J, McInnes, Rosalind, and McKain, Bruce (2000) *Scots Law for Journalists.* Amdover: Sweet & Maxwell.

Boorstin, Daniel (1963) *The Image: Or What Happened to the American Dream.* Harmondsworth: Pelican.

Bourdieu, Pierre (1998) *On Television and Journalism.* London: Pluto.

Boyd, Andrew (2001) *Broadcast Journalism: Techniques of Radio and Television News.* Oxford: Focal.

Boyer, JH (1981) 'How editors view objectivity', *American Journalism Quarterly* No 58. Cited in Watson, James (1998) *Media Communication: An Introduction to Theory and Process.* Basingstoke: Macmillan, p. 98.

Brandenburg, Heinz (2007) 'Security at the source: embedding journalists as a superior strategy to military censorship', *Journalism Studies,* Vol 8, No 6, pp. 948–963.

Brants, Kees (1998) 'Who's afraid of infotainment?', *European Journal of Communication,* Vol 13, No 3, pp. 315–335.

Brants, Kees (1999) 'A rejoinder to Jay G Blumler', *European Journal of Communication,* Vol 14, No 3, pp. 411–415.

Brennen, Bonnie (2003) 'Sweat not melodrama: reading the structure of feeling in *All the President's Men*', *Journalism: Theory, Practice and Criticism,* Vol 4, No 1, pp. 113–131.

Briggs, Asa and Burke, Peter (2002) *A Social History of the Media: From Gutenberg to the Internet.* Cambridge: Polity Press.

Bright, Martin (2000) 'I'm handing nothing over', *Journalist,* May/June.

Bromley, Michael (1997) 'The end of journalism? Changes in workplace practices in the press and broadcasting in the 1990s', in Michael Bromley and Tom O'Malley (eds), *A Journalism Reader.* London: Routledge, pp. 330–350.

Bromley, Michael (ed) (2001) *No News is Bad News: Radio, Television and the Public.* Harlow: Longman.

Bromley, Michael and O'Malley, Tom (eds) (1997) *A Journalism Reader.* London: Routledge.

Bromley, Michael and Stephenson, Hugh (eds) (1998) *Sex, Lies and Democracy: The Press and the Public.* Harlow: Longman.

Brooke, Heather (2007) *Your Right to Know* (second edition). London: Pluto.

Brown, Andrew (2000) 'Newspapers and the internet', in Stephen Glover (ed), *The Penguin Book of Journalism.* London: Penguin, pp. 177–185.

Brown, Maggie (2003) 'Documentary maker's fury at BBC2 revamp of series on Asians', *Guardian,* 30 September.

Brown, Maggie (2005) 'I want to brighten and enlighten', *Guardian,* 24 October.

Calhoun, Craig (ed) (1992) *Habermas and the Public Sphere.* Cambridge, MA and London: MIT Press.

Cameron, Deborah (1996) 'Style policy and style politics: a neglected aspect of the language of the news', *Media, Culture & Society,* Vol 18, pp. 315–333.

Cameron, James (1968) *Point of Departure*. London: Readers Union.

Carlyle, Thomas (1840) *On Heroes, Hero-Worship, and the Heroic in History*. London: Chapman & Hall.

Carroll, Rory (2002) 'Yes, prime minister', *Guardian*, 1 April.

Carter, Cynthia, Branston, Gill, and Allan, Stuart (eds) (1998) *News, Gender and Power*. London: Routledge.

Castells, Manuel (1996) *The Rise of the Network Society. Volume 1 of The Information Age: Economy, Society and Culture*. Oxford: Blackwell.

Castells, Manuel (1997) *The Power of Identity. Volume 2 of The Information Age: Economy, Society and Culture*. Oxford: Blackwell.

Castells, Manuel (1998) *End of Millennium. Volume 3 of The Information Age: Economy, Society and Culture*. Oxford: Blackwell.

Cathcart, Brian (2007) 'Baiting the goody-goody', *New Statesman*, 21 June.

Chalaby, Jean (1998) *The Invention of Journalism*. London: Macmillan.

Chambers, Deborah (2000) 'Critical approaches to the media: the changing context for investigative journalism', in Hugo de Burgh (ed), *Investigative Journalism: Context and Practice*. London: Routledge, pp. 89–107.

Chandler, Raymond (1984) *Raymond Chandler Speaking*. London: Alison and Busby.

Channel 4 (1998) *The Real Rupert Murdoch*, broadcast 21 November.

Chantler, Paul and Harris, Sim (1997) *Local Radio Journalism*. Oxford: Focal.

Chapman, Jane and Kinsey, Marie (eds) (2009) *Broadcast Journalism: A Critical Introduction*. London: Routledge.

Chesterton, GK (1981) 'The wisdom of Father Brown: the purple wig', in *The Penguin Complete Father Brown*. Harmondsworth: Penguin, pp. 244–255.

Chippindale, Peter and Horrie, Chris (1992) *Stick It Up Your Punter! The Rise and Fall of the Sun*. London: Mandarin.

Clement, Barrie and Grice, David (2001) 'Secret ministry email: "Use attack to bury bad news"', *Independent*, 9 October.

Cohen, Stanley (1972) *Folk Devils and Moral Panics: The Creation of the Mods and Rockers*. London: MacGibbon and Kee.

Cohen, Stanley and Young, Jock (eds) (1973) *The Manufacture of News: Deviance, Social Problems and the Mass Media*. London: Constable.

Colston, Jane (2002) 'Reporting restrictions', in Tom Crone (ed), *Law and the Media*. Oxford: Focal, pp. 133–165.

Conboy, Martin (2002) *The Press and Popular Culture*. London: Sage.

Conboy, Martin (2006) *Tabloid Britain: Constructing a Community through Language*. London: Routledge.

Conboy, Martin (2007) *The Language of the News*. London: Routledge.

Cottle, Simon (2000) 'Rethinking news access', *Journalism Studies*, Vol 1, No 3, pp. 427–448.

Cottle, Simon (2001) 'Television news and citizenship: packaging the public sphere', in Michael Bromley (ed), *No News is Bad News: Radio, Television and the Public*. Harlow: Longman, pp. 61–79.

Critcher, Chas (2002) 'Media, government and moral panic: the politics of paedophilia in Britain 2000–1', *Journalism Studies*, Vol 3, No 4, pp. 521–535.

Crone, Tom (ed) (2002) *Law and the Media*. Oxford: Focal.

Curran, James (2000) 'Press reformism 1918–98: a study of failure', in Howard Tumber (ed.), *Media Power, Professionals and Policies*. London: Routledge, pp. 35–55.

Curran, James and Gurevitch, Michael (eds) (1991) *Mass Media and Society*. London: Edward Arnold.

Curran, James and Seaton, Jean (1997) *Power Without Responsibility: The Press and Broadcasting in Britain.* London: Routledge.

Curran, James and Seaton, Jean (2003) *Power Without Responsibility: The Press, Broadcasting and New Media in Britain* (sixth edition). London: Routledge.

Dahlgren, Peter and Sparks, Colin (eds) (1992) *Journalism and Popular Culture.* London: Sage.

Davies, Nick (2008) *Flat Earth News.* London: Chatto & Windus.

Day, Julia (2001) 'Hellier condemns Express "interference"', www.mediaguardian.co.uk, 6 September.

de Burgh, Hugo (ed) (2000) *Investigative Journalism: Context and Practice.* London: Routledge.

de Burgh, Hugo (2003) 'Skills are not enough: the case for journalism as an academic discipline', *Journalism: Theory, Practice and Criticism,* Vol 4, No 1, pp. 95–112.

de Burgh, Hugo (2008) *Investigative Journalism* (second edition). London: Routledge.

Deuze, Mark and Dimoudi, Christina (2002) 'Online journalists in the Netherlands: towards a profile of a new profession', *Journalism: Theory, Practice and Criticism,* Vol 3, No 1, pp. 85–100.

Dewdney, Andrew and Ride, Peter (2006) *The New Media Handbook.* Abingdon: Routledge.

Dixon, Sara (2002) 'The gentle touch', *Press Gazette,* 5 April.

Dodson, Sean (2001) 'Hacks hit in drugs war', *Guardian,* 25 June.

Doig, Alan (1997) 'The decline of investigatory journalism', in Michael Bromley and Tom O'Malley (eds), *A Journalism Reader.* London: Routledge, pp. 189–213.

Dorril, Stephen (2000) 'What is investigative journalism?', *Free Press,* No 116, May/June.

Dorril, Stephen (2002a) 'Secrets and lies', *Free Press,* No 127, March/April.

Dorril, Stephen (2002b) 'Suspicious incidents', *Free Press,* No 126, January/February.

Dovey, Jon (2000) *Freakshow: First Person Media and Factual Television.* London: Pluto.

Downing, John, with Villarreal Ford, Tamara, Gil, Geneve, and Stein, Laura (2001) *Radical Media: Rebellious Communication and Social Movements.* London: Sage.

Doyle, Gillian (2002) *Understanding Media Economics.* London: Sage.

Drabble, Margaret and Stringer, Jenny (eds) (1990) *The Concise Oxford Companion to English Literature.* Oxford: Oxford University Press.

DTLR (2001) *News Release 388: Consultation Begins on Council Allowances.* London: Department for Transport, Local Government and the Regions. September 11 2001.

Economist (2008) *Style Guide.* London: Profile Books.

Eliot, George (1859) *Adam Bede.* Edinburgh: Blackwood.

Engel, Matthew (1997) *Tickle the Public: One Hundred Years of the Popular Press.* London: Indigo.

Errigo, Jackie and Franklin, Bob (2004) 'Surviving in the hackademy', *British Journalism Review,* Vol 15, No 2, pp. 43–48.

Evans, Harold ([1978] 1997) *Pictures on a Page: Photo-journalism, Graphics and Picture Editing.* London: Pimlico.

Evans, Harold (2000) *Essential English for Journalists, Editors and Writers.* London: Pimlico.

Fiske, John (1989) *Reading the Popular.* London: Routledge.

Fleming, Carole (2002) *The Radio Handbook.* London: Routledge.

Foley, Michael (2000) 'Press regulation', *Administration,* Vol 48, No 1, Spring, pp. 40–51.

Foot, Paul (1999) 'The slow death of investigative journalism', in Stephen Glover (ed), *The Penguin Book of Journalism: Secrets of the Press.* London: Penguin, pp. 79–89.

Foot, Paul (2000) *Articles of Resistance*. London: Bookmarks.

Forde, Eamonn (2001) 'From polyglottism to branding: on the decline of personality journalism in the British music press', *Journalism: Theory, Practice and Criticism,* Vol 2, No 1, pp. 23–43.

Fowler, HW (1983) *A Dictionary of Modern English Usage*. Oxford: Oxford University Press.

Fowler, Roger (1991) *Language in the News: Discourse and Ideology in the Press*. London: Routledge.

Franklin, Bob (1994) *Packaging Politics: Political Communications in Britain's Media Democracy*. London: Edward Arnold.

Franklin, Bob (1997) *Newszak and News Media*. London: Arnold.

Franklin, Bob (2005) 'Framing' in Bob Franklin, Martin Hamer, Mark Hanna, Marie Kinsey and John Richardson, *Key Concepts in Journalism Studies*. London: Sage, pp. 85–86.

Franklin, Bob and Murphy, David (eds) (1998) *Making the Local News: Local Journalism in Context*. London: Routledge.

Franklin, Bob, Hamer, Martin, Hanna, Mark, Kinsey, Marie, and Richardson, John (2005) *Key Concepts in Journalism Studies*, London: Sage.

Frayn, Michael [1965] (1995) *The Tin Men*. London: Penguin.

Fresco, Adam, Syal, Rajeev and Bird, Steve (2005) 'Suspect shot dead "had no bomb" – London terror', *Times*, 23 July.

Frith, Simon and Meech, Peter (2007) 'Becoming a journalist: journalism education and journalism culture', *Journalism: Theory, Practice and Criticism,* Vol 8, No 2, pp. 137–164.

Frost, Chris (2000) *Media Ethics and Self-Regulation*. Harlow: Longman.

Frost, Chris (2002) *Reporting for Journalists*. London: Routledge.

Frost, Chris (2007) *Journalism Ethics and Self-regulation*. Harlow: Pearson.

Fry, Don (2004) 'Unmuddling Middles', *Poynter Online*, 16 June, www.poynter.org.

Galtung, Johan and Ruge, Mari (1965) 'The structure of foreign news: the presentation of the Congo, Cuba and Cyprus crises in four Norwegian newspapers', *Journal of International Peace Research,* Vol 1, pp. 64–91.

Gans, Herbert J (1980) *Deciding What's News: A Study of CBS Evening News, NBC Nightly News, Newsweek and Time*. London: Constable.

Gieber, Walter (1964) 'News is what newspapermen make it', in Howard Tumber (ed) (1999), *News: A Reader*. Oxford: Oxford University Press, pp. 218–223.

Gilbert, Harriett (1999) 'Writing reviews', in Wynford Hicks, with Sally Adams, and Harriett Gilbert, *Writing for Journalists*. London: Routledge, pp. 99–123.

Glover, Mike (1998) 'Looking at the world through the eyes of … reporting the "local" in daily, weekly and Sunday local newspapers', in Bob Franklin and David Murphy (eds), *Making the Local News: Local Journalism in Context*. London: Routledge, pp. 117–124.

Glover, Stephen (ed) (1999) *The Penguin Book of Journalism: Secrets of the Press*. London: Penguin.

Golding, Peter and Elliott, Philip (1979) *Making the News*. London and New York: Longman.

Golding, Peter and Murdock, Graham (1979) 'Ideology and the mass media: the question of determination', in Michele Barrett, Philip Corrigan, Annette Kuhn, and Janet Wolff (eds), *Ideology and Cultural Production*. London: Croom Helm, pp. 198–224.

Goodwin, Bill (1996) 'Safe sources', *Journalist*, April/May.

Gopsill, Tim (2001) 'The wages of spin', *Journalist*, April.

Gopsill, Tim and Neale, Greg (2007) *Journalists: A Hundred Years of the National Union of Journalists*. London: Profile.

Gramsci, Antonio (1971) *Selections from the Prison Notebooks*. London: Lawrence & Wishart.

Green, Nigel (2008) 'Insight', *Press Gazette*, 1 February.

Greenslade, Roy (2003a) 'Their master's voice', *Guardian*, 17 February.

Greenslade, Roy (2003b) 'Readers in Ilkley, owners in Virginia', *Guardian*, 1 September.

Greenslade, Roy (2004) *Press Gang: How Newspapers Make Profits from Propaganda*. London: Pan.

Greenslade, Roy (2008) 'The digital challenge', *Guardian*, 7 January.

Griffiths, Dennis (2006) *Fleet Street: Five Hundred Years of the Press*. London: The British Library.

Grundberg, Peter (2002) 'The "new" right to privacy', in Tom Crone (ed), *Law and the Media*. Oxford: Focal, pp. 114–130.

Grundy, Bill (1976) 'Sex Pistols interview', broadcast on *Today*, Thames Television, 1 December 1976, reproduced in *Great Interviews of the 20th Century*, No 8, Guardian News & Media, 2007.

Gurevitch, Michael, Bennett, Tony, Curran, James, and Woollacott, Janet (eds) (1982) *Culture, Society and the Media*. London: Methuen.

Habermas, Jürgen (1989) *The Structural Transformation of the Public Sphere: An Inquiry into a Category of Bourgeois Society*. Cambridge: Polity Press.

Habermas, Jürgen (1992) 'Further reflections on the public sphere', in Craig Calhoun (ed), *Habermas and the Public Sphere*. Cambridge, MA and London: MIT Press, pp. 421–461.

Hahn, Daniel (2004) *The Tower Menagerie: The Amazing True Story of the Royal Collection of Wild Beasts*. London: Pocket.

Hall, Jim (2001) *Online Journalism: A Critical Primer*. London: Pluto.

Hall, Sarah (2002) 'Paper fined for Leeds case error', *Guardian*, 20 April.

Hall, Sarah (2006) 'Doctors enjoy the greatest public trust', *Guardian*, 2 November.

Hall, Stuart (1967) 'People, personalities and personalisation', in Richard Hoggart (ed), *Your Sunday Paper*. London: University of London Press.

Hall, Stuart (1973) 'The determinations of news photographs', in Stanley Cohen and Jock Young (eds), *The Manufacture of News: Deviance, Social Problems and the Mass Media*. London: Constable, pp. 176–190.

Hall, Stuart (1977) 'Culture, the media and the "ideological effect"', in James Curran, Michael Gurevitch, and Janet Woollacott (eds), *Mass Communication and Society*. London: Edward Arnold, pp. 315–348.

Hall, Stuart (1982) 'The rediscovery of "ideology": return of the repressed in media studies', in Michael Gurevitch, Tony Bennett, James Curran, and Janet Woollacott (eds), *Culture, Society and the Media*. London: Methuen, pp. 56–90.

Hall, Stuart (1986) 'Media power and class power', in James Curran, Jake Ecclestone, Giles Oakley, and Alan Richardson (eds), *Bending Reality: The State of the Media*. London: Pluto, pp. 5–14.

Hall, Stuart, Critcher, Chas, Jefferson, Tony, Clarke, John, and Roberts, Brian (1978) *Policing the Crisis*. London: Macmillan.

Hanna, Mark (2000) 'British investigative journalism: protecting the continuity of talent through changing times'. Paper presented to the International Association for Media and Communication Research, Singapore, 18 July.

Harcup, Tony (1994) *A Northern Star: Leeds Other Paper and the Alternative Press 1974–1994*. London and Pontefract: Campaign for Press and Broadcasting Freedom.

Harcup, Tony (1996) 'More news means worse news, conference on media ethics told', *Broadcast*, 27 September.

Harcup, Tony (2002a) 'Conduct unbecoming?', *Press Gazette*, 1 March.

Harcup, Tony (2002b) 'Journalists and ethics: the quest for a collective voice', *Journalism Studies*, Vol 3, No 1, pp. 101–114.

Harcup, Tony (2003) 'The unspoken – said. The journalism of alternative media', *Journalism: Theory, Practice and Criticism,* Vol 4, No 3, pp. 356–376.

Harcup, Tony (2005) '"I'm doing this to change the world": journalism in alternative and mainstream media', *Journalism Studies,* Vol 6, No 3, pp. 361–374.

Harcup, Tony (2007) *The Ethical Journalist.* London: Sage.

Harcup, Tony (2008) 'Learning some lessons at the school of hard knocks', *Press Gazette,* 11 April.

Harcup, Tony and O'Neill, Deirdre (2001) 'What is news? Galtung and Ruge revisited', *Journalism Studies,* Vol 2, No 2, pp. 261–280.

Hardt, Hanno (2000) 'Conflicts of interest: newsworkers, media, and patronage journalism', in Howard Tumber (ed), *Media Power, Professionals and Policies.* London: Routledge, pp. 209–224.

Harris, Paul (2007) 'Why I said "no" to Paris Hilton mania', *Observer,* 1 July.

Harrison, Jackie (2000) *Terrestrial TV News in Britain: The Culture of Production.* Manchester: Manchester University Press.

Harrison, Jackie (2006) *News.* London: Routledge.

Hart-Davis, Duff (1990) *The House the Berrys Built.* London: Hodder & Stoughton.

Hartley, John (1982) *Understanding News.* London: Methuen.

Hastings, Max (2004) 'Never forget that they lie', *Guardian,* 31 January.

Hattenstone, Simon (2007) 'Reflections of a professional stalker', *Guardian,* 8 September.

Hecht, Ben and MacArthur, Charles (1974) *The Front Page.* A U-I film.

Helmore, Ed (2001) 'Meet the enforcer', *Observer,* 3 June.

Hencke, David (2001) 'No news is bad news', *Guardian,* 5 March.

Herman, Edward (2000) 'The propaganda model: a retrospective', *Journalism Studies,* Vol 1, No 1, pp. 101–112.

Herman, Edward and Chomsky, Noam (1988) 'Manufacturing consent', in Howard Tumber (ed) (1999), *News: A Reader.* Oxford: Oxford University Press, pp. 166–179.

Hetherington, Alastair (1985) *News, Newspapers and Television.* London: Macmillan.

Hicks, Wynford (1998) *English for Journalists.* London: Routledge.

Hicks, Wynford (2007) *English for Journalists* (second edition). London: Routledge.

Hicks, Wynford, with Adams, Sally and Gilbert, Harriett (1999) *Writing for Journalists.* London: Routledge.

Hicks, Wynford and Holmes, Tim (2002) *Subediting for Journalists.* London: Routledge.

Hilton, Phil (2007) 'Show us your bids!', *Guardian,* 26 May.

Hobsbawm, Julia and Lloyd, John (2008) *The Power of the Commentariat.* London: Editorial Intelligence.

Hodge, Robert and Kress, Gunther (1993) *Language as Ideology.* London: Routledge.

Hodgson, FW (1993) *Subediting: A Handbook of Modern Newspaper Editing and Production.* Oxford: Focal Press.

Holland, Patricia (1998) 'The politics of the smile: "soft news" and the sexualisation of the popular press', in Cynthia Carter, Gill Branston, and Stuart Allan (eds), *News, Gender and Power.* London: Routledge, pp. 17–32.

Holland, Patricia (2000) *The Television Handbook.* London: Routledge.

Hollingsworth, Mark (1986) *The Press and Political Dissent: A Question of Censorship.* London: Pluto.

Honigsbaum, Mark (2005) 'Brazilian did not wear bulky jacket: Stockwell shoot-to-kill relatives say Met admits that, contrary to reports, electrician did not leap tube station barrier', *Guardian,* 28 July.

Hudson, Gary and Rowlands, Sarah (2007) *The Broadcast Journalism Handbook.* Harlow: Pearson.

IFJ (International Fedesation of Journalists) (2007) '"Tragedy unlimited" says IFJ as killings of journalists in 2007 maintain record levels', 31 December, www.ifj.org/default.asp?Index=5638&Language=EN.

IFJ (2008) *Deadly Stories 2007: Killings of Journalists Touch Record Levels*. Brussels: International Federation of Journalists.

Ingrams, Richard (2005) *My Friend Footy: A Memoir of Paul Foot*. London: Private Eye.

Jack, Ian (2006) 'Things that have interested me', *Guardian*, 5 August.

Jarvis, Jeff (2008) 'Why Twitter is the canary in the news coalmine', *Guardian*, 19 May.

Jeffries, Stuart (2008) 'There's humour in the darkest places', *Guardian*, 18 March.

Jenkins, Simon (2007) 'The British media does not do responsibility. It does stories', *Guardian*, 18 May.

Johnston, Alan (2007) *Kidnapped and Other Dispatches*. London: Profile.

Johnston, Don (2002) 'He wouldn't last long on my desk', letter in the *Journalist*, December.

Journalism Training Forum (2002) *Journalists at Work: Their Views on Training, Recruitment and Conditions*. London: Publishing National Training Organisation/Skillset.

Journalist (2007a) 'Threat came with a bullet', *Journalist*, November.

Journalist (2007b) 'Robin's final triumph as the Lords slam door on NHS Trust', September/October.

Kampfner, John (2007) 'Less stenography and more reporting, please', *Guardian*, 16 July.

Karim, Karim (2002) 'Making sense of the "Islamic Peril": journalism as cultural practice', in Barbie Zelizer and Stuart Allan (eds), *Journalism after September 11*. London: Routledge, pp. 101–116.

Keeble, Richard (1998) *The Newspapers Handbook* (second edition). London: Routledge.

Keeble, Richard (2001a) *The Newspapers Handbook* (third edition). London: Routledge.

Keeble, Richard (2001b) *Ethics for Journalists*. London: Routledge.

Keeble, Richard (2006) *The Newspapers Handbook* (fourth edition). London: Routledge.

Kelso, Paul (2001) 'We have known about this for 15 years. The media should have exposed this man a long time ago', *Guardian*, 23 July.

Kieran, Matthew (ed) (1998) *Media Ethics*. London: Routledge.

Kiley, Sam (2001) 'The Middle East's war of words', *Evening Standard*, 5 September.

Kiss, Jemima (2006) 'Changing media summit: citizen media will unlock the secret society, says Jon Snow', www.journalism.co.uk/news/story1779.shtml, March 28.

Knight, Alan (2008) 'Journalism in the age of blogging', *Journalism Practice,* Vol 2, No 1, pp. 117–124.

Knightley, Phillip (1998) *A Hack's Progress*. London: Vintage.

Knightley, Phillip (2000) *The First Casualty: The War Correspondent as Hero and Myth-maker from the Crimea to Kosovo*. London: Prion.

Knightley, Phillip (2001) 'The disinformation campaign', *Guardian*, 4 October.

Knightley, Phillip (2002) 'The creation of public enemy No 1', *Evening Standard*, 11 September.

Kobre, Kenneth (2008) *Photo Journalism: The Professonals' Approach*. Oxford: Focal Press.

Krajicek, David J (1998) 'The bad, the ugly and the worse', *Guardian*, 11 May.

Kuhn, Raymond (2002) 'The first Blair government and political journalism', in Raymond Kuhn and Erik Neveu (eds), *Political Journalism: New Challenges, New Practices*. London: Routledge, pp. 47–68.

Lagan, Sarah (2007) 'Duped Cumbria papers slam April fool prank', *Press Gazette*, 4 April.

Larsson, Larsake (2002) 'Journalists and politicians: a relationship requiring manoeuvring space', *Journalism Studies,* Vol 3, No 1, pp. 21–33.

Lavie, Aliza and Lehman-Wilzig, Sam (2003) 'Whose news? Does gender determine the editorial product?' *European Journal of Communication*, Vol 18, No 1, pp. 5–29.

Lee, Seow Ting, Maslog, Crispin C, and Kim, Hun Shik (2006) 'Asian conflicts and the Iraq War', *International Communication Gazette*, Vol. 68, pp. 499–518.

Leigh, David (2007) 'Anthony Sampson Chair inaugural lecture', City University, 1 November, http://www.city.ac.uk/journalism/ download_files/01_11_07_sampson_ lecture.pdf.

Leigh, David and Evans, Rob (2008) 'Sources', 17 February, http://www.guardian.co.uk/ world/2007/jun/07/bae18.

Lewis, Justin (2006) 'News and the empowerment of citizens', *European Journal of Cultural Studies,* Vol 9, No 3, pp. 303–319.

Lewis, Justin, Williams, Andrew, and Franklin, Bob (2008a) 'A compromised fourth estate? UK news journalism, public relations and news sources', *Journalism Studies,* Vol 9, No 1, pp. 1–20.

Lewis, Justin, Williams, Andrew, and Franklin, Bob (2008b) 'Four rumours and an explanation: a political economic account of journalists' changing newsgathering and reporting practices', *Journalism Practice,* Vol 2, No 1, pp. 27–45.

Lipton, Eric (2001) 'Toll from attack at Trade Center is down sharply', *New York Times*, 21 November.

Lipton, Eric (2002) 'Death toll is near 3,000, but some uncertainty over count remains', *New York Times*, 11 September.

Loffelholz, Martin and Weaver, David (eds) (2008) *Global Journalism Research: Theories, Methods, Findings, Future*. Oxford: Blackwell.

Ludlam, Joanna (2002) 'Breach of confidence', in Tom Crone (ed), *Law and the Media*. Oxford: Focal, pp. 89–103.

Lule, Jack (2001) *Daily News, Eternal Stories: The Mythological Role of Journalism*. New York: Guilford Press.

Lynch, Jake (2002) 'Reporting the world: how ethical journalism can seek solutions', www.mediachannel.org, 23 January.

Machin, David and Niblock, Sarah (2008) 'Branding newspapers: visual texts as social practice', *Journalism Studies,* Vol 9, No 2, pp. 244–259.

Malik, Shiv (2008) 'Stop police seizing reporters' notes', *Press Gazette*, 23 May.

Manning, Paul (2001) *News and News Sources: A Critical Introduction*. London: Sage.

Mansfield, FJ (1936) *The Complete Journalist: A Study of the Principles and Practice of Newspaper-making*. London: Sir Isaac Pitman and Sons.

Mansfield, FJ (1943) *Gentlemen, the Press! Chronicles of a Crusade: Official History of the National Union of Journalists*. London: WH Allen.

Marr, Andrew (2005) *My Trade: A Short History of British Journalism*. London: Pan.

Marsh, David (ed.) (2007) *Guardian Style*. London: Guardian Books.

Martinson, Jane (2005) 'It's hello, good evening and welcome to *al-Jazeera* for David Frost', *Guardian*, 7 October.

Marx, Karl and Engels, Friedrich ([1846] 1965) *The German Ideology*. London: Lawrence & Wishart.

Mayes, Ian (2000) *The Guardian Corrections and Clarifications*. London: Guardian Newspapers.

McAdams, Mindy (2005) *Flash Journalism: How to Create Multimedia News Packages*. Oxford: Focal Press.

McCafferty, Nell (1981) *In the Eyes of the Law*. Dublin: Ward River Press.

McCafferty, Nell (1984) *The Best of Nell: A Selection of Writings over Fourteen Years*. Dublin: Attic Press.

McChesney, Robert (2000) *Rich Media, Poor Democracy: Communication Politics in Dubious Times*. New York: New Press.

McChesney, Robert (2002) 'The US news media and World War III', *Journalism: Theory, Practice and Criticism*, Vol 3, No 1, pp. 14–21.

McCombs, Maxwell and Shaw, Donald (1972) 'The agenda setting function of mass media', in Howard Tumber (ed) (1999) *News: A Reader*. Oxford: Oxford University Press, pp. 320–328.

McKane, Anna (2006) *News Writing*. London: Sage.

McKay, Jenny (2006) *The Magazines Handbook*. London: Routledge.

McKay, Peter (1999) 'Gossip', in Stephen Glover (ed), *The Penguin Book on Journalism: Secrets of the Press*. London: Penguin, pp. 186–195.

McLaughlin, Greg (2002a) 'Rules of engagement: television journalism and NATO's "faith in bombing" during the Kosovo crisis, 1999', *Journalism Studies,* Vol 3, No 2, pp. 257–266.

McLaughlin, Greg (2002b) *The War Correspondent*. London: Pluto.

McNair, Brian (2000) *Journalism and Democracy: An Evaluation of the Political Public Sphere*. London: Routledge.

McQuail, Denis (1992) *Media Performance: Mass Communication and the Public Interest*. London: Sage.

McQuail, Denis (2000) *McQuail's Mass Communication Theory*. London: Sage.

Media Lawyer (2002) '*S Mirror* fined £75,000 for interview', *Media Lawyer,* No 39, May/June, pp. 18–19.

Millar, Stuart (2001) 'Robot reporter "to write news in future"', *Guardian*, 9 August.

Milton, John ([1644] 2005) 'Areopagitica: a speech for the liberty of unlicensed printing', in John Milton and Granville Williams, *Milton and the Modern Media: A Defence of a Free Press*. Accrington: B&D.

Mirsky, Jonathan (2001) 'In bed with the Reds', *Spectator*, 10 November.

Morgan, Jean (1999) 'Reporter who refused death-knock loses job fight', *Press Gazette*, 17 December.

Morgan, Jean (2002a) '"Lack of humanity" over Soham led to *Herald* sacking', *Press Gazette*, 6 September.

Morgan, Jean (2002b) 'Never ever sign copy deals, says freelance in singer row', *Press Gazette*, 22 March.

Morris, Steven (2007) 'I can't believe the story went so big. I didn't even get any money out of it', *Guardian*, 9 August.

Murrow, Ed (1958) 'Speech at the 1958 RTNDA Convention, Chicago, 15 October, http://media.www.mediaethicsmagazine.com/media/storage/paper655/news/2004/12/31/AnalysesCommentary/Ed.Murrows.Speech.At.The.1958.Rtnda.Convention-833533.shtml.

Ndlela, Nkosi (2005) 'The African paradigm: the coverage of the Zimbabwean crisis in the Norwegian media', *Westminster Papers in Communication and Culture*, Special Issue, November, pp. 71–90.

Neveu, Erik (2002) 'The local press and farmers' protests in Brittany: proximity and distance in the local newspaper coverage of a social movement', *Journalism Studies*, Vol 3, No 1, pp. 53–67.

NGO–EC Liaison Committee (1989) *Code of Conduct: Images and Messages Relating to the Third World,* http://www.globalnews.org.uk/teacher_values.htm.

Niblock, Sarah (2007) 'From "knowing how" to "being able": negotiating the meanings of reflective practice and reflexive research in journalism studies', *Journalism Practice*, Vol 1, No 1, pp. 20–32.

Niblock, Sarah and Machin, David (2007) 'News values for consumer groups: the case of Independent Radio News, London, UK', *Journalism: Theory, Practice and Criticism,* Vol 8, No 2, pp. 184–204.

Northmore, David (2001) 'Investigative reporting: why and how', in Richard Keeble, *The Newspapers Handbook*. London: Routledge, pp. 183–193.

Norton-Taylor, Richard (2000) 'Bombing in Iraq an "undeclared war"', *Guardian*, 11 November.

Observer (2002) 'Talking about my generation', *Observer*, 21 July.

O'Malley, Tom (1997) 'Labour and the 1947–9 Royal Commission on the Press', in Michael Bromley and Tom O'Malley (eds), *A Journalism Reader*. London: Routledge, pp. 126–158.

O'Malley, Tom and Soley, Clive (2000) *Regulating the Press*. London: Pluto.

O'Neill, Deirdre and Harcup, Tony (2009) 'News values and selectivity', in K Wahl-Jorgensen and T Hanitzsch (eds), *Handbook of Journalism Studies*. Mahwah, NJ: Lawrence Erlbaum Associates.

O'Neill, John (1992) 'Journalism in the market place', in Andrew Belsey and Ruth Chadwick (eds), *Ethical Issues in Journalism and the Media*. London: Routledge, pp. 15–32.

Orwell, George (1946a) 'Decline of the English murder', in George Orwell (1965), *Decline of the English Murder and Other Essays*. Harmondsworth: Penguin, pp. 9–13.

Orwell, George (1946b) 'Politics and the English language', in George Orwell (1962), *Inside the Whale and Other Essays*. Harmondsworth: Penguin, pp. 143–157.

Osborn, Andrew (2007) 'These are the faces of the 20 journalists who have lost their lives in Putin's Russia', *Independent on Sunday*, 11 March.

O'Sullivan, Kevin (2001) 'Kate Winslet disappears up her a***', *Daily Mirror*, 27 November.

Palast, Greg (2002) *The Best Democracy Money Can Buy: An Investigative Reporter Exposes the Truth about Globalisation, Corporate Cons, and High Finance Fraudsters*. London: Pluto.

Pape, Susan and Featherstone, Sue (2005) *Newspaper Journalism: A Practical Introduction*. London: Sage.

Pape, Susan and Featherstone, Sue (2006) *Feature Writing: A Practical Introduction*. London: Sage.

Parfitt, Tom (2006) 'The only good journalist…', *Guardian*, 10 October.

PCC (1992) 'Editorial', *Report No 7*, Press Complaints Commission, March, pp. 2–3.

PCC (2008) *The Review 2007*. London: Press Complaints Commission.

Perkins, Anne (2001) 'Hands up who fell off the career ladder as they hit motherhood', *Guardian*, 31 May.

Petley, Julian (1999) 'The regulation of media content', in Jane Stokes and Anna Reading (eds), *The Media in Britain: Current Debates and Developments*. Basingstoke: Palgrave.

Pew Research Centre (2000) 'Self-censorship: how often and why. A survey of journalists in association with Columbia Journalism Review', www.people-press.org/jour00rpt.htm.

Phillips, Angela (2007) *Good Writing for Journalists*. London: Sage.

Philo, Greg (1991) 'Audience beliefs and the 1984/5 miners' strike', in Greg Philo (ed) (1995), *Glasgow Media Group Reader. Vol. 2: Industry, Economy, War and Politics*. London: Routledge, pp. 37–42.

Philo, Greg and McLaughlin, Greg (1993) 'The British media and the Gulf War', in Greg Philo (ed) (1995), *Glasgow Media Group Reader. Vol 2: Industry, Economy, War and Politics*. London: Routledge, pp. 146–156.

Pilger, John (1998) *Hidden Agendas*. London: Vintage.

Pilger, John (2001) 'This war of lies goes on', *Daily Mirror*, 16 November.

Plunkett, John (2003) 'Hello girls', *Guardian*, 22 December.

Politkovskaya, Anna (2008) *A Russian Diary*. London: Vintage.

Ponsford, Dominic (2006) 'Shifting of Sands baffles staff', *Press Gazette*, 10 March.

Porter, Roy (2000) *Enlightenment: Britain and the Creation of the Modern World*. London: Allen Lane.

Powell, James (2001) 'The allure of foreign affairs', www.mediaguardian.co.uk, 30 October.

Press Gazette (2000a) 'PA reporter stops identification ban on dead baby', *Press Gazette*, 28 July.

Press Gazette (2000b) 'On and off the record', *Press Gazette*, 21 January.

Press Gazette (2002) 'Coventry paper wins name-ban challenge', *Press Gazette*, 18 January.

Press Gazette (2004) 'PCC rap for Welsh weekly over story of dog eating dead man', *Press Gazette*, 26 March.

Private Eye (2001) 'Hackwatch: the big story', *Private Eye*, 26 January.

Pulford, Cedric (2001) *JournoLISTS: 201 Ways to Improve Your Journalism*. Banbury: Ituri.

Randall, David (2000) *The Universal Journalist*. London: Pluto.

Randall, David (2005) *The Great Reporters*. London: Pluto.

Randall, David (2007) *The Universal Journalist* (third edition). London: Pluto.

Reah, Danuta (1998) *The Language of Newspapers*. London: Routledge.

Reece, Peter (2005) 'Brian Whittle dies after suffering heart attack', *Hold The Front Page*, 12 December, http://www.holdthefrontpage.co.uk/news/2005/12dec/051212whit2.shtml.

Richardson, John (2001) 'British Muslims in the broadsheet press: a challenge to cultural hegemony?', *Journalism Studies,* Vol 2, No 2, pp. 221–242.

Richardson, John (2005) 'News values', in Bob Franklin, Martin Hamer, Mark Hanna, Marie Kinsey, and John Richardson, *Key Concepts in Journalism Studies*. London: Sage, pp. 173–174.

Richardson, John (2006) *Analysing Newspapers: An Approach from Critical Discourse Analysis*. Basingstoke: Palgrave Macmillan.

Robinson, Sue (2007) '"Someone's gotta be in control here": the institutionalisation of online news and the creation of a shared journalistic authority', *Journalism Practice,* Vol 1, No 3, pp. 305–321.

Rocco, Fiammetta (1999) 'Stockholm Syndrome: journalists taken hostage', in Stephen Glover (ed), *The Penguin Book of Journalism*. London: Penguin, pp. 48–59.

Rose, David (2003) 'Wake up or face privacy law, warns Rusbridger', *Press Gazette*, 14 March.

Rose, David, Smith, Patrick and Ponsford, Dominic (2007) 'Thank Gord, now here's how to make FOI better', *Press Gazette*, 2 November.

Ross, Karen (2001) 'Women at work: journalism as en-gendered practice', *Journalism Studies,* Vol 2, No 4, pp. 531–544.

Roth, Eric and Mann, Michael (1999) *The Insider*. A Forward Pass film.

Rowland, Jacky (2002) 'Milosevic trial: I saw it as my duty', *Ariel*, 3 September.

Roy, Kenneth (2002) 'One pair of eyes: Jon Snow, presenter of *Channel 4 News*, laments the decline and fall of the broadcasting characters', interview published in *The Journalist's Handbook,* No 71, Autumn, pp. 33–38.

Ruddock, Alan (2001) 'Hello! Have redtops said goodbye to politics?', *Observer*, 26 August.

Rusbridger, Alan (2000) 'Versions of seriousness', *Guardian*, 4 November.

Salas, Randy A (2007) 'Wilder's "Ace" is a buried treasure', *Star Tribune*, 16 July, www.startribune.com/459/story/1306175.html.

Sanders, Karen (2003) *Ethics and Journalism*. London: Sage.

Schlesinger, Philip (1987) *Putting 'Reality' Together*. London: Routledge.

Schlesinger, Philip (1990) 'Rethinking the sociology of journalism: source strategies and the limits of media-centrism', in Marjorie Ferguson (ed), *Public Communication the New Imperatives: Future Directions for Media Research*. London: Sage, pp. 61–83.

Schudson, Michael (1978) 'Discovering the news: a social history of American newspapers', in Howard Tumber (ed) (1999), *News: A Reader*. Oxford: Oxford University Press, pp. 291–296.

Schudson, Michael (1989) 'The sociology of news production', *Media, Culture and Society*, Vol 11, pp. 263–282.

Schudson, Michael (1991) 'The sociology of news production revisited', in James Curran and Michael Gurevitch (eds), *Mass Media and Society*. London: Edward Arnold, pp. 141–159.

Schudson, Michael (2001) 'The objectivity norm in American journalism', *Journalism: Theory, Practice and Criticism*, Vol 2, No 2, pp. 149–170.

Seib, Philip (2002) *The Global Journalist: News and Conscience in a World of Conflict*. Oxford: Rowman & Littlefield.

Sergeant, John (2001) *Give Me Ten Seconds*. London: Macmillan.

Sheridan Burns, Lynette (2002) *Understanding Journalism*. London: Sage.

Shoemaker, Pamela (1991) 'Gatekeeping', in Howard Tumber (ed) (1999), *News: A Reader*. Oxford: Oxford University Press, pp. 73–78.

Shukman, David (2000) 'Watching them watching me', *Independent*, 7 November.

Silver, James (2007) 'Hillary brought to book', *Guardian*, 25 June.

Singer, Jane (2004) 'Strange bedfellows: diffusion of convergence in four news organisations', *Journalism Studies*, Vol 5, No 1, pp. 3–18.

Singer, Jane (2005) 'The political blogger: "normalizing a new media form to fit old norms and practice"', *Journalism: Theory, Practice and Criticism*, Vol 6, No 2, pp. 173–198.

Sissons, Helen (2006) *Practical Journalism: How to Write News*. London: Sage.

Slattery, Jon (2002) 'Journalism must halt drift into "unintended apartheid"', *Press Gazette*, 12 July.

Slattery, Jon (2005) 'Never mind the corporate bollocks – what about the future?', *Press Gazette*, 2 December.

Smith, Patrick (2007) 'Investigators share BAE bribery expose on the internet', *Press Gazette*, 20 July.

Spark, David (1999) *Investigative Reporting: A Study in Technique*. Oxford: Focal.

Sparks, Colin (1992) 'Popular journalism: theories and practice', in Peter Dahlgren and Colin Sparks (eds), *Journalism and Popular Culture*. London: Sage, pp. 24–44.

Sparks, Colin (1999) 'The press', in Jane Stokes and Anna Reading (eds), *The Media in Britain: Current Debates and Developments*. Basingstoke: Macmillan, pp. 41–60.

Specter, Michael (2007) 'Who's killing Putin's enemies?', *Observer*, 25 February.

Staab, Joachim Friedrick (1990) 'The role of news factors in news selection: a theoretical reconsideration', *European Journal of Communication*, Vol 5, pp. 423–443.

Stabe, Martin (2008) '*Times* milks web search benefits', *Press Gazette*, 16 May.

Stevens, Mary (2001) 'The new doorstep challenge', *Press Gazette*, 15 June.

Stevenson, Nick (2002) *Understanding Media Cultures*. London: Sage.

Sugden, John and Tomlinson, Alan (2007) 'Stories from planet football and sportsworld: source relations and collusion in sport journalism', *Journalism Practice*, Vol 1, No 1, pp. 44–61.

Sullivan, Andrew (2002) 'Out of the ashes: a new way of communicating', *Sunday Times*, 24 February.

Susman, Gary (2001) 'Tales of the junket', *Guardian*, 5 October.

Telegraph (2008) *Telegraph Style Book*, http://www.telegraph.co.uk/news/main.jhtml?xml=/news/exclusions/stylebook/nosplit/SBintrostyle.xml.

Temple, Mick (2006) 'Dumbing down is good for you', *British Politics,* Vol 1, pp. 257–273.

Tench, Dan (2001) 'Don't pull the dog's teeth', *Guardian*, 23 July.

Thom, Cleland (2007) 'Researchers need a reality check', letter published in *Press Gazette*, 5 October.

Thomas, Lou (2006) '"I was never going to work for the *Telegraph*, put it that way"', *Press Gazette*, 23 June.

Times (2005) 'Questions for the Met – the shoot-to-kill policy must have more safeguards', *Times* leader, 18 August.

Tomasky, Michael (2007) 'Newsreader strikes a blow for journalistic integrity, but Paris packs a stronger punch', *Guardian*, 30 June.

Tomlin, Julie and Morgan, Jean (2001) 'Poll voted a turn-off by viewers and readers', *Press Gazette*, 8 June.

Tuchman, Gaye (1972) 'Objectivity as a strategic ritual: an examination of newsmen's notions of objectivity', *American Journal of Sociology*, Vol 77, No 4. Reprinted in Howard Tumber (ed) (1999) *News: A Reader*. Oxford: Oxford University Press, pp. 297–307.

Tumber, Howard (ed) (1999) *News: A Reader*. Oxford: Oxford University Press.

Tumber, Howard (ed) (2000) *Media Power, Professionals and Policies*. London: Routledge.

Tunstall, Jeremy (2002) 'Trends in news media and political journalism', in Raymond Kuhn and Erik Neveu (eds), *Political Journalism: New Challenges, New Practices*. London: Routledge, pp. 227–241.

Tutek, Edwin Andres Martinez (2006) 'Undocumented workers uncounted victims of 9/11', *Newsday*, 7 September, http://www.newsday.com/news/local/newyork/am-gone0907,0,5880980.story.

UK Metric Association (2002) *Measurement Units Style Guide*, available from: www.metric.org.uk.

Ursell, Gill (2001) 'Dumbing down or shaping up? New technologies, new media, new journalism', *Journalism: Theory, Practice and Criticism,* Vol 2, No 2, pp. 175–196.

Vasterman, Peter (1995) 'Media hypes', www.journalism. fcj.hvu.nl/mediahype/mchype/hype_article.html (article first published, in Dutch, in magazine *Massacommunicatie*, September 1995).

Wahl-Jorgensen, K and Hanitzsch, T (eds) (2009) *Handbook of Journalism Studies*. Mahwah, NJ: Lawrence Erlbaum Associates.

Walker, David (2000) 'Newspaper power: a practitioner's account', in Howard Tumber (ed), *Media Power, Professionals and Policies*. London: Routledge, pp. 236–246.

Walker, David (2002) 'Low visibility on the inside track', *Journalism: Theory, Practice and Criticism*, Vol 3, No 1, pp. 101–110.

Ward, Mike (2002) *Journalism Online*. Oxford: Focal.

Waterhouse, Keith (1993) *Waterhouse on Newspaper Style*. London: Penguin.

Waterhouse, Keith (1994) *English Our English (and How to Sing It)*. London: Penguin.

Watkins, Alan (2001) *A Short Walk Down Fleet Street: From Beaverbrook to Boycott*. London: Duckbacks.

Watson, James (1998) *Media Communication: An Introduction to Theory and Process*. Basingstoke: Macmillan.

Waugh, Evelyn (1943) *Scoop*. London: Penguin.

Weitz, Katy (2003) 'Why I quit the *Sun*', *Guardian*, 31 March.

Wells, Matt (2001a) 'ITN cuts jobs and shifts towards lifestyle news', *Guardian*, 22 November.

Wells, Matt (2001b) 'BBC's "brighter" news to beat rising rival, *Guardian*, 18 January.

Wells, Matt (2005) 'Paxman answers the questions', *Guardian,* 31 January.

Welsh, Tom, Greenwood, Walter, and Banks, David (2005) *Essential Law for Journalists.* (eighteenth edition). Oxford: Oxford University Press.

Welsh, Tom, Greenwood, Walter, and Banks, David (2007) *Essential Law for Journalists* (nineteenth edition). Oxford: Oxford University Press.

Welsh, Tom and Greenwood, Walter (2001) *Essential Law for Journalists.* London: Butterworths.

Welsh, Tom and Greenwood, Walter (2003) *Essential Law for Journalists.* London: Butterworths.

Westerstahl, Jorgen and Johansson, Folke (1994) 'Foreign news: news values and ideologies', *European Journal of Communication,* Vol 9, pp. 71–89.

Wheen, Francis (2002) *Hoo-Hahs and Passing Frenzies: Collected Journalism 1991–2001.* London: Atlantic Books.

Whitaker, Brian (1981) *News Ltd: Why You Can't Read All About It.* London: Minority Press Group.

White, David Manning (1950) 'The gatekeeper: a case study in the selection of news', in Howard Tumber (ed) (1999), *News: A Reader.* Oxford: Oxford University Press, pp. 66–72.

Williams, Francis (1959) *Dangerous Estate: The Anatomy of Newspapers.* London: Arrow.

Williams, Granville (1996) *Britain's Media: How They are Related.* London: Campaign for Press and Broadcasting Freedom.

Williams Granville (2009) (ed) Shafted: *The Media, the Miners' strike and Aftermath.* London: Campaign for Press and Broadcasting Freedom.

Williams, Kevin (1992) 'Something more important than truth: ethical issues in war reporting', in Andrew Belsey and Ruth Chadwick (eds), *Ethical Issues in Journalism and the Media.* London: Routledge, pp. 154–170.

Williams, Raymond (1980) *Problems in Materialism and Culture.* London: Verso.

Wilson, John (1996) *Understanding Journalism: A Guide to Issues.* London: Routledge.

Winch, Samuel P (1997) *Mapping the Cultural Space of Journalism: How Journalists Distinguish News from Entertainment.* Westports, CT: Praeger.

Winchester, Simon (2001) 'My tainted days', *Guardian*, 22 May.

Wu, H Denis (2000) 'Systemic determinants of international news coverage: a comparison of 38 countries', *Journal of Communication*, Vol 50, pp. 110–130.

Wykes, Maggie (2001) *News, Crime and Culture.* London: Pluto.

Younge, Gary (2001) 'Bradford needs hope, not teargas', *Guardian*, 10 July.

Younge, Gary (2002) 'Temples for tomorrow', *Guardian*, 9 December.

Younge, Gary (2006) 'Take a potshot at the powerless, and you too can win a medal of valour', *Guardian*, 6 March.

Zelizer, Barbie (2004) *Taking Journalism Seriously: News and the Academy.* London: Sage.

Zelizer, Barbie and Allan, Stuart (eds) (2002) *Journalism after September 11.* London: Routledge.

index